Effective SEO and Content Marketing

The Ultimate Guide for Maximizing Free Web Traffic

Nicholas Papagiannis

WILEY

I dedicate this book to my friends and family, especially my late father and my mother.

About the Author

Nick Papagiannis is a Chicago-based SEO and content consultant, currently working at Cramer-Krasselt. He has been in the industry for 20 years and has focused on search engine marketing for most of those years. After graduating from the University of Illinois at Champaign-Urbana, Nick worked at several consultancies and marketing agencies, including Accenture, Razorfish, and iCrossing before joining Cramer-Krasselt. He has done SEO and website work on several notable brands, including Coca-Cola, GM, Cetaphil, Sears, Lands' End, State Farm, and ADT.

He has spoken at several notable conferences, including South by Southwest, and has written for many trade publications, including *PR Daily* and *Direct Marketing News*.

In his free time, Nick enjoys running and working out, traveling to his home country of Greece, spending time with his friends and family, and watching his beloved Chicago sports teams.

About the Technical Editor

Sandy Writtenhouse is a writer and editor with a background and education in the field of technology. After obtaining her bachelor of science degree in information technology, she worked for many years managing people and projects.

Sandy has had a love for writing since she was a young girl scribbling down stories in a notebook. When writing manuals and business requirements for IT projects was no longer enough to fulfill her passion, she decided to leave the daily grind to pursue her dream of working for herself as a full-time freelancer.

Now, you can find Sandy's articles on many technology- and Apple -related websites. She concentrates on technologies that make life easier and work more productive. This includes writing tutorials and how-to articles that help others.

Along with her own writings, Sandy has gained proficiency in SEO and works as an SEO editor to assist her clients in setting and meeting their SEO initiatives and goals. In addition, she manages and participates in additional web projects for her clients.

When Sandy is not pounding away at her keyboard, you can find her enjoying time with her husband, family, and dogs in the sunny state of Florida. After spending most of her life growing up and living in the Midwest, she now makes the most of the warmer climate in the South.

Sandy's personal motto is: live, laugh, write. These words motivate her each day to live every moment, laugh uncontrollably, and write because she loves it.

Acknowledgments

Though I loved writing growing up, I never thought I would be in a position to write a book. I never thought of myself as a writer, but life and career choices had their way of putting me in this place. I'd like to thank my family for helping me over the years. On top of being raised in a great family and around friends who preached education and staying away from career complacency, with the help of my good friends from my childhood, I ventured into a college major and career that was still forming and in high demand: digital marketing.

I kept in touch with close friends, including Jonathan Tauber, whom I've known since sixth grade, and saw him succeeding and moving ahead in this industry. He was the first person I knew in the digital marketing industry and one of the most influential people in my career life, who directed me toward a high-demand career path that was still emerging. Jonathan, you are not only a lifelong friend, you are a brother, and I'm happy our paths crossed that day during little league tryouts. Thank you so much for all your guidance and input through the years.

After getting some experience as an analyst in the industry, I came across my mentor who would become one of my best friends, John Doyle. I can't thank him enough. John, you are a gem of a person and knowing you has truly changed my career and life. Thank you so much for everything you've done.

I would also like to thank those who have contributed their feedback via interviews, specifically Max Cheprasov, Gary Opp, Nitin Himmady, Andrew Furman, Christian Dodd, and Caleb Gonsalves.

Contents

Introduction

This book came about after many intensive hours in the digital marketing, content, and SEO spaces. I've been in the industry for 20 years and have had all kinds of experiences, clients, and projects: some good, some not as good. This book is designed to offer modern-day marketers the templates, processes, education, and other resources to help them execute free traffic initiatives through effective search engine optimization (SEO) and content marketing. I've seen many wasted hours on projects that didn't meet goals, and this book outlines how to ensure your program runs as optimally as possible. SEO and organic content are often underutilized and overlooked across the marketing realm. SEO is not merely trying to improve your website ranking on Google. SEO can spark and optimize ideas, and organic content can be the form for those ideas.

SEO is no longer a stand-alone discipline; it has evolved beyond a simple marketing tactic that should be applied throughout the marketing process. I would argue it should be used to inform and regulate the complete marketing process in an effort to optimize free traffic levels to your brand.

In my opinion, maximizing your organic (free) traffic channels should be a top priority, and this book provides insight on how to do that. This is the most effective way to spend total marketing efforts and dollars. From working with social media influencers to steering creative ideas and campaigns, modern-day SEO requires a full-service perspective of marketing and processes. To date, it's hard to find a book that provides a comprehensive view on how to incorporate SEO throughout each marketing discipline and the broader marketing delivery process.

Currently, many books on the market focus mainly on the basics of SEO but fail to demonstrate how and why SEO needs to be integrated into each marketing competency (social media, PR, creative teams, etc.) for the best return on total marketing investment.

The following are the key areas of this book:

- General education on SEO and organic content execution, and marketing
- Important search engine strategies and analytic reports
- Understanding which search engines to focus on
- How SEO and content can solve business problems
- Building a new brand through SEO and content
- Identifying who your true competitors are
- How to establish research channels that can inform your business initiatives
- Building personas and audience purchase journeys
- Prioritizing locations, demographics and countries
- What needs to be in place to maximize free traffic levels to your brands assets
- Understanding all the key tasks and attributes for an effective content program
- Data-Driven Content: Detailed instruction on how to use data to inform content responses, ideas, and asset types
- Understanding different content asset types from standard items like articles to highly advanced assets like films, podcasts, white papers, and other assets
- Calculating ROI for SEO and Content initiatives
- Building an SEO and Content vision through your company with the right content principles, team structure and processes
- Small business marketing via content and SEO and having the right small business mindset for success
- Website and content design considerations (accessibility, principles of marketing)
- Optimizing for the future and looking at other search venues
  - Amazon Optimization
  - YouTube Optimization

- App Store Optimization (ASO)
- Podcast Optimizations
- Optimizing Blogs and other off-site content)
- Prepping and optimizing for the newest technologies, including voice search, artificial intelligence, and content discovery vehicles
- How to build an optimization path and programs that drive results and manage risks

The book aims to provide an exponential return on investment by optimizing marketing budgets across paid and owned content via nonpaid tactics like SEO and organic content marketing. It also aims to bring the readers up to speed on the latest and emerging SEO tactics and factors, content marketing principles, and processes. It also provides quizzes for each chapter, checklists, templates to get started, and interviews with industry leaders.

For more information on the author, book, contact information, consulting services, and other valuable free content (discussion forums, news) please visit http://www.effectiveseoandcontentmarketing.com.

CHAPTER

1

Getting on the Same Page

The goal of this book is to provide marketers and business leaders with an understanding of how to gather and optimize free traffic to their brand. This book is designed to offer an exponential return on investment. If you follow the tactics laid out in this book, I am confident that you will see significant increases in traffic and revenue.

The ensuing chapters of this book will provide a roadmap and understanding of how to best optimize your overall web presence through search engine optimization (SEO) and content marketing, as well as how to raise your organic traffic footprint and performance. There are many books on the market that speak to SEO and content marketing, but they do not speak to both. SEO and content marketing depend on each other these days. This is because of the way Google's algorithm works and the way digital marketing and user experience have evolved. Do not focus on one without the other.

This book is essentially a guide for how to leverage both sciences to create a higher amount of free traffic to your brands. It is a framework that modern-day marketers should know, and it's a low-cost way for business owners and marketers to gather a basic understanding and skill set and learn how to provide exponential traffic and marketing effectiveness to their clients and businesses.

Free Traffic

Capturing free, high-quality, high-qualified traffic is a core function and goal of an effective digital marketing strategy. Getting free traffic is not an easy thing. There are many levers that need to be pulled and optimized. Free traffic can benefit an overall marketing program in a lot of ways, especially if there are paid or media tactics involved. The levers of free traffic can help boost paid media performance as well. There are many instances where applying organic optimization techniques through SEO, user experience, content, and other organic strategies can yield a better sales conversion process, more search engine keyword rankings, and stronger traffic levels.

However, it's not easy to make all the free traffic cylinders work well together. There are several things that are required.

Responsive Teams

You need a cooperative IT and website management team. This is necessary so that optimization recommendations can be quickly implemented and rolled live. Oftentimes, IT cán prove to be a hindrance in implementing recommendations that ultimately fueled better website performance and traffic. The more responsive the IT team is in making changes quickly, the better the performance output can be.

Strong SEO

You also need a strong SEO expert. Over the years, I've come across many different types of SEO experts. Some were strong technically and only technically, while some were strong on the content side. Some are not strong in either and are generally unhelpful. As we will discuss later in this book, the SEO strategist is the quarterback for a lot of the tactics that generate free traffic. It's important you have a strong quarterback who bridges the gap between technical and content opportunities. Additionally, SEO experts should be well-versed in emerging search channels like social media sites, Amazon, and other platforms beyond your website.

User Experience Expertise

It's extremely important to have a well-seasoned and strong user experience expert. A lot of the conversion or sales process online can be hindered by bad user experience techniques. As the user experience transforms from devices to other things like voice or conversational commerce, it's important to have a strong user experience expert who is well-versed in these channels and can stay in tune with emerging channels to better position your site for changing user behavior and dates.

Ongoing Content Production

Content production is critical. Having a strong content team that is able to create content quickly and effectively is paramount to having a successful free traffic or organic traffic program for your brand. Content, as we'll get into later, essentially creates your free traffic footprint and is necessary for capturing organic traffic. Think of content as a fishing net. The larger it is, the more fish you're going to catch. It's no secret that news sites tend to drive the most traffic because they are constantly pushing out new content and have a strong content discovery and promotional strategy in place. All these things help sites with a large amount of content and web pages capture the most free traffic around. Back in the day these were called *content farms*, but now many of those low-quality content farms have dissolved, and high-quality websites that offer a broad spectrum of quality content tend to capture the most free traffic these days.

Strong Analytics

Digital marketers require strong analytics. Data-driven initiatives and content have become the norm nowadays. For a marketer to showcase their effectiveness, there have to be data points and evidence around performance. Strong data analytics and experts are critical to the organic and free traffic process. This book will discuss the different processes needed for achieving strong SEO and content marketing results. A core lever to the organic traffic process is having strong analytics with a frequent cadence of reporting to inform the types of content users are interested in and the effectiveness of your brand's content. It also shows whether the traffic coming to your side is incrementally growing from free channels as a result of good SEO and effective content marketing. Without analytics, you will be a ship lost at sea.

Data-Driven Culture

We live in a data world, and it's imperative that creative ideas and concepts begin with data. Data should inform the ideation stage, and the analytics team should provide this to help ideation and creative concepting.

Process Management

Marketing projects live and die depending on process management. Marketing projects have gotten more complex and technical, which require detailed planning, communication, and process execution. Brands need dedicated and strong project or process managers.

If you're a brand that cannot provide these levers, it is better to wait on free content initiatives like SEO and content marketing, whose results will be severely impacted and compromised. Instead, I would increase the budget for paid media and paid advertisements and focus more on a paid traffic strategy. Paid strategies are clearly more costly, but they do work and provide short-term workarounds until you get your free traffic levers and infrastructure in place.

Learning SEO

I remember my first foray into a search marketing agency, where I was initially a project manager. Search engine optimization seemed so complicated and foreign to me. My manager at the time said some people get it, but most people don't. He rolled his eyes and I felt like taking a gulp, little did he know I thought I was destined to be one of those people who don't get it. At the time I felt I would never understand all the different terminology, the algorithm factors, the definition of content, and the different website management systems. It seemed so overwhelmingly complex, and I was discouraged. I started being thankful that I was a project manager and not the actual subject-matter expert who was in charge of compiling deliverables and educating clients on how it all works. It took me a year of intensive client meetings, several walk-throughs of deliverables, and many repetitions of executing an SEO program to get a comfortable high-level understanding of what it's all about. I am so thankful for that overwhelming time because it not only gave me a thorough knowledge of search engine optimization, but it gave me a great perspective and understanding of how to simplify it and spoon-feed it to the common marketer who is first learning about it.

I also recall the first time I saw a website that I was working on rank #1 for a broad product term, *women's swimwear,* and the thousands of website visits and sales it yielded. It was an unbelievable, homerun feeling. That was more than 13 years ago, and the core fundamentals of good SEO have not changed.

It might be surprising to know, but SEO is actually not that complicated on a strategic level. Understanding the vision that search engines hold is a great first step in understanding the system of how search engines work.

"Google's mission is to organize the world's information and make it universally accessible and useful." Google: https://about.google/

As this quote says, it's Google's mission is to **organize** all the world's information so users can universally **access** it and are provided with the most **useful** information. We can dissect each key term in that quote to the following areas:

- *Organize* relates to Google's algorithm, which ranks and organizes content for search results.

- *Access* relates to conduction web crawls, which are essentially programs that scour the Internet to discover websites and content and then provide users with links via the search page to the content.

- *Useful* describes the content Google finds, which is also the most trustworthy and authoritative around a given subject.

How Search Engines Work

Search engines are constantly seeking new information on the Web. They have their own software programs that scour or crawl the Web looking for information. These are sometimes also called *spiders* or *bots*. They go from site to site and collect information. They use a *ranking algorithm* that determines which sites to rank and in what order (Figure 1.1). This is done to provide users with the most relevant and useful content and with an experience that allows users to easily consume content. If you aren't providing that as a brand or website, you are likely not ranking or visible to search engine users. If that's the case, it is time to educate yourself and/or employ a search engine optimization expert to help provide services that help you. Google provides its own "Starter Guide" for websites looking to learn about SEO, but I would argue that you should always employ a search engine expert who understands SEO on a very detailed level and whose job it is to stay up-to-date on the latest Google algorithm processes to help you build and maintain a strong presence on the search results page. Also, it's important to think beyond the technical and HTML code aspects of SEO. It's evolved into much more of a comprehensive game that requires a longer view around tech, content, and popularity aspects. In fact, according to Andrey Lipattsev, search quality senior strategist at Google, high-quality content and link building are the two most important signals used by Google to rank your website for search (source: Search Engine Watch, 2016; `https://searchengineland` `.com/now-know-googles-top-three-search-ranking-factors-245882`).

Figure 1.1: How search engines work

Executing Search Engine Optimization

Whether you are a brand marketer with the benefit of having an SEO subject-matter expert on hand to provide you guidance or a small business owner who is trying to do SEO themselves, it's important to understand the key levers that are needed to affect and optimize your search engine presence and rankings. It's actually quite simple; the science and art of search engine optimization can fall into three pillars that must be executed together and in order (Figure 1.2).

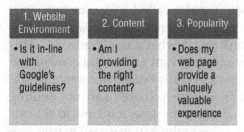

Figure 1.2: The three pillars of good SEO

An SEO initiative should provide guidance on how to drive and optimize these three areas of website environment, content, and popularity. Let's dive into each of these because they are essential to understanding and executing the right SEO program that will get you ranking higher in search results for most search engines.

Priority 1: A Great Website Technical Environment

A sound and fully optimized website technical environment is critical and the top priority when it comes to SEO and capturing strong organic traffic levels. If you don't have your website technology set up correctly, your content will not get crawled, so it's useless and pointless to not focus on your website technology first and foremost. Websites are usually managed via a content management system housed on a website server. Both the content management system and website server have important influence on how search engines crawl your content when reaching your website. Most SEO crawling tools and SEO platforms look at these key areas as part of their auditing features. Typically, they crawl the site and pull a list of issues around the following topics into a report.

There are some important areas that must be "set up" correctly to ensure the ideal crawling of your website. While not an exhaustive list, these are typically the most critical:

- **Redirects:** Redirects are used when a page has been moved to a different location or URL. These can be temporary or permanent. There are many kinds of redirects, but it's important to know that search engines recognize and pass SEO value only for permanent redirects. These are also called *301 redirects* (whereas temporary ones are called *302 redirects*). Both are managed through the web server. As a website, you almost always want to use permanent redirects because pages are rarely moved temporarily (a few days). SEO audits typically scan your website to identify the kinds of redirects your site is using. If you are using a redirect for temporary purposes, it should be flagged and evaluated as to why you are using it and for how long. Otherwise, an SEO subject-matter expert will likely instruct your IT team to change it to a 301 permanent redirect so SEO value is transferred to the new location of the page.

- **URL structures:** URLs are an important area for search engines. The actual URL string provides a unique identification for the page, almost like what a Social Security number does for a person. Additionally, URLs are a key area search engines look to when identifying what the page is about. In fact, it is critical that URLs and their folder structures include keywords. It's also best to use hyphens when separating terms. For instance, this is the number-one ranking for the search *men's adidas shoes*: https://www.adidas.com/us/men-shoes. The terms are all in the URL and spaced out by hyphens. Hyphens communicate to search engines to separate out the terms versus merging them and ranking them for the merged phrase search results. Additionally, the closer to the root folder of the URL, which is the folder closest to the .com, the more emphasis the keyword gets. The more competitive and general the search ranking you might be trying to rank for, the closer the phrase should be to the root folder. Additionally, it's critical to use only one URL for a page throughout your website. Some sites use variables to track users or to display dynamic content based on where the user clicks throughout the site, which is generally bad for SEO performance results and rankings and, in the case of creating duplicate content, may result in ranking penalties from search engines.

■ **Web page and website load time:** How quickly a web page loads, or page speed, is one of the most important ranking factors right now. The top search engine ranking is typically dominated by faster-loading pages, especially on mobile devices that are at the center of Google's design. Furthermore, quick-loading pages positively affect user experience and may increase your conversion rates. According to a study by the Aberdeen Group, every one-second delay in load time equates to a 7 percent drop in conversions. Google will reduce your search engine rankings if your site or web page loads slowly. Slow load time is typically attributed to your server performance and the density of your web page's HTML code. Keep code simple, clean, and easy to process. If your server is causing the issue, work with your website host to determine why and/or consider moving to a different provider that may be closer in distance to your target audience and your location.

■ **XML sitemap and robots.txt files:** XML sitemaps and robots.txt files are files that allow you to communicate to search engines the web pages that should get into the search results and rankings. Be sure to leverage your CMS tools to build a complete XML sitemap and robots.txt files and have them validated and submitted via Google's Search Console tool.

■ **Broken pages or 404 errors:** A 404 error page means that a web page is not accessible or no longer there. This is usually a result of a broken link or a link using the wrong URL for a web page. The 404 error hampers the user experience by preventing a user from connecting to a desired page. Because of this, websites that produce many 404 errors can lead to a drop in SEO rankings and traffic.

- **Duplicate content:** Duplicate content was one of Google's original spam checks and part of its algorithm early on. Web pages are considered duplicates if their content is 80 percent or more similar. Sites that have duplicate content are usually significantly affected by penalties and lower search engine rankings. Sometimes duplicate content happens by accident due to CMS or URL structuring reasons, so it's important to ensure there is only one URL created for a web page.

- **Page linking:** Page linking within a website is extremely important. Search engines follow them while crawling the site, and the anchor text that links use are another area search engines look to for determining what a page is about (also called *relevancy*). Every page should have at least one internal link pointing to it and should include the term that you'd like the page to rank for in the anchor text. It's also recommended that the number of links to a page from within a site (not external sites) be no more than 3,000.

- **SEO meta tags:** HTML tags are extremely important to search engines. They explain what your site is about, what to display in the search engine result copy it ranks for, and what type of page it is (recipe, product page, etc.). Each page should have its own unique set of tags. Similar to duplicate content, tag duplication can be a big hinderance to search engine rankings. Be sure to keep tags within the right character limits, and be sure you have an ongoing tag management strategy that uses the latest Schema. org tags, which are constantly changing.

- **HTTPS encryption:** Providing users with a secure website has become a top priority to search engines. Security has become part of the search engine ranking algorithm. Google says, "HTTPS is an internet communication protocol that protects the integrity and confidentiality of data between the user's computer and site" (https://developers.google.com/web/fundamentals/security/ encrypt-in-transit/why-https). Websites that do not support HTTPS connects should expect a lower ranking in search engine results and be surpassed by sites that are using HTTPs in search results.

- **Global SEO elements:** Global brands understandably need to have multiple versions of their website for each country and language. Ideally countries should have a different ccTLD for each country (Amazon.com for the United States versus Amazon.ca for Canada), which is the preferred method to tell search engines which content to rank in each country. If that's not possible, another option is to use a subdirectory (spotify.com/fr). Once you determine your URL style, be sure to use hreflang tags (rel="alternate" hreflang="x") on each page as they communicate to search engines which pages should be shown to web page visitors based on their location. Also, if you offer multiple languages in the same country (e.g., a Canadian site that offers French and English content for respective audiences), it's even more important to use this tag.

- **Page layout and text usage:** The top-ranking pages typically offer long-form content, so it's important that your pages have a lot of text around a given subject. Search engines tend to reward fast-loading pages that offer a lot of basic text copy (some even more than 500 words) with the top rankings. Be sure your web pages offer a lot of text, especially in the "above the fold of the page" area, or the area at the top of the page that is initially displayed upon loading, without scrolling. Copy that's within an image does not count since search engines have a difficult time reading the image and typically just scan a page and extract basic HTML text.

These are the key "website environment" areas that take top priority before moving to the content pillar of good SEO. Be sure these are set up and implemented correctly before moving to the next step: content.

Priority 2: Creating the Right Content

During my early days in the SEO world, and still to this day, I remember constantly hearing the saying "Content is king." This is still the case today, but I believe this applies across all of marketing. I believe the marketing world is still trying to define what good content means and what's included when it comes to defining content types. I will break down content in much more detail in Chapter 5, "Data-Informed Creative." In my opinion, the list of marketing content is vast. It's not just a blog article or website landing page. Content can mean a lot of things in the marketing world, and SEO can help inform and regulate its creation so it gets the most views possible.

Content is extremely critical to the SEO process because content allows you to rank for the searches you are targeting. Unlike a paid search, to show up for an organic search, a website must typically have a piece of content with the phrase you are targeting. For example, a brand may consider itself an auto insurance provider, and their site solely uses the term *auto insurance*. They task their team with ranking for *car insurance* or *motorcycle insurance* as well as their core term, *auto insurance*. To rank for car insurance or motorcycle insurance, the brand would have to build content on their site that specifically mentions and is optimized around those terms. For the best chance at ranking, a brand should build a dedicated web page for each search term they'd like to rank for. There are a few exceptions to this, and sometimes content will rank without specifically mentioning the term, but it's rare, usually a fluke, and does not last.

Creating the right content takes a lot of research and understanding of your audience, and that effort is worth it only if you have a sound, SEO-friendly technology environment to house it. If you follow the top-priority tech environment tips discussed earlier, you should be in good shape.

Identifying content ideas can come in many ways, but in general there is nothing like the insight search keyword data provides. I would argue that it's the best way to identify what content you should create. The process is fairly simple, and there are many keyword tools available on the market for purchase. Google also provides keyword data in its AdWords Keyword Planner tool. Once you identify what phrase or category of phrases you'd like to rank for, you need to identify what kind of content you'd like to create.

If you are looking for your website to rank for a phrase, you need to create a long-form piece of content that speaks to that phrase in several key areas, including the URL, the title of the page, throughout the copy, and the link text on the page. Figure 1.3 shows an example of an actual page for *diamond buying guide* that ranked #1 for the term.

As time has gone on, it's even more important to have long-form content, especially for search terms that are extremely common and competitive and have a lot of content already ranking in search engines. The average Google first-page result contains 1,890 words (source: Backlinko, 2016).

The example in Figure 1.4 for *best car insurance* is a page that has more than 4,000 words and 12 mentions of the exact phrase. The phrase is also in the URL and SEO HTML tags (like the earlier example).

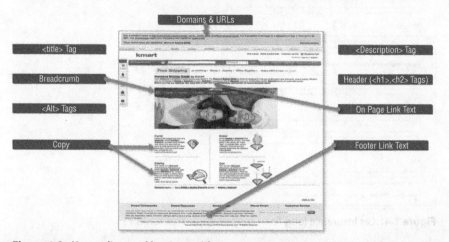

Figure 1.3: Kmart diamond buying guide

Figure 1.4: Car Insurance long-form copy example that ranks #1

For extremely general and common search phrases, a more comprehensive content approach may be necessary. This will be outlined in Chapter 5. The key takeaway is to provide an SEO-optimal web page for each term you'd like to rank for.

Priority 3: Popularity of Your Web Page and Website

The third pillar of good SEO, popularity, is the most difficult to affect. Oftentimes, search engines find your website and web pages through links from other sites. They assign a "trust factor" or quality factor to those links to determine whether a piece of content is popular and should be trusted. Links from .gov or .org websites are traditionally looked at as having even more power and quality because they are looked at as strong authorities and very trustworthy due to their affiliation with the government or an association.

As often as a few years ago, brands could easily manipulate the link factor. There were all kinds of link networks and vendors that you could subscribe to that would essentially allow you to "rent" links in their website network. In essence, you were buying links artificially. There have been several algorithm updates since then, and search engines have penalized sites that seem to be acquiring links from low-quality sites. The best way to build links to your site is do so organically and to be deserving of them by providing useful, high-quality content. This requires long-term, strategic thinking. It also requires a combined approach that leverages online assets a brand may create outside of their website on other high-traffic websites and to embed links in those assets that go to their content (that they're trying to rank).

Additionally, brands need to be vigilant and regularly monitor that low-quality sites aren't pointing links to them; these are also called *toxic links*. Fortunately, search engines provide a link disavow option via their Google Search Console or webmaster website monitoring tools, which allow you to mark incoming links as low quality and instructs them to "disavow" or essentially ignore them. Many SEO tools have a feature that checks the quality of links pointing to your site and provides you with a list that you can upload into each search engine's platform to disavow poor-quality links.

To boost links, nothing works better than offering useful and unique content. I once had an automotive brand that we were working with that was looking to build links. When we started working with them, their site had only about 1,200 links pointing to it. This is incredibly low considering many websites in their industry had more than 1 million links pointing to them. We were at a major disadvantage to ranking well and leapfrogging the competition. We conducted a content and search term analysis to determine what topics people were searching for and provided a gap analysis to show where they were missing content. We built many "how to" and other types of help content.

As a result, the link counts increased significantly. Within two years, the link count went to more than 100,000. When we dove deeper, we found that a huge number of local auto dealers were linking to their site and content because they found it useful and complementary to their dealer sites. Additionally, we saw that other channels were driving a lot of traffic to them, email and social media in particular. As a result, we saw our total website rankings increase exponentially. Table 1.1 shows the dos and don'ts of building links.

Table 1.1: The Dos and Don'ts of Building Links

DO	DON'T
Aim for getting links from high-quality sites, especially `.org` and `.gov` websites	Get links from low-quality sites
Point links to your home page and other important pages that you are trying to rank	Just link to your home page
Include the term that you are trying to have your website rank for in the anchor text of the link pointing to it	Use a general anchor text like "click here"
Consider *content promotion* tactics to help boost awareness of your content	Forget to use the search term in the anchor text that you would like to have the page rank for
Use a link quality tool to run monthly checks to determine if your links are low quality and disavow them using Google Search Console	Buy or rent links

The key is to understand that acquiring links should be done organically, by providing high-quality content that other sites link to. There are some additional organic ways to build awareness of your content and links.

- **Paid media:** Paid search or content promotion vehicles can drive a significant amount of traffic to your content, which can yield links or shares of your content.

- **Custom content strategies (bloggers, influencers, publication sites):** Custom content pieces are often collaborative and allow brands to provide an "assignment brief" where they can discuss the guidelines for the project. When soliciting proposals and completing assignment briefs, brands can often ask for links in the copy to important web pages of the brand website. This can increase the awareness of your content and could increase links as well.

- **Social media updates:** Sharing content on social media channels (Twitter, Pinterest, Facebook, etc.) can be a great way to bring awareness of your content, particularly if you have a robust following.

- **Email newsletters:** For brands that publish email newsletters and have a large email list, adding a link to a new article can be a great way to build awareness and attract views of content that may lead to links. See Figure 1.5.

- **Digital news releases:** For brands that drop online press releases, consider using a newswire service like PR Newswire. These services push out your release to hundreds of news publications at once and typically allow for embedding links to content and other owned media assets that you are trying to increase links to in the release. Including search terms in the anchor text is an excellent way to build links. It's a really quick and passive way to bring awareness of your content and your site.

- **YouTube videos:** YouTube is considered the second most popular search engine according to the *New York Times*. For brands that have videos on YouTube or a program on YouTube, they should employ SEO best practices (to be discussed later) to maximize free views of video content. They should also include a link to a relevant web page for each video.

While the factors that affect search engine rankings are constantly changing, I've found that the three pillars of good SEO that I just outlined have lasted since the beginning of Google. I am confident that if brands focus on optimizing the three pillars of good SEO and optimizing the factors underneath them, they will see significant improvements to their organic traffic levels and search engine rankings.

Figure 1.5: Example of rich newsletter promoting content on website from mrporter.com

Focusing on Google First

The big three search engines (Google, Yahoo, Bing) focus on most of the same elements of a web page but weigh them a little differently. This makes it difficult to optimize around all three search engines at the same time, so we recommend focusing mostly around Google since it controls the largest share of users by far. See Figure 1.6.

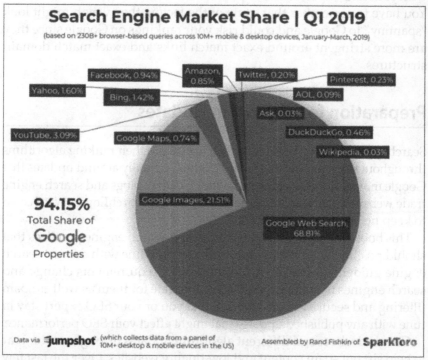

Figure 1.6: Search engine share study, Jumpshot 2019

At the end of the day, Bing and Yahoo look at page, domain, and link quality but weigh them slightly differently. If you are not ranking well on Bing or Yahoo but are ranking well on Google, consider looking at the following factors:

- **Your domain characteristics:** Bing and Yahoo favor older domains with keywords in them, for example, if your target search term is in your domain (www.mensshoes.com).
- **Link quality:** Yahoo and Bing weigh links from .edu, .org, and .gov websites and exact match anchor text more heavily.

- **On-page elements:** Yahoo and Bing favor web pages that include the specific phrase you are targeting in key web page areas like the header, title, web page copy, and description tags.

- **Social media signals:** Bing has come out and said that it factors social media factors into its results, so content that is shared more on Facebook, Twitter, and other channels typically will rank better.

If you are concerned about a lack of rankings on Bing or Yahoo, work with your SEO expert to craft a plan specific to ranking on those engines. You have to remember that some of the factors they weigh might look "spammy" to Google and could risk your rankings on Google since they are more stringent around exact match links and exact match domain structures.

Preparation for Algorithm Updates

Search engines typically make several updates to their ranking algorithms throughout the year. The most news chatter is usually around updates that Google makes. It's important to monitor Google's blogs and search engine trade websites like SearchEngineLand.com and SearchEngineWatch.com to keep up with the latest news.

This book provides general usability and search engine practices that should position your site to rank well and be in line with current search engine guidelines. However, since usability requirements change and search engines make updates to accommodate for them as well as spam filtering and security needs, be sure that you or your SEO expert stay in tune with any published updates that might affect your SEO performance.

Google does several different algorithm updates throughout the year to help sift out spam content and low-quality websites. Over the last few years Google has done several updates every few months, including the following through June 2019:

- **August 2017:** Google did the Hawk local algorithm update. Google was trying to force similar businesses that were near each other to be filtered out of local search results. Google then followed up that update to essentially correct it and put businesses near each other even if they're similar.

- **November 2017:** There were rumors that Google did another update in November 2017. It decreased the search engine ranking on many small sites with minimal content that offered ads. Essentially,

Google penalized sites that were trying to rank for search results to capture traffic and solicit advertisements to that traffic.

- **December 2017:** Google confirmed that it did an update that targeted websites that had way too many limited landing pages targeting different keyword derivatives, as well as sites with too many ads or thin content on them. This update essentially targeted spam sites.

- **March 2018:** Google representatives confirmed that they did a ranking algorithm update but did not disclose what exactly they penalized.

- **April 2018:** Google representatives again confirmed that they did a core algorithm update and gave no significant feedback as to what they filtered out. Many sites did not see a significant impact from this update.

- **August 2018:** Google representatives confirmed that they released a major search algorithm update to reward quality websites with higher search engine ranking results. According to Google, the update was not focused on demoting low-quality content but rather providing more relevant results to users that offer high-quality comment content.

- **September 2018:** Google representatives confirmed that they released a minor search algorithm update on the company's anniversary, September 27. They did not disclose any details regarding the impact of this update and the types of content it penalized or rewarded.

- **March 2019:** Google representatives confirmed that there was a broad algorithm update dubbed the Florida2 update because it was discussed at the Pub Conn Florida conference. Since it was a broader update, they didn't disclose any specific changes or impacts to look out for. In general, it was rumored to just focus on the quality of search results and how well content how well content is mapped to search query or phrase.

- **April 2019:** Google confirmed that there was a glitch in its algorithm and the company had to do an update because it led to some websites and content being in the index and removed from search engine results. The update was essentially to fix the indexing issue. Normal sites were typically not impacted unless they were deindexed.

- **May 2019:** There was rumored to be another algorithm update because Google had issues indexing new content. This update was rumored to be a fix for that issue.

- **June 2019:** Google rolled out the well-publicized domain diversity update. It was aimed to improve search results in that instance where a single domain dominated all the search results for a search phrase. As Google says, going forward, it will generally not show more than two URLs (listings) from the same domain as a result of this update.

The big takeaway from this timeline is that Google *frequently* updates its algorithm that ranks content and websites. It's extremely important that marketers pay attention to the latest news on Google algorithm updates because they can severely impact your websites and content performance. These updates could compromise free traffic as well and decrease the overall return on investment (ROI) of your web assets. In my opinion, it's extremely critical to have an experienced SEO expert on hand at all times to ensure your website is positioned well to handle the turbulence that comes out of these frequent search algorithm updates. Google is constantly tweaking its ranking algorithm and rewarding users with a better user experience by molding irrelevant content and low-quality sites. It's critically important that brands stay ahead of the curve by offering high-quality content and a great user experience.

Quiz

1. What redirect type is best for SEO?
   a. 302 meta refresh redirect
   b. 301 permanent redirect
   c. 301 meta refresh redirect
   d. 404 permanent redirect

   Answer: b

2. What are the three pillars of good SEO?
   a. Content, website environment, trust
   b. Technology, linking, copy

    c. Copy, website environment, linking

    d. Content, website environment, popularity

    Answer: d

3. True or False: Google's mission is to optimize the world's information and make it universally accessible and useful.

    Answer: True

4. True or False: For good SEO, links should be high-quality *and* numerous.

    Answer: True

5. Content should be:

    a. Unique

    b. Long-form

    c. Useful

    d. Search informed

    e. All the above

    Answer: e.

6. True or False: Typically, link building is the toughest of the three pillars to affect.

    Answer: True

7. Which of the following is not a good example of a content promotion tactic to build awareness and links to content?

    a. Influencer strategies

    b. Partner content: custom content on a partner site

    c. Placing links to brand web pages in the YouTube description of highly viewed videos

    d. Social media sharing

    e. Adding a link to your content from a website's XML sitemap file

    Answer: e

8. If you are trying to get a page to rank for *black shoes*, where should you include the exact search phrase that you would like to have the page rank for?

    a. HTML title tag (page title)

    b. Header tag (or h1, h2)

    c. The URL

    d. Anchor text

    e. Image/alt tags

    f. In the page copy

    g. All the above

    Answer: g

9. To have a free-traffic oriented marketing program, which of the following do you *not* need?

    a. Analytics

    b. Content production process

    c. SEO expert

    d. News-writing expert

    e. User experience expert

    f. Data-driven creative team members

    g. All the above

    Answer: d

10. How often does Google conduct algorithm updates?

    a. Several times a year

    b. Once a year

    c. Every few years

    d. Once a week

    e. Every day

    f. Every few days

    g. All the above

    Answer: a

Your Website

Search engine optimization and other digital marketing channels are reliant on a brand's website, so it's important that you think about your website as the centerpiece to your program.

Why Your Website Is Critical

The benefits of a website cannot be overstated. From a search engine optimization perspective, a website is the critical piece to strong business performance. Many brands neglect their website from many different areas or fail to properly monetize and optimize their website to rank well. A website can provide many brand and marketing benefits.

Improves Search Engine Rankings

A website can provide search engine rankings, which are comprised of web pages and content from websites. A brand's website gives them an opportunity to dictate what search engine rankings say and how high that content ranks. A strong website can help you boost the number of search rankings a brand ranks for and thereby the amount of traffic it can collect. The more quality rankings you have in search engine results, the better your free traffic levels will be.

Communicates Brand

A website allows brands to tell their story and describe their products and the benefits of their offerings. Once a user enters a brand's website universe, the user is taken through a brand experience that communicates what the brand is about, what it offers, and how it could help the user. Also, the user learns what products or promotions the brand offers as well as answers to any questions the user might have. The website essentially allows brands to communicate with an audience interested in their brands and products. It allows brands to control their communication and engage users with their story and utilities.

Provides Information About Audience

A website allows for a brand to learn more about their audience. If a website has adequate analytics tracking set up, it will be able to provide brands with very valuable information about what website visitors are interested in and what they engage with. This data can help inform several areas of marketing and research. It is critical for brands to properly set up analytics so that the website's benefits can be leveraged. As we get into the next chapters, we will learn how to help inform marketing and content initiatives.

Captures Customer Relationship Management Inputs

A website allows for brands to capture contact information of their audience that can be used for remarketing purposes. Customer relationship management is an established area of digital and traditional marketing. Websites can help feed customer relationship management (CRM) strategies by collecting contact information of audiences. Contact information can be as little as an email, which can be collected by offering valuable content such as a white paper or an ongoing newsletter. Users are typically open to sharing their contact information in exchange for valuable content or content that offers utility and entertainment.

Provides Traffic Monetization Opportunities

The most obvious benefit to our website is traffic monetization opportunities. Whether it's a purchase, lead generation, click to call a business or other sales conversion types, websites offer brands a channel to create sales and orders of their products and services. Most brands build websites for this purpose. It is important to determine how to best monetize your website. A monetized website provides marketers with a means to assign a return on investment to their marketing initiatives. A website that is not monetized properly will fail to inform and measure the effectiveness of marketing initiatives.

Search Engine Optimization Process for Your Website

When it comes to your website, it's important to understand what the ideal SEO process is for an effective program and what activities fall under each step. Generally, SEO and marketing are most effective if they are process-driven. Having a process in place assigns ownership, ensures certain steps happen, and enables the final product to be the highest quality possible. For SEO, the process also should address the three pillars of good SEO. Figure 2.1 shows a general high-level process flow to follow when executing an effective SEO process on your website. (Chapter 3 will have a much more detailed project process for a comprehensive SEO and content program, so please stand by for that.)

Figure 2.1: General process flow

This chapter contains a breakdown of each step to help you employ an effective SEO stand-alone program for your website.

Step 1: SEO Technical Audit: Identify Technical Roadblocks

The SEO technical audit is the first key deliverable that needs to be completed when executing an SEO program. This deliverable is typically technical, can take many shapes, and outlines many areas of technical issues your website might be having. Typically, this deliverable is done in a presentation format, if a vendor is compiling it. If you are doing an audit for your own site, you can do something informal like a simple list of issues with their respective URLs. The goal of the audit is to identify technical roadblocks and issues that are comprising search engine rankings and indexing. When summarizing an issue on a site, it's important to know how to fix it. So, each audit issue should have a corresponding description of the issue, the URL, and how to fix it. This should be submitted to the website team for fixing. If you are not an SEO expert, you might want to discuss the issues with the website team to figure out how to fix them. There are many audit tools on the market that provide several features to make your life easier when doing SEO audits. Consider leveraging them. One popular website auditing tool is called Screaming Frog, and it's free to use for free websites. Consider downloading this for your use on your website at https://www.screamingfrog.co.uk.

Screaming Frog offers a free website crawl, and it pulls technical information into its platform and assesses it. Once you download it and log in, all you have to do is input your website URL at the top (Figure 2.2).

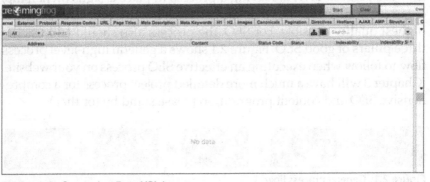

Figure 2.2: Screaming Frog URL input

Once you put in the URL you would like to crawl and click Start, the program runs, crawls your website, and begins to populate the interface and tabs with specific information about your website.

If you click through each tab, you can see a list of the URLs on each tab. See the example of Nike.com in Figure 2.3.

The first tab, Internal, is a combined view of all other tabs except for External, Hreflang, and Custom Tabs. This gives you a comprehensive view of the website data that you can export and analyze further if needed.

The next tab, External, is essentially a list of outbound URLs that Screaming Frog found referenced on the website. You can view details for the external links such as status and crawl depth. Typically, there aren't many issues to look for on this tab.

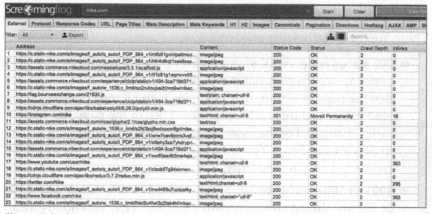

Figure 2.3: Screaming Frog output

From an SEO audit point of view, the important tabs are the Response Codes, Page Title, Meta Description, Meta Keywords, H1, H2, Images, and Canonicals.

Response Codes Tab

The Response Codes tab offers the list of page URLs and the response code for each page (Figure 2.4). The response code is a code that is returned by a web server when a website visitor makes a request to access a web page. The response code is typically three digits and can mean different things. Some response codes are positive for SEO, and others are negative.

Figure 2.4: Response Codes tab

SEO Positive Response Codes

These are the positive response codes:

- **200 status code:** A 200 code is good and means that the web server will provide a direct and successful response with the page information that you were expecting.

- **301 status code:** A 301 code is also good but indicates the page has moved permanently. It will forward your request to the new page and provide you with the page information you were looking for.

SEO Negative Response Codes

These are the negative response codes:

- **302 status code:** A 302 status code is tricky. It can be bad for SEO performance if a page has permanently moved because it indicates that the page is temporarily redirected, and it may not pass along SEO value. Use this code only if the URL of the page has temporarily changed. For the most part, 302 codes are something to note in Screaming Frog. You should verify the page is meant to be redirected only temporarily.

- **400+ or 500+ status codes:** Status codes 404, 401, 403, 410, and 500 or 503 are almost always negative for SEO. They essentially mean the web page or URL is no longer available, there's an error, or the user is not allowed to access it. You don't want to see any of these in your Screaming Frog data.

If you see any negative status codes, you should take up the issue with your website hosting company and quickly resolve the issue in one of several ways.

- Change them to a correct, live URL and removing all website references/links to the broken or dead URL across your site.

- If a 404 response code is used, put a custom 404 error page together that includes the navigation and a friendly error message for the user (Figure 2.5 and Figure 2.6).

- Set up 301 permanent redirects from the erroneous URL to the live, appropriate URL.

The other item you should look at on the Response Codes tab is the Response Time column (Figure 2.7).

This metric essentially indicates how long it takes for the server to respond when a user requests a page. This is a critical metric since search engines now penalize sites with slow load times. Google's research claims that the chance of a user leaving your site increases 32 percent when your load time is longer than one second. Try to keep response times as low as possible and definitely less than one second. If you have a response time that's higher than one second, you should consider reaching out to your website hosting company to see whether there's anything they can do. You should also consider testing the page on Google's Page Speed tool and resolving any other issues with your website developer or the person who programmed your website. Try the tool here: https://developers.google.com/speed/pagespeed/insights/.

Figure 2.5: Set up a page like this. . .

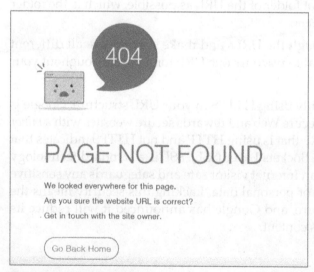

Figure 2.6: . . .instead of this

Address	Content	Status Code	Status	Indexability	Indexability Status	Inlinks	Response Time
http://nike.com/	text/html; charset=iso-8859-1	301	Moved Permanently	Non-Indexable	Redirected	0	0.05
https://www.nike.com/	text/html; charset=utf-8	200	OK	Indexable		16	0.04
https://www.nike.com/us/en_us/c/innovation/react	text/html; charset=utf-8	200	OK	Indexable		324	0.12
https://www.nike.com/ruhl_nl	text/html; charset=utf-8	200	OK	Non-Indexable	Canonicalised	15	0.14
https://www.nike.com/ckida_ds	text/html; charset=utf-8	200	OK	Non-Indexable	Canonicalised	15	0.16
https://store.nike.com/us/en_us/pw/mens-big-tab?pw21tam		301	Moved Permanently	Non-Indexable	Redirected	201	0.09

Figure 2.7: Response Time column

Address Column

Take a look at the Address column on the Response Codes tab in Screaming Frog to assess whether the site has good SEO (Figure 2.8). URLs are extremely important for SEO.

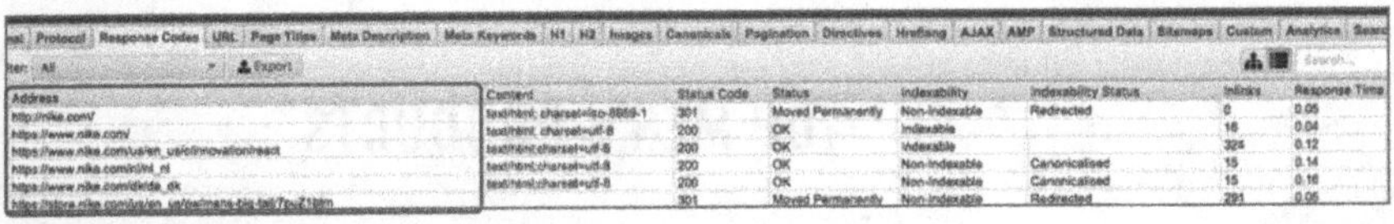

Figure 2.8: Address column

- As mentioned in Chapter 1, the actual URL string provides a unique identification for the page, and URLs are a key area where search engines look when determining the page content.

- Be sure that your website URLs and their folder structures include keywords instead of numbers. It's also best to use hyphens when separating terms.

- Make sure the term you'd like to target the page to rank for is as close to the root folder of the URL as possible, which is the folder closest to the .com.

- Also sort through the URLs and make sure they're all different since it's critical to use only one URL for a page throughout your website.

Be sure you are only using HTTPS in your URL structure. Google is pushing for a more secure Web and rewards secure websites with a *minor* ranking boost. A URL that is using HTTP and not HTTPS indicates that it's not using Secure Sockets Layer (SSL). SSL is a standard technology that is used to keep an Internet visitor safe and safeguards any sensitive data, such as logins or personal data. Lacking this security means the website isn't as secure, and Google has announced it will reduce its ranking for the site's content.

Page Titles Tab

The Page Titles tab is an important tab in Screaming Frog because it indicates what the title tag in the HTML is for each page (Title 1) and the character length of the title (Title 1 Length). Figure 2.9 shows these columns.

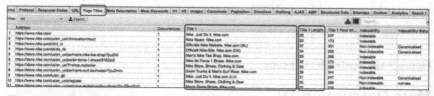

Figure 2.9: Page Titles tab

It's important to look at each of these columns to make sure you don't have title tags that have the same copy on multiple URLs. Additionally, it's important to keep character length within 45 to 65 characters to have an effective message displayed in the search results because this tag is typically the top blue part of a search engine result. A title tag greater than 65 characters runs the risk of getting cut off, as shown in Figure 2.10.

> Nike Statement on Forced Labor, Human Trafficking and Modern ...
> https://www.nike.com/help/a/supply-chain?cid=4942550... ▾
> Nike Statement on Forced Labor, Human Trafficking and Modern Slavery for Fiscal Year 2018.

Figure 2.10: Long title tag

When looking at your titles, it's also important to look for duplicate content on different URLs. Be sure to look for any duplications by checking for duplicate title tags, which are a sign of it.

Also, be sure to check for duplicate title tags in general, as they are also potentially negative because the title tag is the first place search engines look when discerning what the page is about and what search terms to rank it for. Having duplicate title tags can result in multiple pages competing for a search ranking, which can waste SEO value. Good title tags are less than 65 characters and clearly state what the page is about, which can increase click-throughs on the search results page. Place the targeted search phrases as close as possible to the beginning of title tags. Be sure to target only one phrase for very competitive searches and no more than two for other terms. Figure 2.11 shows an example of a great title tag that ranks #1 in Google for *mortgages*, which is a competitive search phrase. Figure 2.12 shows the corresponding HTML code.

> Mortgages - NerdWallet
> https://www.nerdwallet.com/blog/category/mortgages/ ▾
> Buying a home can be complicated. That's why NerdWallet provides clarity at each step of the mortgage process, empowering you to make the best decisions ...

Figure 2.11: NerdWallet title

```
<head>
    <meta charset="utf-8">
<title>Mortgages - NerdWallet</title>
<meta name="viewport" content="width=dev:
```

Figure 2.12: NerdWallet title code

Meta Description Tab

The Meta Description tab pulls the meta description tag and its character length for each page (Figure 2.13). This tag is extremely important because it provides the copy on the search engine result page below the URL (black font in Figure 2.14).

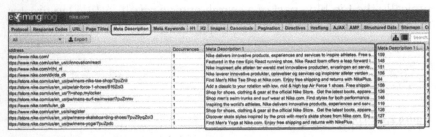

Figure 2.13: Meta Description tab

Nike Statement on Forced Labor, Human Trafficking and Modern ...
https://www.nike.com/help/a/supply-chain?cid=4942550... ▾
Nike Statement on Forced Labor, Human Trafficking and Modern Slavery
for Fiscal Year 2018.

Figure 2.14: Nike description tag

This copy should be 160 characters or fewer. It can be looked at as a form of advertising; it should include brand messaging and a call to action and should mention the topic of the page.

Meta Keywords Tab

Though no longer important to SEO rankings, I still consider using keyword tags a best practice whenever possible. The keywords tag is a tag that's typically found in the HTML of most pages and was originally a place where search engines also look to determine relevance or for the search term to use for ranking a web page. In Screaming Frog, the Meta Keywords tab essentially outlines what the keywords tag is for each page (Figure 2.15). Remember, it's not important to have a keywords tag from an SEO standpoint, but it's still a best practice to include one. Try to have one for each page, whenever possible.

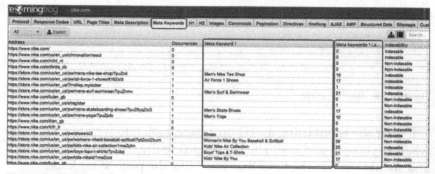

Figure 2.15: Meta Keywords tab

H1 Tab

The H1 tab indicates whether a head tag or an H1 tag is being used on the page. Every page should be using an H1 tag, since it's a key area where search engines look to determine what the page is about. The tag is important too from a website visitor's standpoint because it's usually displayed on the page as the page header (Figure 2.16).

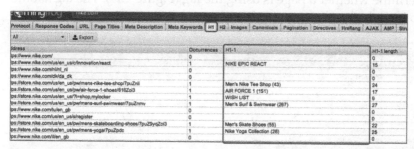

Figure 2.16: H1 tab

Figure 2.17 shows an example of a page header (h1 tag).

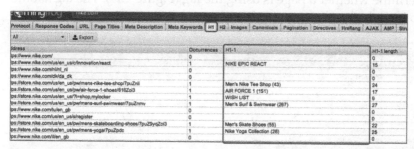

Figure 2.17: Nike H1

Figure 2.18 shows the HTML code where the H1 is.

```
<div data-component-container="true" class="
<header class="nike-cq-title-component">
<h1>NIKE EPIC REACT</h1>
</header>
</div>
```

Figure 2.18: Nike H1 code

If your site is not using an H1 on a page, look into why to determine whether you can add one. The tag doesn't really have a character limit and should include the term that you'd like the page to rank for.

H2 Tab

While not as valuable as the H1 tag, the H2 is another page header tag search engines look at when determining what to rank a page for. Most sites fail to use H2 tags because they are already using an H1 tag and they might think it's unnecessary or they don't have enough copy on the page that's relevant. Look for the H2-1 column in Screaming Frog to determine whether a page is using the tag (Figure 2.19). The tag should also include the phrase you'd like the page to rank for.

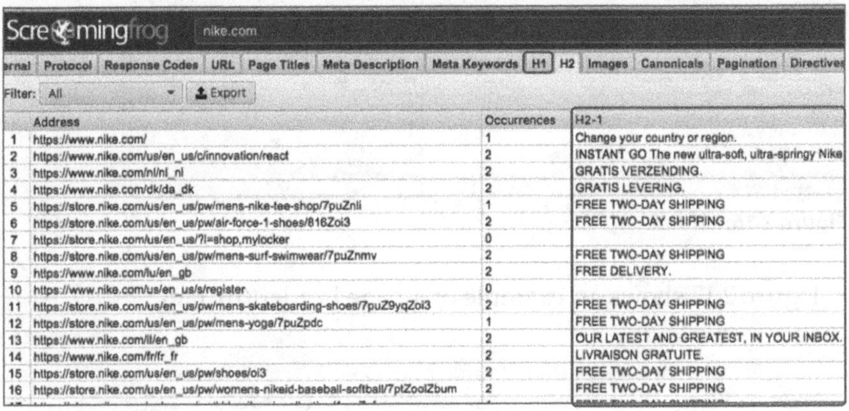
Scre mingfrog
nike.com
ernal
Protocol
Response Codes
URL
Page Titles
Meta Description
Meta Keywords
H1
H2
Images
Canonicals
Pagination
Directives
Filter: All
Export
Address
Occurrences
H2-1
1 https://www.nike.com/ 1 Change your country or region.
2 https://www.nike.com/us/en_us/c/innovation/react 2 INSTANT GO The new ultra-soft, ultra-springy Nike
3 https://www.nike.com/nl/nl_nl 2 GRATIS VERZENDING.
4 https://www.nike.com/dk/da_dk 2 GRATIS LEVERING.
5 https://store.nike.com/us/en_us/pw/mens-nike-tee-shop/7puZnli 1 FREE TWO-DAY SHIPPING
6 https://store.nike.com/us/en_us/pw/air-force-1-shoes/816Zoi3 2 FREE TWO-DAY SHIPPING
7 https://store.nike.com/us/en_us/?l=shop,mylocker 0
8 https://store.nike.com/us/en_us/pw/mens-surf-swimwear/7puZnmv 2 FREE TWO-DAY SHIPPING
9 https://www.nike.com/lu/en_gb 2 FREE DELIVERY.
10 https://www.nike.com/us/en_us/s/register 0
11 https://store.nike.com/us/en_us/pw/mens-skateboarding-shoes/7puZ9yqZoi3 2 FREE TWO-DAY SHIPPING
12 https://store.nike.com/us/en_us/pw/mens-yoga/7puZpdc 1 FREE TWO-DAY SHIPPING
13 https://www.nike.com/il/en_gb 2 OUR LATEST AND GREATEST, IN YOUR INBOX.
14 https://www.nike.com/fr/fr_fr 2 LIVRAISON GRATUITE.
15 https://store.nike.com/us/en_us/pw/shoes/oi3 2 FREE TWO-DAY SHIPPING
16 https://store.nike.com/us/en_us/pw/womens-nikeid-baseball-softball/7ptZoolZbum 2 FREE TWO-DAY SHIPPING

Figure 2.19: H2 tab

In the page shown in Figure 2.20, the "Tiger Woods" link was marked as an H2. You can see this in the HTML code shown in Figure 2.21.

Figure 2.20: Nike H2

```
         <h2 class="nike-cq-subtitle-headline nike-cq-subtitle-headline-level-
2 nike-cq-subtitle-styled-header"><span class="nike-cq-subtitle-line-1 nike-cq-
title-line nike-cq-line1 nsg-text--dark-grey nike-cq-font16px nike-cq-nospacing
nsg-font-family--base">Tiger Woods</span></h2>
```

Figure 2.21: Nike H2 code

Directives Tab

The Directives tab has one column that is important to SEO, the Meta Robots 1 column, which indicates whether a web page has a noindex tag (Figure 2.22). This tag essentially tells search engines to not rank the page at all in the search engine results. If you see a page in a Screaming Frog column that says "no index," make sure you want it to not be ranking, because it's likely not. If you want it to rank, edit the tag by removing the "no" so that it says "index."

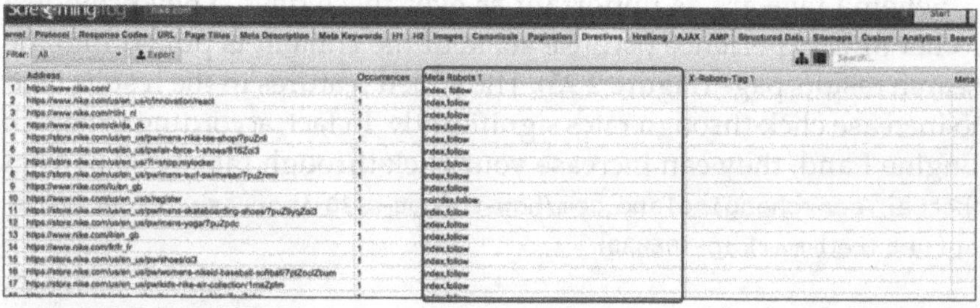

Figure 2.22: Directives tab

After using Screaming Frog for the previous basic checks, it's important to view the HTML of your website for specific opportunities that require a manual view of the code (Figure 2.23). These consist of checking for schema.org tag opportunities, language and country designations, and sitemap.xml files.

```
<meta http-equiv="X-UA-Compatible" content="IE=edge" />
<meta name="viewport" content="width=device-width, initial-s
<meta name="robots" content="noindex,follow" />
<meta http-equiv="content-language" content="en">
```

Figure 2.23: Robots tag indicating to not rank the page

Schema.org Tags

Schema tags are advanced HTML tags that provide additional details for search engines and users. They offer a way to communicate to search engines what type of page you have. Some examples are "product page," "recipes," or "review" pages (Figure 2.24). For the most part, these tags require a basic tag element to be implemented on each respective page.

```
<div class="clear"></div>
        <ol class="rankings_list" id="rankings-list">
<!--product -->
        <li class="row shoe_list rp no_prices "
        data-match="1" itemprop="itemListElement" itemscope itemtype="http://schema.org/Product"
    >
        <div>
            <meta itemprop="url" content="https://runrepeat.com/nike-air-zoom-pegasus-35">
            <meta itemprop="brand" content="Nike">
                    <div itemprop="AggregateRating" itemscope="" itemtype="http://schema.org/AggregateRating">
            <meta itemprop="bestRating" content="5"/>
            <meta itemprop="worstRating" content="1"/>
            <meta itemprop="ratingValue" content="4.7"/>
            <meta itemprop="ratingCount"
                    content="1203"/>
        </div>
                    <div itemprop="offers" itemscope></div>
            <span itemprop="description" itemscope itemtype="http://schema.org/Text"></span>
            <a href="https://runrepeat.com/nike-air-zoom-pegasus-35"
```

Figure 2.24: `Schema.org`

Schema tags are as important as ever these days. They provide a richer SEO experience because some of the content is pulled into the search results page (Figure 2.25). The added features in the results tend to increase click-through rates significantly. In fact, according to Search Engine Land, they can increase your click-through rate by 30 percent (https://searchengineland.com/how-to-get-a-30-increase-in-ctr-with-structured-markup-105830).

125 Best Nike Running Shoes (April 2019) | RunRepeat
https://runrepeat.com/ranking/rankings-of-nike-running-shoes ▾
★★★★★ Rating: 4.7 - 1,203 votes
All 125 Nike running shoes ranked by the best – based on reviews from 646 experts & runners. The ultimate list. Updated April 2019!

Figure 2.25: Reviewing the search result

Additionally, `Schema.org` tags are extremely helpful in getting your site to rank for voice search results. It's important that you consider which schema tags need to be used for your website so that the site is set up as well as possible in traditional and voice search engine results.

For a detailed list of the pages and their respective code to use, visit `https://schema.org/docs/schemas.html`.

Language and Country Designations

If you have a website that serves multiple countries and/or languages, it's important that they are set up the best way possible to rank in search results in those countries and languages.

The `hreflang` (`rel="alternate" hreflang="x"`) attribute is an HTML tag on a web page that helps search engines understand which page should be shown to visitors based on their location. Utilizing this attribute is necessary if you're running a multilingual website and would like to help users from other countries find your content in the language that is most appropriate for them.

Be sure that you are using the correct country code to avoid any problems with `hreflang` links. We recommend that you review any `hreflang` tags on your website to ensure you are using the correct ISO 639-1 language code and the correct ISO 3166-1 alpha-2 country code. Click the page on your website aimed for foreign visitors and make sure the tag has a designation. Figure 2.26 shows an example of a website using the `hreflang` attribute on the French version of its website.

```
<!DOCTYPE html>
<!--[if lt IE 7]> <html class="no-js ie ie6 fr_fr"
xmlns="http://www.w3.org/1999/xhtml" xml:lang="fr_fr" lang="fr_fr"
xmlns:fb="http://ogp.me/ns/fb#"> <![endif]-->
<!--[if IE 7]>    <html class="no-js ie ie7 fr_fr"
xmlns="http://www.w3.org/1999/xhtml" xml:lang="fr_fr" lang="fr_fr"
xmlns:fb="http://ogp.me/ns/fb#"> <![endif]-->
<!--[if IE 8]>    <html class="no-js ie ie8 fr_fr"
xmlns="http://www.w3.org/1999/xhtml" xml:lang="fr_fr" lang="fr_fr"
xmlns:fb="http://ogp.me/ns/fb#"> <![endif]-->
<!--[if IE 9]>    <html class="no-js ie9 fr_fr"
xmlns="http://www.w3.org/1999/xhtml" xml:lang="fr_fr" lang="fr_fr"
xmlns:og="http://opengraphprotocol.org/schema/"
xmlns:fb="http://ogp.me/ns/fb#"  ><![endif]-->
<html class="no-js fr_fr" xmlns="http://www.w3.org/1999/xhtml"
xml:lang="fr" lang="fr">
<head>

<script type="text/javascript">(window.NREUM||(NREUM={})).loader con
```

Figure 2.26: `hreflang` attribute

XML Sitemaps

A website should have two forms of a sitemap. First, it should have a standard web page linked at the bottom of the page that provides links to all the pages of the site (Figure 2.27).

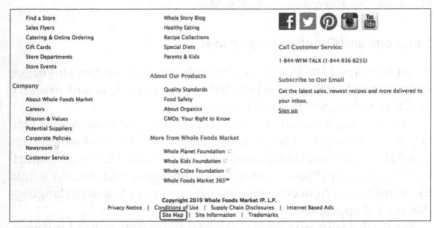

Figure 2.27: HTML sitemap

Also, a sitemap in an XML file is needed. Be sure your website is providing an XML sitemap since search engines reference this when crawling your URLs. It helps provide guidance to the search bots with regard to which URLs you'd like to get scanned and ranked in search engine results. The sitemap is typically located in the root folder and is usually publicly reachable by simply typing your domain (www.abc.com) and attaching sitemap.xml at the end of it (www.abc.com/sitemap.xml).

Figure 2.28 shows an example of the sitemap for Whole Foods.

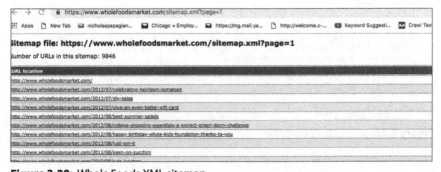

Figure 2.28: Whole Foods XML sitemap

Be sure your website uses a sitemap that lists all the URLs of your website to ensure their visibility in search engine results.

robots.txt File

The robots.txt file is the first page search engine bots visit when crawling your website. The file is a simple text file that resides in the root folder. To examine the one for your site, type your domain and add /robots .txt at the end of it, for example (abc.com/robots.txt).

This file allows you to prevent some URLS from getting crawled and indexed. For the most part, unless you want specific URLs crawled, your robots.txt file should look like this, which allows *all* web crawlers access to all content:

User-agent: *

Disallow:

If you would like to block URLs from a section of your website (this sometimes happens for various reasons), you can use this language in it:

User-agent:*

Disallow: /*subfolder you want blocked*/

As part of your audit, check your robots.txt file to take note of any pages being blocked by simply typing your URL and robots.txt after that. Verify you'd like these pages blocked from ranking in search engine results. Figure 2.29 shows an example of a comprehensive robots.txt file that's blocking many different subdirectories on Wholefoods.com.

Image Filenames and alt Tags

The alt attributes within img tags are referenced by search engines to understand what your image is about. It's essentially the text that goes after the alt= in an image tag that's right next to each image in the HTML code.

If you neglect alt attributes, you may reduce your ranking in image results and regular search results. Not using the image alt attribute is also a failure for visually impaired users who depend on the image results. Be sure your site is using alt tags for each image and the text explains what the image is about.

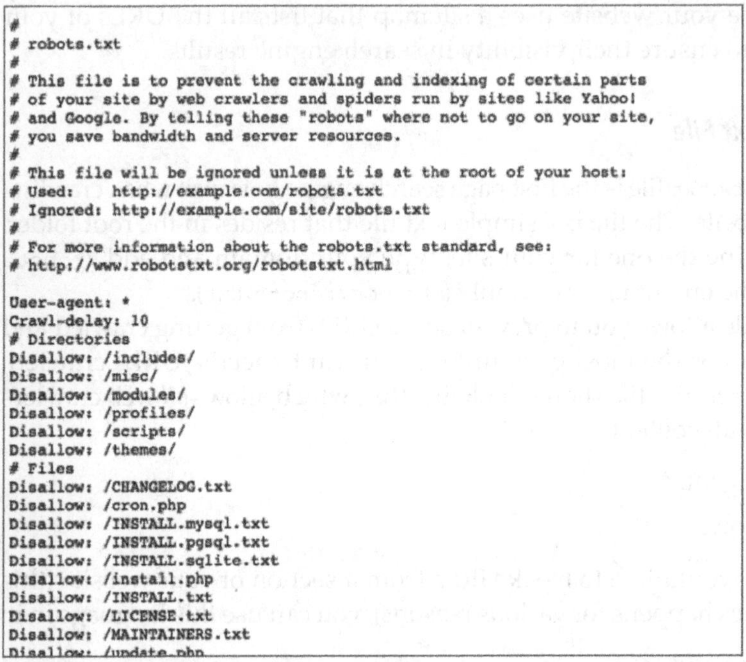

```
#
# robots.txt
#
# This file is to prevent the crawling and indexing of certain parts
# of your site by web crawlers and spiders run by sites like Yahoo!
# and Google. By telling these "robots" where not to go on your site,
# you save bandwidth and server resources.
#
# This file will be ignored unless it is at the root of your host:
# Used:    http://example.com/robots.txt
# Ignored: http://example.com/site/robots.txt
#
# For more information about the robots.txt standard, see:
# http://www.robotstxt.org/robotstxt.html

User-agent: *
Crawl-delay: 10
# Directories
Disallow: /includes/
Disallow: /misc/
Disallow: /modules/
Disallow: /profiles/
Disallow: /scripts/
Disallow: /themes/
# Files
Disallow: /CHANGELOG.txt
Disallow: /cron.php
Disallow: /INSTALL.mysql.txt
Disallow: /INSTALL.pgsql.txt
Disallow: /INSTALL.sqlite.txt
Disallow: /install.php
Disallow: /INSTALL.txt
Disallow: /LICENSE.txt
Disallow: /MAINTAINERS.txt
Disallow: /update.php
```

Figure 2.29: `robots.txt` file blocking

Also, be sure to include the search term you'd like to rank for in the name of the image file. So, if you want the image to rank for ABC Company's logo searches, be sure to include that in the filename. Here's an example of a file that's optimized with alt tags and filename to rank for *ABC company logo* searches:

```
<img src="abclogo.jpg" alt="ABC Company's logo">
```

These are the key areas to examine in your website audit. It's important to review each line of these to ensure you are utilizing these elements correctly and that the technology of your website is up to par for search engine rankings.

Step 2: Improve Conversions

Whether it's a sale, an email submission, or a call to your business link, a conversion can come in many forms. Follow these steps to ensure the most conversions and the best possible return on investment.

Having Effective Site Navigation for SEO

One of the most important areas of a website is the navigation element. The navigation summarizes, organizes, and provides the hierarchy of a website's content. It's one of the first areas a user sees when they reach your website, and it's typically part of the main website template and visible on every page of your website. The better this is organized, the better the user experience. A better user experience usually means more sales.

It's also important to know that search engines reference your navigation when populating the sublinks of your result for your brand terms (Figure 2.30). Creating an optimal navigation that provides great page categorization and organization will help you garner more traffic and engagement with your site.

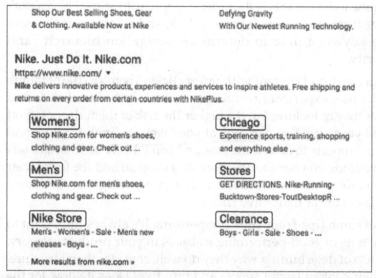

Figure 2.30: Nike navigation

There are some key practices to consider when determining the navigation of your website.

- **Keep the top-level structure simple and intuitive:** Think about the user first coming to the website. Ask yourself, what are their possible needs? What are the various sections of content they may be looking for? Start from the top level and keep the navigation to the topmost popular/content categories. If you are selling shoes, consider dividing up the shoes by the key categories, men's shoes, women's shoes, kid's shoes, etc., and then drive users down from there.

- **Use search data to determine terms to use and which pages to include:** Use a keyword tool to determine which terms to use in the copy of your navigation. For instance, if you had a shoe website, pull together a list of the top related searches in the shoe category and around your brand. Go line by line to see which terms have the most search frequency or volume to prioritize navigation choices. If the term *men's shoes* has more search volume, be sure to put that ahead of *kid's shoes* in your navigation. Start your navigation priority from the top or left side of the page, and go with the terms that have the most searches first. So, for the top categories, if search volume indicates this is the order of popularity, start with *women's shoes*, have *men's shoes* as the next link, and *kid's shoes* as the next. Use keyword data to determine navigation hierarchy and priority.

- **Help users find content with fewer clicks:** There's a rule of thumb in the user experience world: the more a user has to click to find what they're looking for, the higher the risk of them dropping off from your site. You can look at your website analytics tool and funnel reports to determine this, and you'll likely see that as users move along on your site, the more they drop off and the fewer their visits. Keep that in mind when designing navigation and keep things to fewer than three clicks.

- **Take some tips from your competitors:** It's always important to take note of good-performing websites in your product category. On top of determining why they do well, consider their structure. Is their content layout simple and intuitive? Does it allow for the user to find their content relatively easily?

- **Use breadcrumb navigation:** Breadcrumbs are small subnavigation elements that are visible on each page of your site. They are an added feature to a good user experience and offer a subtle way to help the user navigate through your site. They also offer direct SEO benefits since they help build keyword relevance. This is why the most popular websites use them, particularly ecommerce sites. Be sure to use them on your site and use the same terms that are in your other navigation links to keep things simple and consistent for the user. Figure 2.31 shows an example of Amazon using breadcrumbs.

Figure 2.31: Amazon breadcrumbs

■ **Use a website search widget:** Website search features a variety of uses, one of them being user experience. It enables a user to input exactly what they're looking for and enhances the user experience. This is critical, especially for ecommerce sites, which need to leverage every visit as a potential sale (Figure 2.32).

Figure 2.32: Nike search widget

Keyword Research

Keyword research is a critical task that provides information, which can be utilized for your website content and for other content ideas, outside of your website. There are many keyword tools available, and if you subscribe to an SEO program platform like SEMrush, BrightEdge, and Ahrefs, you likely have a keyword research tool available. The process should be pretty similar regardless of the tool. For our example, we will use the Google Keyword Planner tool. This tool is traditionally a keyword information tool for running pay-per-click ads or paid search ads; it's free to anyone who has set up a Google AdWords account. Here's how it works:

1. Once you set up a Google AdWords account and log in, click the Tools button on the top right of the page and access the Keyword Planner tool in the top navigation on the Planning tab (Figure 2.33).

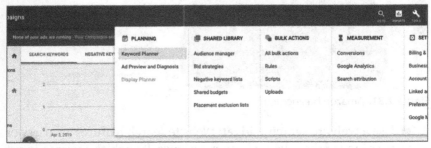

Figure 2.33: Keyword Planner tool

2. Click Get Search Volume And Forecasts (Figure 2.34).

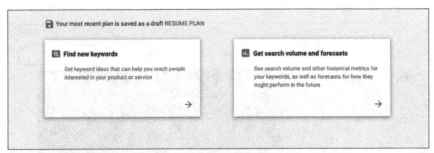

Figure 2.34: Getting the search volume and forecasts

3. Input the types of keywords or topics you'd like to find data about. Then click Get Started (Figure 2.35).

4. Click the top-left Keyword Ideas button, type in the topic you'd like to find data about, and click Get Results. In this example, I entered **running shoes** (Figure 2.36).

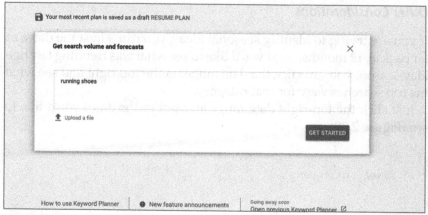

Figure 2.35: Input keywords field

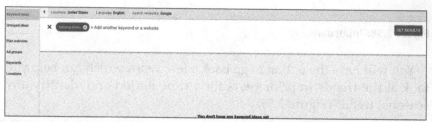

Figure 2.36: Getting results

5. Analyze the data (Figure 2.37). You can see how many searches the keyword topics get on average per month in the Vol. column. Additionally, the competition in the third column for that term (indicative of how many paid search ads are running) can also apply to the number of sites vying to rank for that term organically.

Figure 2.37: Search term data

Other Considerations

If you are trying to identify seasonal ideas, you can adjust the dates as far back as 12 months. So, if you'd like to see what was trending last holiday season, you can click the date range on the top right and see what the top searches were for that category.

Just click the top-right date range and put in the dates you'd like to see (Figure 2.38).

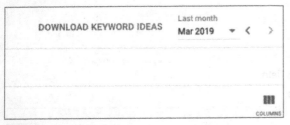

Figure 2.38: Input date

You will have the option to go back a few years, which can help you look at the trends in prior years for a time period and identify any seasonal trends (Figure 2.39).

Figure 2.39: Input data range

Location Targeting

If you are looking for information in a specific market, you can edit the location at the top left to find specific keyword topics for a city or metro area (Figure 2.40).

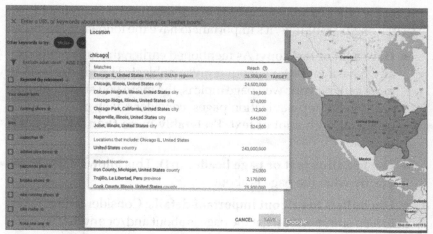

Figure 2.40: Specifying a location field

Optimal Web Page Layout

An optimal page layout can mean different things depending on your goals. If you are not concerned with ranking on search engine results, which I would argue goes against your best interests, you should design solely to move a user to a sale. The Nielsen Norman Group did a study several years back that indicates users tend to consume content from the top left outward (Figure 2.41). Keep that in mind when building content, since the most important areas of the page are in those areas.

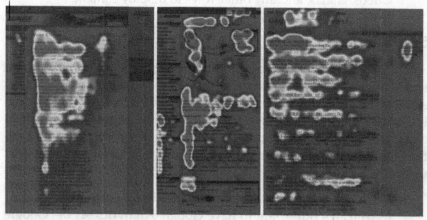

Figure 2.41: Content consumption study visual
Nielsen, Jakob. *F-Shaped Pattern For Reading Web Content (original study)*. (April 16, 2006). Retrieved from: https://www.nngroup.com/articles/f-shaped-pattern-reading-web-content-discovered/

If, on the other hand, your goal is mainly focused on ranking higher in search engine rankings, it's important to have the following attributes:

■ **Have a lot of text copy:** As mentioned earlier, the top results usually have a lot of text about a given subject. The higher level or more general your web page topic is, the more you should plan on writing. For top navigation pages, consider a web page template or layout with a lot of text. Preferably more than 500 words if possible.

■ **Use headline text or page header (h1):** This allows users to see exactly what the page is about.

■ **Use bullets to call out important details**: Consider using bullets to help summarize what the page is about and/or any key features. This will allow you to call out important points to the user.

■ **Use a responsive design**: When mobile visits and website traffic have surpassed desktop devices, be sure to create a web page that loads quickly on mobile devices. Longer load times can result in worse performance, as mentioned earlier.

■ **Include social sharing buttons:** This will help users share content and encourages more views of your web page.

■ **Use images and other content types:** Depending on the focus of the page, it's important to offer different types of content that can make the page more visually attractive. Consider adding images, videos, charts, and any other ways to display content.

Strong Analytics

Analytics are the backbone of your SEO and content programs. Without sound analytics, you will not perform as well as possible. From an SEO standpoint, analytics can mean many things. There are two key analytics tools that should always be installed and regularly monitored either directly through the interface or through a compiled report via the SEO expert and analytics teams. Be sure to have the following set up on your site:

■ **Google Analytics or other website analytics programs:** For your website, it's important to have Google Analytics set up. Google Analytics provides a user-friendly navigation structure. Look at the different channel reports to drill down to SEO channel data where you can drill further down into landing pages and specific performance data for that page (Figure 2.42). If you have a sales page or other important transaction pages, from here you can pull how many visits are coming from SEO and other channels.

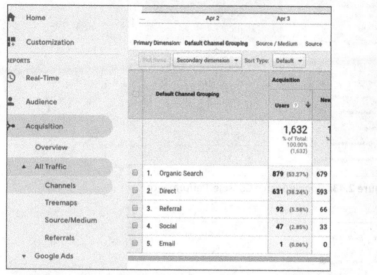

Figure 2.42: Google Analytics

- **Google Search Console:** Search Console is another type of analytics tool that Google offers for free, mainly for website managers (and SEO teams) to install and use. It's often overlooked by marketers, but it should be installed and used because it offers many important features to your website program. It even allows you to communicate with Google to an extent. These are the key features of Search Console to look at once you have it installed:

  - **Performance tab information:** This tab allows you to view the total clicks in any time period you'd like, impressions, average click-through rate, and average position for all rankings of your website (Figure 2.43). These are important to view regularly and can provide a great window into how you are doing from a search engine standpoint.

  - **Sitemaps feature:** This feature is critical and allows you to add a new XML sitemap file (discussed earlier) and to see whether your sitemap file is successfully read (Figure 2.44). This is critical to make sure your pages get crawled by search engine bots and ensures your web page's ranking.

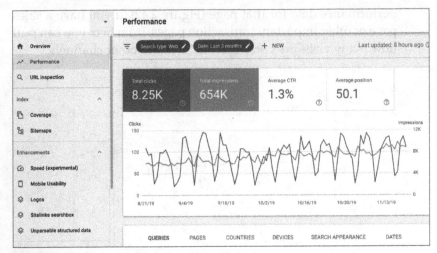

Figure 2.43: Google Search Console, Performance

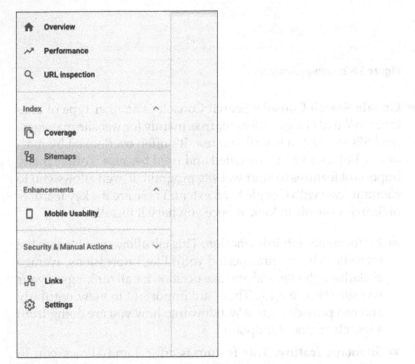

Figure 2.44: Google Search Console, Sitemaps

■ **Links tab:** The Links tab provides insights into how many links are pointing to your website, what pages are the most linked, and what sites are linking to you the most (Figure 2.45). It's important to stay in tune with these key areas because a link's quality and numbers can have a detrimental effect on your search engine rankings.

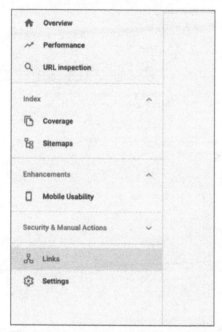

Figure 2.45: Google Search Console, Links tab

If you are seeing links come from low-quality sites or getting warning messages in your Search Console inbox, Google provides a link disavow tool here as well, which enables you to tell Google to ignore the links from these poor-quality sites. Once logged into Search Console, visit www.google.com/webmasters/tools/disavow-links-main to upload a text file that includes details of the sites you'd like disavowed (Figure 2.46).

Your SEO expert should be tasked with doing this, and uploading the file, but for learning purposes, I have provided a sample link disavow text file in Figure 2.47.

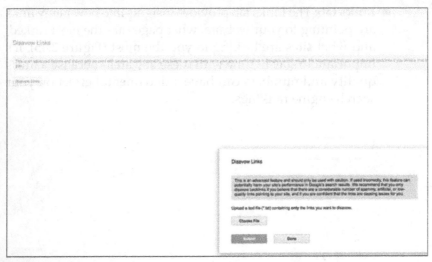

Figure 2.46: Disavow Links dialog

```
# domains
domain:www.earth.shopping
domain:www.airbnb.com.bo
domain:advertisewebpages.com
domain:web.diamonds
domain:advertising.clothing
domain:advertise-estate.com
domain:the-globe.today
domain:dolcevita.over-blog.com
domain:globe.market
domain:local.tourmake.al
domain:theearth.tv
domain:internets.shopping
domain:advertise.enterprises
domain:elsalvadornegocios.com
domain:www.theworld.money
domain:www.advertisewebpage.net
domain:advertise-internet.com
domain:advertise.center
domain:seek.rocks
domain:www.airbnb.com.hn
domain:theglobe.clothing
```

Figure 2.47: Disavow links file example

SEO Key Performance Indicator Metrics

Analytics are a critical part of your success, and there are several to monitor for a successful SEO and content program. You should be monitoring these at least every month, if not more. Also, trend these each time period to see whether they are increasing or decreasing each reporting period. Several reporting periods that indicate decreased performance should be addressed by re-auditing your website and content and overall marketing strategies as these can also affect your general brand searches and direct traffic to your site. Work with your SEO expert to help diagnose where the issues are coming from. For now, here are some good KPI metrics to monitor:

In Google Analytics and Most Website Platforms

- **Organic/SEO traffic:** This report shows what your SEO traffic was for a time period. It's important to watch trends happening with this. Look as far back to the same time period as last year and see whether there are any seasonality trends or increases/decreases from year to year. If you are adding content to your site and fixing SEO issues identified in the audit phase outlined earlier, you should see some increases in traffic from the prior year or time period.

- **Conversions:** Conversions can take many shapes. They can be sales, orders, visits to find a location page, or submitting or signing up for an email. Work with your analytics resource or decide for yourself what the most important user actions are for your site. Maybe it's a visit to a page, or maybe you need to configure the ecommerce function on Google Analytics to report sales and transactions. Regardless of what it is, be sure to figure out how to pull that information from Google Analytics. Your end goal is to increase traffic and conversions.

- **Engagement:** You can see how long website visitors stayed on your site or individual web pages and how many other pages they clicked through to discover content on your site. Almost all analytics tools report on engagement in some way. In Google Analytics, this data is available in the Behavior ➪ Site Content ➪ Landing page report (Figure 2.48). These KPIs are called Bounce Rate, Pages/Session, and Average Session Duration. You want a lower bounce rate because that indicates what percentage of visitors immediately left your page before it even loaded (less than zero seconds). The higher the duration and pages per session numbers are, the better. A good bounce rate, higher number of pages per session, and session duration indicate a better site experience and more engaged users. Figure 2.48 shows the reporting data.

Behavior		
Bounce Rate ⓘ	**Pages / Session** ⓘ	**Avg. Session Duration** ⓘ
77.35% Avg for View: 77.35% (0.00%)	**1.17** Avg for View: 1.17 (0.00%)	**00:00:43** Avg for View: 00:00:43 (0.00%)
77.25%	1.18	00:00:48

Figure 2.48: Google Analytics engagement data

In Google Search Console

- **Organic impressions:** Organic impressions data that is summarized in the Performance report can be extremely valuable (Figure 2.49). It basically indicates how many times your website was shown in organic search results (not clicked). This can be an extremely important indicator of website SEO health and of whether there are any new issues resulting in fewer search engine rankings. Be sure to monitor this closely, since this is likely tied to overall website traffic.

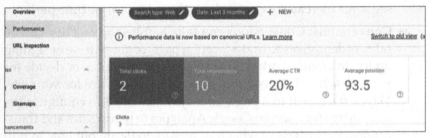

Figure 2.49: Google Search Console impression data

- **Organic click-through rate:** Click-through rate is important to monitor because it demonstrates what percentage of users clicked each of your search result positions. With improved title tags and meta descriptions and URLs, your search engine result will be cleaner and have better messaging, likely increasing your click-through rate.

- **Valid pages indexed:** This report is available in the "Coverage" section of Google Search Console and shows how many valid website pages are getting indexed or ranking in Google search results (Figure 2.50). It's important to keep the number flat or trending up. A decrease in valid pages loaded can indicate pages getting blocked or not crawled, resulting in fewer search engine rankings.

- **Link report:** As we mentioned, the number and quality of the links pointing to your site is one-third of the SEO equation. You need numerous, high-quality links to rank for important searches. Ideally links should be increasing each month as you employ link building and content promotion tactics. This will benefit your site and increase your search engine results. It's important to monitor and trend how many links are pointing to your site and where they're coming from (Figure 2.51).

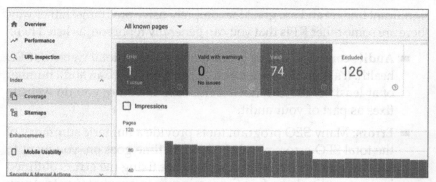

Figure 2.50: Valid pages' indexed data

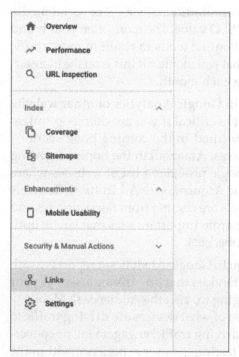

Figure 2.51: Link data

Other Data Sources

There are other data sources to consider monitoring, too, if you or your SEO expert are using an SEO program management tool, like SEMrush (my recommendation). These tools have significant price differences. In my opinion, the best low-cost one is SEMrush. In the higher-priced range, there are Brightedge, Conductor, and some others that require a significant budget and are great for comprehensive programs. Either way, there are some other KPIs that you can generally report on, as listed here:

- **Audit score:** Audit score is a summary of your total website's SEO health. It's typically a scale of 100. You want to see an audit number of at least 70/100 and have it increase the more you do website fixes as part of your audit.

- **Errors:** Many SEO program tools provide a numeric summary of the total SEO errors a website has. As time goes on, you want to see this number decrease since you are fixing the errors outlined in your audit phase (via Screaming Frog or whatever tool you might use).

- **Mentions:** Brand mentions are traditionally a PR or social media metric but are now proving SEO value. The more often your brand and website are mentioned online tends to result in more traffic and links, so it's important that you monitor if this is on the increase. Ideally, it will be increasing each month.

- **Referral report (available in Google Analytics or other website analytic tools):** This report is critical if you are doing optimizations on other websites outlined in the coming book sections (YouTube, blogs, press releases, Amazon) in the hopes of getting traffic back to your site. Google provides a list of websites where users are clicking from in the Acquisition ⇨ All Traffic ⇨ Referrals report. Trend how many visits are coming from referring sites and list individual traffic trends from important sites that you're optimizing (for example, YouTube, etc.).

- **Device or operating system:** In Google Analytics, a report is available that provides a list of devices that are driving users to your site (Figure 2.52). Upon logging in, visit the Audience ⇨ Mobile ⇨ Devices report to get an idea of what devices are driving traffic to your site. If a device is not driving traffic, engagement, or conversions, you should consider testing the user experience within the device to see whether there's an issue.

Reporting on these metrics often is important. Typically, I recommend pulling these KPIs into a trended report at least on a monthly basis. I've seen some sites do a report every week or every quarter. It's up to you and your expectations and goals for SEO. The higher the expectations, the higher frequency of reporting you should consider.

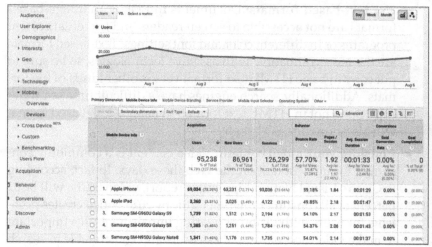

Figure 2.52: Google Analytics Device report

Step 3: Consider Accessibility: SEO Design Considerations

Having an accessible site is still important for users with disabilities and SEO. There's some overlap in providing content effectively for users that also allows for search engine bots to crawl and index content effectively. What's great is that if you use the recommendations in this book, some of the key areas of accessibility are covered.

Focusing on accessibility is important because the Internet has significantly evolved in the way people consume and seek content. Content should appeal to all users and website visitors. Google seems to agree; in fact, following some of its recommendations tends to equate to more and better search engine rankings. Here are the key areas outlined by ADA.gov that promote good SEO and accessibility on websites:

- **Use descriptive image tags:** As we outlined earlier, image alt tags provide an area to input copy explaining what the image is about. This benefits your site by explaining to search engines what the image is about and what to rank it for. Additionally, screen readers or refreshable Braille displays that are used by visually impaired visitors rely on alt text. Also, consider using the longdesc= tag for more complex images that require a longer description.

- **Use text-based formats:** Documents in PDF or in image-based formats are not accessible to screen readers and text enlargement programs or in different color and font settings. Text-based formats are the most compatible with assistive technologies, so be sure to put copy in basic HTML text format versus other kinds of file formats. Additionally, search engines have a difficult time scanning copy that's not in HTML text format, so using a text-based format will also provide SEO benefits.

- **Consider your video content:** Video content is a commonly consumed form of content on the Web these days. In fact, according to Cisco's Visual Networking Index report, video traffic will be 82 percent of all consumer Internet traffic by 2020. Video creates problems for users with vision or hearing impairments. It's important to make video accessible to these users and consumable to search engines, which also have a difficult time consuming content that's within a video. Consider adding audio descriptions of image changes (changes in setting, gestures, and other details) for visually impaired users and provide text captions for users with hearing impairments. Also consider adding the transcript of the video in the description or in the HTML text.

- **Use SEO tags:** HTML tags that are commonly used for search engine optimization also benefits accessibility. Providing concise and complete title, meta descriptions, header, and `schema.org` tags, as outlined earlier, help search engine bots as well as readers and other assistive technologies.

- **Use a website sitemap:** Be sure to use a sitemap in case your navigation is too difficult for readers to pick up. This will provide an alternative way for readers pick up all the pages of your website.

- **Other considerations to improve accessibility:** Accessibility can affect the overall user experience, which can affect SEO performance in the long term. Be sure to consider these additional tactics to make your site even more accessible:

  - Include a telephone number, chat, or email for visitors to request more information in an accessible manner.
  - Conduct periodic testing with disability groups to provide feedback on any content readability issues.
  - Make sure your website is designed to be displayed using the color and font of settings of a visitor's browsers and operating system to cater to the needs of visitors who need enhanced visuals.

Step 4: Set Up a Good Site Architecture

When setting up a website architecture, there are key rules to consider for user experience and SEO success. It's important to follow these core principles when kicking off design discussions for your website and web page templates. A website and web page should be

- **Easy to discover:** Make content and web pages easy to find through clear navigation that requires as few clicks as possible to find desired content and good search engine optimization, which links users directly to the most relevant content.

- **Relevant to a user's needs:** Consider the user's intent and needs. In addition to standard product content, build content that answers common questions around your brand and product category. Consider what kind of content is likely needed for each stage of the conversion funnel.

- **Easy to share**: Share ability is an extremely important facet of good architecture for a few reasons.

  - It can help garner more views and links.

  - It can reach users who aren't coming to your site or haven't been there before, which can build awareness and help other marketing tactics (retargeting, etc.).

- **Device agnostic:** Designs should be mobile device–centered and should also be optimal for other platforms to consume content. The list of devices that users are using to reach your site has grown from traditional desktop devices to mobile phones, tablets, and even smart TVs. As time goes on, be sure to create a design that's responsive to different screen sizes and platforms.

- **Easy to change:** Social media and search engine keywords provide for almost real-time feedback on your brand and product category. It's important to build templates that are flexible and easy to modify, should content needs and types change.

- **Enabled with an SEO-friendly content management system:** Have a content management system or website platform that follows the following SEO best practices and standards:

  - **Supports mobile friendliness:** We're in a mobile-centered world, and a modern-day CMS must provide flexibility for multiple devices.

- **Supports canonical tag on all pages:** This reduces the risk of duplicate content.

- **Allows for custom 301 redirects:** This provides the ability to redirect SEO value from old pages to new ones.

- **Has SEO-friendly and custom URL structures:** Page URLs are able to be customized on a per-page basis and use page-relevant/targeted search phrases separated by hyphens (-) to give you the ability to create URLs that offer the best chance of ranking high on search engines.

- **Supports a custom robots.txt file:** This allows you to block certain folders and pages from getting indexed ranked in search results, in case you need it.

- **Has automated XML sitemap creation:** For sites that add or remove pages frequency, this allows for automatically updating which pages get listed on the URLs/pages provided to search engines.

- **Allows for plain HTML text navigation rendered in plain HTML text:** This makes sure that search engines can follow and crawl through navigation links.

- **Has title, description, and header tags that are customizable on a per-page basis:** This allows for SEO teams to go in and implement the most optimal tags for the web page.

- **Supports ability to create content pages "outside" of ecommerce/retail category and product pages:** This is useful for creating specialized landing pages for SEO and other channels to use.

- **Supports a custom 404 page (autogenerated but "friendly" is OK):** Instead of a broken plain page, this allows you to create a custom page that offers a friendly error message and your global navigation and/or links so users don't hit a dead end and leave your website.

- **Supports separate location pages:** Having location pages that are able to be indexed at the individual store-level (for multiple physical store locations) allows for greater exposure and listings in local search results.

- **Caters to more than one location or language (if applicable to your business):** This is in case you are creating a website or web pages that target different languages and/or countries.

- **Accommodates custom `Schema.org` tags (structured data) that result in richer search snippets:** This is increasingly more critical for ranking voice search results and also provides for a richer/visual search experience for users.

- **Is set up for quick page speed:** This is absolutely critical to ranking high on search results and offering a great mobile user experience. Some CMSs allow for the automatic creation of accelerated mobile pages (AMPs). These are special versions of web pages explicitly designed for fast loading and ranking in mobile search results.

- **Supports breadcrumbs on e-commerce category, subcategory, and product pages:** Breadcrumbs are a great practice that offer user experience benefits, increase content findability, and offer another link for search engines to crawl and index content.

- **Supports product ratings and reviews (or at least inclusion of a third-party rating/review system):** Ratings are critical if you offer product pages on your website, so be sure your CMS offers a way to integrate outside product rating systems and/or offers product rating features. Additionally, product ratings should be able to utilize `Schema.org` tags, which automatically pull ratings into search results.

- **Supports inclusion of social sharing buttons on all pages:** This is extremely important for content pages that encourage social sharing. Sharing promotes content discovery and offers linking benefits, which is good for SEO rankings.

This list of good architecture practices is not exhaustive and will likely change with time, but it's a great start. If you can accommodate each of these when employing new design or technical architecture, you will find your site able to change with the agility that's needed for brands to succeed in today's rapidly changing world.

Here is a list of questions to ask if you aren't ranking for a search phrase:

Website Environment

- Is my page getting crawled and indexed in Google (type the exact URL in Google)?
- Do I have the page URL in the XML file?
- Is the page being blocked in the `robots.txt` file?
- Does the page load too slowly?

- Does the page have many and/or the wrong types of redirects pointing to it?
- Did the URL of the page recently change and/or was it recently taken down?
- Am I using all the correct SEO tags?
- Am I using the right language tags?
- Is the page a duplicate, or are there duplicates of this page?
- Do any pages of my site rank?
- Does the page have any links pointing to it?
- Does my site use HTTPS (versus HTTP)?

Content

- Do I have a dedicated page that mentions that *exact phrase* throughout the copy, URL (close to the root folder), and HTML tags?
- Does my web page have at least 500 words of copy (long form)?
- Is my content original and useful?

Popularity

- Does my web page have a lot of links from other sites pointing to it?
- Do the links from those sites have the phrase that I want to rank for in the anchor text?
- Do I have a lot of toxic, low-quality links pointing to the page and my site in general?
- Is my site new?
- Am I using outside assets to bring awareness of my content?
- Do I have a content promotion strategy?

Creating a New Website or Replacing an Old One

Websites are not only a critical part of your content and SEO marketing strategies; they are a critical part of your own media and overall marketing program. Typically, there are two big causes for creating or replacing a website. If a new brand is launching, creating a website is one of the important first steps in that process. If a brand has been around for a long time and its website has become outdated, particularly from a technical perspective, it makes sense to replace the old website with something new.

There are important actions on the SEO side that marketers must take to reduce risk and ensure good performance when either creating a new website or replacing an old one. When creating a new website, consider the following recommendations:

- **Do your research:** It's critical to understand how a website fits into your marketing strategy and what its role is. Consider doing a competitive analysis and looking at what your competitors are doing from a website perspective and what they are offering users on the content, technological experience, and SEO sides.

- **Understand what the user is looking for and what to provide on your site:** As we'll discuss later, it's important to understand the user journey and your consumer needs when building a website. This information can help inform what users are looking for, how to engage them, and ideally how to convert them. Each of these can be done with the content on your website and the website itself.

- **Follow the latest technical guidelines and search engine best practices:** This should go without saying, but a website that is not search engine friendly or following SEO best practices will not perform well. It's important that early in your planning stage, you build out requirements that inform your website developers what is needed to make your website beneficial and adherent to the latest technical guidelines from search engines, accessibility, and user expectations. When creating a new website, it's important that you focus on these key SEO areas specifically.

- **Have the right words in your domain:** Search engines still look at the key words that are used in a website's URL. So, when choosing a domain, consider opting for one that includes your product category or other important search terms that you want your website to rank for (e.g., abcplumbers.com will help the site rank for *plumbers*).

- **Establish the link value of your new website:** Since Google's algorithm is driven largely by the number and quality of links pointing to your website, a new website can take some time to rank for competitive search phrases. Once your website is live and out of the gate, consider conducting an intensive link-building campaign to build links to your website. The more links you get to your site, the better and quicker or rank for nonbranded searches.

- **Submit your XML sitemap file for crawling:** Once your website is up and live, it's important to notify search engines about it. The first step is to submit your XML sitemap file to the search engines via the Google Search Console and Bing webmaster tools. Set up a free account for each, and you will see the feature that allows you to submit your sitemap for crawling.

- **Follow all the SEO best practices laid out earlier in the chapter:** We have laid out all the current SEO best practices for websites. Be sure to follow each of them and their principles to ensure your website is set up as well as it can be to rank in search results and capture traffic.

- **Set up tracking and reporting tools:** There are two big analytics and data reporting tools that are critical to set up when you're building a new website: Google Analytics (or a similar tool) and Google Search Console. Both tools will provide you with important data about how your website is performing and how it's connecting with users and your audience. You will not know how successful your website is without these tools, and they should be set up immediately.

- **Conduct quality assurance:** Unfortunately, even in this day and age, quality assurance testing is not always performed when websites are rolled live. It's extremely important that you conduct multiple levels of website testing throughout the development of your website. This includes testing in your development environment, in your staging environment, and immediately in your live environment when it goes live.

- **Monitor performance and consider doing periodic website updates:** Once tracking and reporting vehicles are set up, it's important to pool reports at least every month about your website and how it's performing. If performance is not satisfactory, consider conducting an analysis to understand why that's the case. Sometimes technical, content, and SEO fixes can significantly improve performance.

When replacing an old website, consider the following recommendations:

- **Identify which pages are driving the most traffic and ranking the best in organic searches:** This step is critical and can make or break your website redesign. Using either Google Search Console or Google Analytics, list your top-performing URLs from an organic traffic and impression perspective. It's important that these get redirected to their respective new page or URL to ensure that SEO value is immediately passed through to your website so that you do not see a dip.

- **Incorporate SEO in design stages:** When building new navigation, site architecture, landing pages, user research, layouts, templates, content, and features, be sure to include SEO reviews and inputs on each of these. At the end of the day, doing so will result in an SEO- and user-friendly website.

- **Ensure proper tagging:** HTML tagging is critical even when rebuilding a website. Be sure to roll over the tags of high-performing pages to your new website. Also be sure to incorporate the latest schema tags that can help search engines better index your website's content.

- **Set up the right redirects:** As mentioned, identifying your top-performing pages from an organic and even a paid search side is critical to maintaining and carrying over that performance into your new website. Be sure to take the list that you identified earlier and set up 301 permanent redirects immediately after the website is launched. This will prevent your website from seeing a search engine ranking drop.

Bonus: Interview with Website Experience Expert

To get a better idea of how websites and brands are working through challenges today, I've interviewed my friend and former colleague, Christian Dodd, who is an experienced leader at Ford Motor Company. Christian has almost 20 years' experience in the marketing and web industry. The full interview appears next, but here are the key takeaways of the interview:

- Brands need to formalize a website strategy with a clear understanding of the purpose of their website.

- When looking to bring an offline behavior to an online channel, brands must thoroughly understand how consumers are currently performing that action offline.

- Brands need to involve their website developers early on, especially in the design stages to ensure the final product vision is feasible.

- Brands, particularly ones that have been around for a long time, should have a long-term vision of their website needs to prevent any limitations that legacy systems might cause to functionality added later.
- With data privacy now a top priority, brands should look at finding other ways to provide personalized messaging and value.

Here is the interview:

Nick Papagiannis: Thanks for taking time out today from your busy schedule. Can you say what your current role is and the types of experience you've had over the years?

Christian Dodd: I am currently head of experience design for global experiences at Ford Motor Company, specifically the Ford Pass and Lincoln Way mobile apps. But prior to this, I spent the majority of my career in digital marketing advertising design agencies, usually focused on UX [user experience] and digital strategy, with a little bit of time in hardware product design.

NP: Are there any UX best practices brands or users should think about as they're building out a website or even just a content hub?

CD: I think the first thing is being focused on the intent of the site or the contents. It's easy for a company to say we're going to build a website for our company or we're going to build a website for this product or we're going to build a website for this store, but I think if you flip it around and think about why anyone's going to get there, it should be that we're going to answer this question or we're going to sell this thing—really focusing on the action that you hope that the site elicits. So is it a purchase? Is it to answer a question? Is it to reduce call volume? What are you really trying to do? And then as you go through designing, developing that design experience, and making technical decisions, you're really focused on what you're trying to accomplish, not just on creating a thing for its own sake.

The second area that I try to get people to focus on is really about once you've decided what an experience is supposed to do, get an idea of how people actually do that experience today. It's rare that we're doing something totally revolutionary or at least something that doesn't already have an analog in someone's life. Are they shopping for shoes? Are they shopping for a new insurance provider? Are they looking for a financial advisor? Are they shopping for a car? Are they checking on the status of their vehicle? I think that thinking about how people do that today can really help you develop something that matches their current experience.

If you don't really look at how it's happening today, it's easy to get pulled into things that seem novel and fun and exciting or maybe revolutionary. But those things, unfortunately, in my experience, have a lot lower chance of success if they're not grounded in the way someone is doing it right now so that the overall behavior pattern feels comfortable, or right, to the user. They're not having to learn how to do it. So I think reduction in new learning is super key.

Finally, I've lived through a lot of product development methodologies, from what I would consider extreme waterfall to what is called extreme programming and sort of the opposite end of very agile approaches. I'm not a real adherent of any specific methodology, but I can't speak highly enough of working closely with your developers early on as you're working through a concept. Another pitfall that I think people still fall into is developing to a very high degree of fidelity: lots and lots and lots and lots of screen comps or really thinking through what this thing is going to look like before they think through how it works. Even though everything you do might be technically feasible, if you're not working tightly with developers, you might be making relatively arbitrary decisions about how things work that have a real dramatic impact on performance, which translates into a really negative impact on the actual user experience.

So, you could have something that's like really gorgeous with tons of groovy animations and a beautiful video, but it's so slow that no one is ever going to see it because they're going to go to the next site. So, doing that prototyping consistently as you're working through stuff and as you're answering questions, and trying it out to see what the impact is going to be on performance, is going to be super critical. It's also critical to choosing the technology you use to build it, because if you have a general idea of what you want, a developer can help you pick the right backend solution so you're starting on the right foundation.

NP: The next question is more about content and content development. We're going to get into journeys and personas in the next chapter, so I would love for you to just talk about some best practices around creating a journey or creating a persona and some things for brands to think about and ask themselves.

CD: When you're creating a journey or persona, again it's good to think about what you are trying to get out of this. When you start, I definitely live, just like with development methodologies, through different phases of journey and persona development. When I started, personas were really tactical. So, a persona wouldn't be Dave who's 35 years old and lives in the suburbs and has two kids, and here are his hopes and dreams and aspirations. A persona was an administrator or an end user; they were super tactical.

I think that has some benefits. I mean, the intent there was that when you're developing in a very rudimentary way, like for a software developer, when you're developing something that you at least acknowledge all the people who are going to use the system and think about those, the functionality that's going to be required for each of them. At the other end of the spectrum, we did things that were emotional and very focused on really creating this whole person. I would say that while I believe there is value in creating some of that in rounding it out and building some empathy with a person, I don't think that the end document, this persona, particularly if it's just a paper document, is ever really going to do that. So, I like to break personas. It's just you can't really convey empathy through a PowerPoint slide.

So to me, there are two pieces of this. One is figuring out how can I create the personas with the team that's going to develop this project in a way that builds empathy? So, it's less the persona itself that becomes useful, but the act of its creation and the act of going out and meeting real people. So instead of saying, well, we're all going to sit down and we're going to put a PowerPoint slide together, it's, well, let's go meet five people who we think are our target customer. We're going to see how they shop, and we're going to figure out how they do the thing we want them to do so that we can gain that empathy. But it's really about meeting them, not so much the document that comes out the other side.

I think the document that does come up and come out of the other side is more useful when it's more tactical. It's not useful to think, "Hey, by the time you're developing and doing those things, like look at a slide that says the person read *Dwell* instead of *Architectural Digest*." It's not that useful, at least it hasn't been for me.

But it is useful to say, "Here are the top five things based on meeting these people they're really interested in doing." That's a useful ongoing tool.

NP: Does that apply for journeys you're saying as well?

CD: Yeah, I would say journeys are similar in the approach to trying to get that empathy in the real world and then building a document that's useful. I think there are a couple of different watch outs with journeys. With journeys, I think there's a tendency to be comprehensive, so you want to show off all these possible interactions somebody might have with your product and your site or your content. And in doing so, you tend to create something that's pretty artificial, and you also tend to obfuscate the natural priority of things.

So, you end up in a situation where you're like, "Well, they look at this thing and then they talk to their Alexa and they ask it something and then they look at their Apple Watch and then they do this other thing," and somehow then all of a sudden all those things are just as important when really they're going to use their mobile website or maybe the mobile app 20 times or 100 times for every time they're going to use that same thing on the watch. That's not universally true, but it is for a lot of things. But if you're looking at that whole journey like, "Oh, here are the 12 things we absolutely have to do with Apple Watch before we launch," then they become extremely useful. . .

NP: Makes sense.

CD: The important thing to be careful with on journeys is just to really be cognizant of what are the real things, what are the things that somebody is really going to do, and what are the things that they might do or are going to do really infrequently.

NP: In general with design and just websites, we've mentioned some challenges, but are there other challenges that you're seeing friends dealing with today?

CD: Yeah, there are lots of challenges. One challenge, again, depending on sort of the size and age of the brand, is dealing with legacy systems. It doesn't seem like a direct concern, but it definitely is. Again, for that real experienced UX, it might not have a huge effect on the kind of screens you can design and what they look like.

But it can have a huge impact on how they perform. How reliable they are, how fast they are, how I'm able to personalize things. Am I able to? Any of those things.

I work at a big company now that's been around for well over 100 years, so that's definitely an issue we deal with every day, but I think even for small businesses, they may have a legacy system or they may have a system, even a subscription service or a software subscription, that isn't really built for what they want to do on the Web.

It's not something that's easy to fix retroactively. But I think, particularly with small businesses or new businesses, the more you can look at infrastructure type things when you're buying them. For example, you might be buying systems that are going to manage content and if you say, "You know, that might be something that I eventually want to put on a website or in social or mobile or whatever," you need to be sure that you're choosing things that are flexible enough for the future that are using a very standard technology, versus getting something that's unique and unflexible to repurpose. It may be that it sounds like it's perfect to solve your needs today, but if it's super unique and you're the one of 10 people using it, there's a much lower probability that you'll be able to find a developer or find another system that's going to plug into that in the future.

The more you can try to stick with standard technologies and platforms that a lot of people are using on the Web and in social media and in the places where you want to put your content, you'll be a lot better off.

NP: Are there any big tech changes you see affecting user experience/ design in the next few years that brands need to be aware of?

CD: One thing that we deal with here is an increase in digital privacy. So much of what digital marketers have done in the past has been dependent on a relatively free flow of data that allowed pretty good personalization and optimization data to users. And I think we're seeing more and more of those things starting to either shut down or be restricted inside specific platforms like Facebook. Finding ways to get your message out, and get your content out in any sort of personalized way given new privacy requirements, is definitely a challenge.

The other opportunity is autonomous vehicles and autonomous experiences. It's still several years away from any real mass adoption, but it will open up this new place where media and content will be consumed in this sort of new way, or at least in a slightly new context that has a lot of opportunity. You know, there's obviously as many opportunities for pitfalls as there are positive opportunities, but it is definitely something to put into long-term plans and start thinking about for lots of businesses, not just those in the mobility space.

NP: So you're talking autonomy across industries, not just transportation?

CD: Yeah, I spend the most time thinking about autonomy in transportation, but it is happening all over the place, and it's tightly coupled with advances in AI. We have a little bit of this converse of increased privacy with increased capability to do facial recognition answers, and super personalized stuff. So, it's an interesting tension.

Quiz

1. Fill in the blank: A website is _____ for optimal SEO performance

    a. Unnecessary

    b. Critical

    c. Nice to have

    d. Optional

    Answer: b

2. What are the brand benefits to having a website?

    a. Communicates brand story, exchanges information with users, provides monetization, collects data to provide user insight

    b. Communicates brand story, exchanges information with users, addresses a basic marketing tactic, collects data to provide user insight

   c. Gives marketers something to do, helps guide users to brand biased content, collects data on users, provides monetization

   d. Provides content, helps users find what they are looking for, communicates what the brand is about, bypasses privacy obstacles

Answer: a

3. Which of the following should a website NOT be?

   a. Easy to discover

   b. Relevant to user needs

   c. Easy to share

   d. Device agnostic

   e. Updated and optimized only every few years

Answer: d

4. True or False: The response code is a code that is returned by a web server when a website visitor makes a request to access a web page.

Answer: True

5. Fill in the blank: The response code is typically ____ digit(s) and can mean different things.

   a. 1

   b. 2

   c. 3

   d. 4

Answer: c

6. True or False: Good title tags are less than 25 characters.

Answer: False

7. True or False: You should aim to place the targeted search phrases as close as possible in the title tags.

Answer: True

8. Which HTML SEO tag is NOT critical for today's SEO world?

   a. Title tag

   b. Meta description tag

   c. Meta keywords tag

   d. H1 header tag

   Answer: c

9. Which of the following are SEO best practices for structuring URLs?

   a. URLs and their folder structures should include keywords instead of numbers

   b. Use hyphens when separating keywords in URLs

   c. Make sure the term you'd like to target the page to rank for is as close to the "root folder" of the URL, which is the folder closest to the .com

   d. Use HTTPS in your URL structure

   e. All the above

   Answer: e

10. Which is NOT a characteristic of a good, SEO-friendly content management system?

    a. Supports mobile friendliness

    b. Allows for canonical tag on all pages

    c. Allows for custom URL structures

    d. Automates XML sitemap creation

    e. None of the above; all are good characteristics

    Answer: e

What Brands Are Missing to Optimize Organic Traffic

The main reason I decided to write this book is to save brands and marketers time and money. Over the years I've seen many disconnects, underutilization, and lack of integration of SEO and the content creation process, which made brands lose money.

I would broaden that even beyond SEO and content marketing projects. There are many reasons why working programs fail, and they are hard to sum up in one book. In my 20 years of experience, while limited, I've seen many programs not work. Although my book is mostly from an SEO and content point of view, I feel like the post-mortem learnings can apply across marketing disciplines. It can be difficult to see a program fail when you put a lot of effort, time, and thought into it. This is why it's extremely difficult to be a marketer these days. There are many cylinders required to work, and the competition is quicker and the market more saturated than ever. Marketing today requires strong processes, strong communication, thorough research, and flawless execution.

Those brands recently entering the marketing world must understand that they will be held to higher expectations, including a more precise performance reporting and capability, plus endless data to inform programs. The marketing and digital science has evolved quickly and much more comprehensively from yesterday's world. Consumers have higher expectations, more resources, more paths, and more touch voids influencing sales and brand experiences. Unfortunately, many brands are still practicing yesterday's marketing science and processes. Part of this is because of leadership's lack of modern skill set, outdated processes, and uncertainty of where marketing is going.

Being in the marketing world as a marketing expert, we are problem solvers. Today's marketing requires first and foremost a problem-solving mind-set. There are many types of problems that we are seeing today and must resolve. These problems include the following:

- **Poor business sales:** Brands aren't meeting sales goals.

- **Brand and target audience disconnections:** Brands and target audiences are not connecting effectively in the way of expectations, purchase processes, and other areas.

- **Lack of awareness and consideration:** Brands fail to be top of mind during the awareness and consideration phases.

- **Poor processes and process management:** Brands lack the processes needed for effective execution of marketing programs.

- **Stale skill sets:** Team members don't evolve their skill sets and end up with stale skill sets, resulting in a compromised output.

- **Heightened competition:** Competition, especially online, has become extreme. Competitors come in many forms as well. This results in lost business for brands.

- **Endless platforms that users are on:** Whether e-commerce, social media, or content platforms, consumers have seen endless options to satisfy their needs.

- **Poor research and lack of data insights:** Flawed research and data can misdirect brands and compromise marketing strategies.

- **Uninformed creative concepts and campaigns:** It's still quite common for creative strategies and campaigns to build campaigns without solid data.

- **Unoptimized and non-search-friendly content:** Brands are still creating content that's not optimized for search engines and are missing a large and impactful traffic opportunity.

- **Brand and consumer disconnect in the way of content and dialogue:** Brands still fail to understand how to reach and speak to prospects and consumers.
- **Irrelevant and mistargeted content:** Similar to the previous point, brands are failing to provide the right content and content types to users.

These are just some of the issues we are seeing today. There are many more not listed. Brands must conduct a little soul-searching to determine what areas they must focus on in the way of consumers in process. They also must consider what platforms they are active on, from Amazon to blogs to LinkedIn; the list is expanding quickly. They must figure out how to best optimize their presence on these platforms in order to effectively market and connect with their audiences.

Since this book is limited and focused on search engine optimization and content marketing, we will explore the current state and best means to employ those tactics through process, team structure, and outputs or deliverables. It's important to remember that many of the gaps between users and brands can be solved with content and process. Content can effectively become the bridge that connects the gap between user needs and brand needs. It's important that brands utilize these three items when conducting an internal analysis and strategies around their marketing tactics and goals.

Why Brand Initiatives Fail

It's hard to pinpoint why brand marketing programs fail these days. There are a number of reasons and factors. Whenever a marketing campaign or program initiative ends, the team should hold a post-mortem meeting to discuss the learnings and successes of the program. This can help bring to light issues that may have contributed to a compromise or failed program. The post-mortem meeting doesn't happen often, unfortunately, from what I've seen. Particularly in the SEO and content marketing space, post-mortem meetings are rare.

When I got my project manager professional (PMP) certification, it was a little frustrating to see that the other processes and standards that I learned in the PMP process were typically not used in the marketing industry. There are a lot of reasons for this, but lately it's because marketing initiatives tend to move quickly and have budget restrictions that can limit the ideal and nice-to-have practices that are recommended in the project management arena. I have seen many programs fail in and outside the SEO and content world, for a variety of reasons. Some of these reasons include the following:

- **Lack of process and ineffective project management:** Project planning and process planning are poor, so tasks are not completed effectively and in a timely manner, leading to a compromised overall program.

- **Poor data collection and planning:** Data informs strategy, opportunity, performance, optimization opportunities, and project learnings. Compromised data results in ineffective programs.

- **Inadequate skill sets:** Unfortunately, sometimes team members are in roles that they aren't suited for or good at. Skill sets should be strong, and roles should be defined.

- **Too aggressive timelines:** Many projects were due "yesterday" and don't have the adequate time allocation for team members to do a quality and thorough job.

- **Budget restrictions:** Obviously budgets are part of any marketing initiative, but sometimes they can be too small and don't allow for a quality and thorough initiative that results in quality results. You get what you pay for, so if you have high expectations, you need to allocate strong budgets to get the best resources and highest quality output.

- **Bad research or lack of customer and audience understanding:** Data also informs a brand about a target audience and personas. It's important to have statistically significant data and a thorough and certain understanding of your audience, their needs, and what they'll likely respond to.

- **Poor key performance indicator (KPI) choices:** Brands should understand what performance metrics indicate actions that lead to their ideal result. If you are judging or basing a marketing program on poor KPIs, they likely won't indicate or steer a program toward success.

- **Lack of creativity:** In today's world, creative solutions win. This is true across all of marketing and SEO. While basic content and

SEO have their purpose, it's important that brands think deeply and creatively about solutions and content. This helps brands break through the noise and content saturation that exist on the Web and on platforms.

- **Lack of enthusiasm:** Some brands are boring and offer boring products. Many marketers try to avoid working on those kinds of brand projects. It's important to have a team that's enthusiastic and looking to elevate even boring brands. If not, marketing programs will continue to be boring and ineffective.

- **The wrong people making the decisions:** Sometimes there are clients and internal team members who have limited skill sets and expertise but have the clout to make powerful decisions. This can result in poor decisions and hamper creative solutions.

- **Limited knowledge of user platforms:** The list of platforms is expanding exponentially, and users are using many different channels to digest and seek out content and ultimately make purchases. It's important that teams understand the list of platforms that users are on.

- **Lack of understanding the competitive landscape and competitive factors:** Competition has grown exponentially. In the old days, product category leaders just needed to be big spenders to crowd out competition. Nowadays, competition online can come from established companies or smaller companies, which are more numerous. It's important to understand the competitive landscape and who your competitors truly are. Not understanding this can result in the wrong tactics or chasing after the wrong competitors.

- **Not understanding marketing disciplines:** I've seen this firsthand as an SEO expert in my early days in the marketing world. Many marketers tend to focus on just their own expertise and fail to understand the different marketing disciplines and how they work and how to best work with them. This can result in lack of resource involvement, poor processes, and inefficiencies that result in poor performance.

- **Lack of implementation:** Finally, as an SEO expert, I see this across the board and often when it comes to implementing website recommendations. Brands must implement recommendations regardless of tactic; otherwise, performance will be compromised.

The Modern-Day Marketer's Skill Set

Today's consumer universe requires a modern skill set and profile for marketers to possess. There are many areas that marketers have to be knowledgeable about these days and understand the complementary relationship different disciplines have with each other.

For instance, content marketing and SEO should be married and fully integrated to help brands capture the highest return on investment and brand success. For marketers to be successful and effective in today's age, I recommend they possess the following characteristics:

- **Constantly learning:** Technology and platforms are expanding at a fast pace, so a good marketer stays in tune with emerging platforms and how they work.

- **Open minded:** Every client issue requires its own solution. There is no template for problem-solving, since every problem and circumstance is unique. A good marketer is open to new ideas.

- **Process-driven:** Processes evolve and weed out problems and inefficiencies that can eliminate risks and save time.

- **Data-focused:** We are in a data-driven world, so solutions must be data and evidence based. It's no longer a shot in the dark. Data can increase the chance of a successful campaign.

- **Collaborative:** There are many marketing disciplines in this day and age. A good marketer will be able to work across disciplines and understand how they can be leveraged to provide the most effective solutions.

- **Technically savvy:** Technology is changing, but it's important that a good marketer understands the basics of websites, platforms, and programming.

- **Generalists as well as specialists:** Just because a marketer is an expert at SEO or CRM, they should be able to understand creative, planning, and media initiatives, and vice versa.

- **Humble and honest:** Attitude is everything, and it is important to understand that a diverse set of experts and points of view provides better marketing solutions than just one person. A marketer must be humble and honest about their limitations and understand that solutions are typically beyond just their capacity.

- **Content diversified:** As we'll get into it later on in this book, content can mean many things and comes in many forms.

While these lists are long, they aren't all inclusive. Brand and marketing teams should always work to evolve their programs to include post-mortem learnings to understand why certain projects fail and certain ones work.

Why SEO and Content Projects Fail

Over the years I've seen so many disconnects and underutilization of SEO and content creation, which made brands lose money. As an SEO subject-matter expert and enthusiast, it was hard to not take personally so many claims that SEO was bunk science and didn't work; yet when I'd probe, I'd realize the person saying that never implemented all the recommendations their SEO vendor provided. Marketers have to remember that the effort for effective SEO is just about 50/50, client to vendor, unlike the 20/80 paid search or social media split, where you can turn ads on and immediately be running programs pretty easily. SEO requires constant cooperation with IT and ongoing implementation. It's best suited to be an undercurrent of each marketing discipline so that all things work together. SEO is no longer just a website thing; it requires coordination and optimization of all your owned media online and even offline. Figure 3.1 shows an example of what SEO was when I first started.

Figure 3.1: Early SEO scope

Figure 3.2 shows SEO today. The growth in off-site optimization has been exponential. The job has gotten much more difficult and requires a vast knowledge and coordination of resources and executions. It also requires ongoing monitoring of the latest and greatest software and tools on the market to help with optimizations.

From what I've seen, the traditional SEO process is no longer suitable to address each of the areas that are required for wholistic SEO optimization. Additionally, clients still don't understand how absolutely critical it is to implement recommendations. Figure 3.3 shows the typical SEO process that's still being practiced by some teams today.

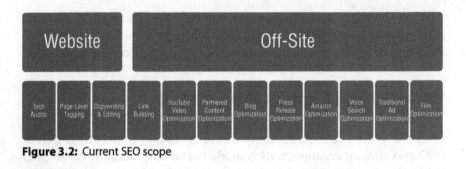

Figure 3.2: Current SEO scope

Figure 3.3: Traditional SEO process

It's extremely website-driven (which is still needed), but it doesn't account for all the nonwebsite optimization opportunities that offer additional ways to boost brand organic performance in the ways of consumer traffic, engagement, and even sales. Furthermore, it does not hold the client accountable for their 50 percent, providing input along the way and implementing all recommendations. Now, not all recommendations can always be implemented. It's the SEO expert's job to articulate which recommendations are the highest priority and can provide the best return on investment. The new SEO process should be much more comprehensive and wholistic and address all website and off-website-brand website assets. Figure 3.4 shows a sample program plan to use for reference.

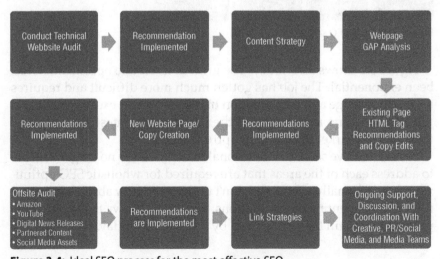

Figure 3.4: Ideal SEO process for the most effective SEO

As you can see, it's much more comprehensive and meant to address all areas of digital marketing and introduces SEO into assets and processes outside the website. Good SEO is used throughout the marketing process and supports and optimizes across content venues. This process is meant to serve as a starting point or reference to executing SEO across venues.

Modern-Day SEO Deliverables and Analysis

As discussed in the previous section, SEO has evolved and grown in complexity, and so have the necessary deliverables. These are the types of deliverables a marketer should compile or receive when running an SEO initiative either yourself or via an SEO partner.

Deliverables for Website Optimization

The following are deliverables for website optimization. These deliverables aim to improve the website from search engine crawling and indexing along with providing more relevance around your targeted search terms.

Technical Audits

An SEO technical audit provides an overview of your website's SEO health by pointing out items that are negatively impacting search engine spiders with corresponding recommended "fixes." A site audit checks for dozens of SEO issues, ranging from surface-level issues such as duplicate content and broken links to technical issues such as HTTPS implementation and other technical attributes. The audit deliverable typically provides a walk-through of each issue, priority level, and possible resolutions.

HTML Tag Optimization

This document or deliverable contains edits to existing HTML metadata. The document will be developed based on search volume estimates and keyword targets defined in an earlier stage. The document can also sometimes provide SEO best practices metadata and also delivered with copy recommendations.

Copy Editing and Optimization

This document will contain edits to existing content (web page copy). It can also provide recommendations on new website content areas and themes that could help build new traffic to a client's site, if you aren't getting a content strategy document. The document can also sometimes provide SEO best practices for writing copy.

Landing Page Design Consultation

Websites oftentimes add new web page templates and landing pages. This deliverable can provide feedback on potential new page layouts to ensure SEO friendliness and adherence.

Analytics Reporting and Monitoring Deliverables

The following are deliverables for analytics reporting and monitoring. These deliverables are critical to help inform the progress of your program, the performance impact of initiatives, and the identification of improvement opportunities.

Monthly/Quarterly Reporting

Regular SEO reporting is *critical* to an SEO program. It helps provide insight into the success of the SEO program and its tactics. Additionally, it helps keep traffic drops on the radar should there be any search engine algorithm updates, which happen frequently. Depending on which SEO platform tool you use, the report will provide keyword ranking, organic search traffic, and conversion tracking.

Google Search Console Monitoring

Google Search Console and Bing Webmaster Tools are website management tools that can help communicate to search engines about website and SEO. It's important that you or your SEO team regularly monitor these tools for alerts, issues, or any performance changes.

Competitive Insights: SEO Competitive Analysis

A competitive analysis typically measures two of your direct competitors, defined by you, to assess their SEO presence. Using a variety of tools, it looks at organic keyword rankings, pages indexed, coding analysis, link popularity, and other items that are important to search engine spiders. The analysis will provide best-in-class examples of SEO if available.

Website Redesign Consultation and New Website Consultation

This deliverable can be one whole deliverable or be comprised of several. The goal of this deliverable is to help a brand team and website team create a new website that is as SEO optimized as possible. There are various web development deliverables that SEO teams can provide feedback on including wireframes, sitemaps, content ideas, page names, navigation, web page layout, HTML tagging, copywriting, URL structures, Redirect consulting and implementation assistance, quality assurance, and search console or webmaster tools monitoring.

Content Marketing Deliverables

The following are deliverables for content marketing. These deliverables help identify the content you should be creating, how it should take shape, and how it should be deployed.

Keyword Research

Using various keyword tools, this deliverable provides a list of relevant keyword terms in your category and about your brand. The list is typically fewer than 100 terms but could be more if necessary. The list is comprised of "critical" terms that aim to boost rankings, which in turn boost SEO performance. In my opinion, the tasks of keyword research and creating keyword or search term target lists represent the most important SEO tasks there are, so this deliverable should be formal and thorough.

Keyword research should provide the keyword terms, how often they're searched, and how competitive they are (Figure 3.5).

A	B	C	D
Keyword	**Avg. monthly searches**	**Competition**	**Where do we currently rank?**
microdermabrasion	60500	High	-
acne treatment	33100	High	12
spray tan	27100	High	13
sunscreen	18100	High	10
lip gloss	12100	High	-
concealer	12100	High	-
puffy eyes	12100	High	-
sesame oil	9900	Medium	-
eye shadow	9900	Medium	-
dark circles	9900	Medium	-
eyeshadow	9900	Medium	-
psoriasis scalp	8100	Medium	-
acne medication	8100	Medium	-
dandruff shampoo	8100	Medium	-
skin care products	8100	Medium	-
shaving cream	6600	Low	-

Figure 3.5: Example of a keyword research deliverable

Content Audit

When undertaking any content program, it's important that you work with the brand team or client to conduct a content audit. The content audit essentially lists all content assets available on the website and outside on the Web. It can be as simple as a spreadsheet that lists the content's URL, the title, a description of the content, and the type of asset (webpage, article, infographic, decision tree, etc.).

These are the steps of the content audit process:

Step 1: Conduct the audit and compile the spreadsheet.

- Be sure to log all the pages you can find and their details.

Step 2: Analyze the content.

- Analyze the data to determine if it's ranking well in a search, if it has links pointing to it, and if you have access to analytics for the site; also review engagement, traffic, and other metrics.

- In the spreadsheet, mark or score the content, and note if you'd like to keep it.

Step 3: Edit the content.

- Edit the content according to your goals or to satisfy any other content needs and optimizations.

Step 4: Update your content audit spreadsheet.

- Perform this process periodically to ensure your brand content is performing well and on par with brand guidelines.

Content Strategy

Content strategies can range in terms of complexity, but in general the aim is to provide a complex view of what organic content types and topics should be created or written. The content strategy deliverable can vary depending on what type of role or team member creates it. The content strategy deliverable is meant to address content need states, to identify audience needs, and to address them by providing relevant content to solve those needs (Figure 3.6).

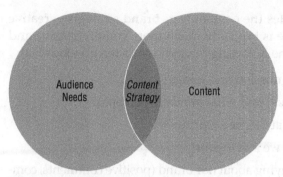

Figure 3.6: Content strategy

If an SEO person creates it, then it typically is smaller, search marketing–centric, and outlines the following:

- What search terms are popular in the category?
- What search terms are popular around the brand?
- How competitive are those search terms?
- What content venues do users use on their journey?
- Is there a gap between what content we're publishing or have and what users are asking for?
- What kind of assets are we providing currently? Do they adequately address user need and the competition/demand for it?
- What kind type of content responses and assets should we provide?
- What's the content publishing schedule and cadence?
- What's the content promotion strategy?
- What are the success factors for content (e.g., engagement, traffic, sales)?
- Copy and brand guidelines:
    - What person (first, third) should the content in?
    - What's the brand voice/tone?
    - What's call to action?

If a broader role creates the content (e.g., brand strategist, creative director), the deliverable is typically much more comprehensive and typically also answers the following (in addition to the previous list):

- What is the brand mission and image?
- Who is our audience, and what are their personas?
- What is the target audience's journey?
- What problem are we solving for?
- What are people saying about our brand (positive comments, complaints, needs)?
- What are people saying about the category?
- How often are we talking to them?
- What media channels are they on? Are we on those?
- What messages are they looking for?
- Are there disconnects with our target audience and our brand? If so, how can content fix it?
- What are the data points that are included to support the answers to these questions?

  - Social listening exercises
  - Quantitative and qualitative surveying
  - Search term analysis
  - Competitive intelligence
  - Website analytics (e.g., website search, surveys, and chat/help reports)

Content Calendar Consultation

This deliverable is typical for existing content initiatives (PR, social media, etc.) that use content calendar to schedule copywriting topics for each month or time period. You or the SEO expert can provide feedback on the exact terminology and keyword targets that go into the content calendar (Figure 3.7).

Content Title	Content Description	Type	Content Venue (YouTube, Brand Website, Facebook, etc)	January	February	March
1 Hydration Infographic	Image that shows how much water you need each day for optimal health	Infographic	Website Resource Pages	1/15/19		
2						
3						
4						
5						

Figure 3.7: Example of a content calendar deliverable

Copywriting

Copywriting is a critical part of SEO. This is usually scoped for new content. It's usually a custom approach based on the type of assets you are looking to create. Normally, a copywriter will handle this task, and the format will depend on the type of content being created. Here are some copywriting considerations, depending on the type of asset you are creating:

Article and Website Copy (Figure 3.8)

- Write content for humans, not search engine robots.
- Using two to three keyword terms per page is a safe recommendation.
- Use at least 300 words in each piece of content, if nonbrand search ranking is a priority.
- Ideally, the body copy of a web page should begin with a keyword phrase, as well as contain a keyword near the end of the content on the page.
- Include targeted terms in all HTML, header, and keyword tags.
- Make content easily shareable.
- Include a call to action.

Video or YouTube Copy

- Include targeted keywords in video title, description, tags, and file name.

Figure 3.8: Example of a relatively SEO optimized article that ranks high for 'How much do you need to retire?' searches

- Keep video titles to approximately 70 characters. If you use the full limit of 100 characters for YouTube videos, your title will be truncated.

- Video descriptions can be up to 5000 characters, so use this opportunity to provide detail about the video. Try to use the keyword in the first sentence and at least once more.

- Place links within the description of the video to the site to help encourage click-throughs.

- Ensure the video script includes the targeted keyword phrase at least once per 200 words.

Infographics (Figure 3.9)

- Consider the reader's frame of mind and understand they likely know very little about the subject (that's why they're researching it).

- Use a process to take a user through and highlight important statistics and phases of the process.

- Be visual and highlight important parts of the process with different text, colors, and other highlights.

- Technical considerations:

  - Be conscious of file size as it may slow load time. Make the file size of your infographics as small as possible without losing quality.

  - As mentioned previously, ensure all images have the alt tag attribute. Save all images in JPEG format for the best outcome. Include in the alt tag all text that's within the image so that search engines can read it.

  - Use the keyword in H1 headings of the infographic where it fits.

  - Be sure to include the keyword in the URL for the infographic.

  - Include the subject and keyword in the file name, e.g., `www.abc.com/retirement-infographic.jpg`.

  - Have an SEO-friendly landing page that houses the infographic image.

  - Promote the image on your social media channels.

Figure 3.9: Example of an infographic

Link Building

The following are link building deliverables that aim to build link popularity to your website and other platforms. These deliveralbes provide immediate links to your website or provide strategies that can help build links to it long-term and on an ongoing basis.

Media Buy Integration

This deliverable or input provides feedback and guidance for custom content agreements that media or PR teams typically provide. The goal of this deliverable is to provide guidance on the content venue, its SEO friendliness, and the content project in general to assure its SEO optimization. This typically begins at the proposal stage.

Press Release/Article Reviews

Press releases or other articles that are put together by the PR team require SEO oversight to ensure they're using the right keywords in important places (Figure 3.10). This leads to more impressions, news site pick-ups, and more links to your website. As discussed, links to a web page are an extremely important factor to ranking for SEO. Additionally, press releases can be used to capture traffic around certain phrases and offer additional exposure for your brand. For these reasons, SEO should be part of the review process for these types of content.

Release Title

- Include target search phrase, and stay within 100 characters. Between 65 and 80 characters is optimal for Google.
- Give a one- to two-sentence release summary, including target search phrase if possible.
- Keep the release summary to fewer than 240 characters.

Body

- Include standard release language.
- Make it at least 300 words. One page is preferable; two pages tops.
- Include target search phrase throughout the release at a ratio of 3 times for every 100 words.
- Include some links for high-priority terms (and target search phrase) and their landing pages throughout the body.
- Use no more than three links or one for every 100 words.
- Include a call to action either in the body or in the boilerplate.

Boilerplate

- Include key business offerings and link them to landing pages on your brand website.
- Try to keep it to less than 150 words.

Figure 3.10: Example of an SEO-optimized press release

Link Building Strategy and Execution

We will talk more about links in later chapters, but this deliverable is typically a strategic deliverable aimed at building more authoritative links to your website. It outlines potential partnerships, "vote worthy" content, and key landing pages that are worth a link to your website. Depending on which SEO tools you have, it could also identify what kind of sites your competitors are getting links from and what their most linked content is. It should also list the general health and spam risks of the links pointing to your site. If you have a lot of toxic or spam sites linking to your site or are overusing the same anchor text, you should outline that in your link strategy and plan. After the strategy and plan are formalized, the team should move toward link execution, which is typically an ongoing piece where you or an SEO team member reaches out to sites to add links or have them edit links; this is typically done every day.

Links can be labeled as "nofollow" or "follow." Sites can add a descriptor in the HTML code called a nofollow attribute. It looks like this: `rel="nofollow"`. It is next to the link anchor text in the HTML.

```
<a href="" rel="nofollow">ABC Link</a>
```

It's almost always best to aim for sites that don't use nofollow attributes so the SEO value is passed to your page and content. Nofollow attributes should be reserved for links coming in from spam or low-quality websites. Be sure your link strategies aim for building numerous high-quality links that don't use the nofollow attribute.

New SEO Areas

There are new areas that provide SEO opportunities for brands. Improving your brand's presence on each of them should be part of your program and deliverables. These include:.

Amazon SEO

As we'll discuss later, Amazon is a critical product search engine. Brands that offer products on Amazon need to make sure they are leveraging organic tactics as much as possible to ensure cost efficiency. This deliverable typically looks at what can be done to improve SEO rankings and traffic.

Voice Search

As we'll discuss later, voice search has become a critical part of the user journey and is yet another key type of search behavior your brand or website needs to rank for. This deliverable aims to look at what kind of content and tags you need to help rank for those searches.

Link Detoxification

Link toxicity or links pointing to your website is a big issue for SEO. Depending on what SEO tool you are using, a link quality audit should be done to identify which links or websites pointing to your website are low quality. Once that list is identified, the SEO expert should work within Google Search Console to disavow or instruct Google to ignore those links. This should be done on an ongoing basis (e.g., quarterly).

Other Nonwebsite Optimization

As we've been saying, improving the free traffic through SEO and content marketing isn't limited to your website. The following initiatives are areas of focus that should have deliverables tailored to their optimization.

YouTube Optimization

We will talk about YouTube later, but in general, YouTube is considered to be the second most popular search engine according to the *New York Times*. If you are spending money creating video content and ads on YouTube, it's important to spend efficiently by maximizing your organic standing. This deliverable is typically comprised of a list of your videos and suggested changes to the title, description, YouTube tags, and hashtags of each video to help improve rankings and traffic to your website from Google.

Reputation Management

We will walk through this in detail later, but making sure you have positive rankings on your brand search results (at least the first page) is extremely important from a brand image or trust point of view. If you are facing negative press or a controversy or negative rankings, this deliverable will provide suggestions to help offset negative rankings and content on the Web that is ranking in search results.

App Store Optimization

We will discuss this more thoroughly later, but many brands have their own smartphone app these days. There are tactics that can be done to improve your ranking on app stores and if and how they are being pulled into Google's general search rankings. This analysis provides feedback on what, if anything, you can improve or fix to help boost rankings across channels.

Social Media Optimization

Depending on the social media channels you are on, a quick run-through of how they rank and how you rank for searches on Google or on those channels should be conducted. Most of them are difficult to affect, but there may be some basic modifications to your presence and programs on them that an SEO expert can identify to improve your ranking (e.g., using the right hashtags, etc.).

The list of deliverables is constantly evolving. It's important to keep tabs on new technologies and how they can help. Whether you are trying to do SEO yourself or have enlisted an SEO team for help, these are the kinds of deliverables and actions you need today to move the performance needle in the way of SEO.

Common SEO Issues

There are many common SEO issues that I've seen time and time again over the years that can severely compromise SEO performance and rankings. They typically can be bucketed into the following main categories.

Bad HTML Coding

HTML coding is the code that's behind each web page. It essentially helps to configure what is visually presented on a web page. Google is heavily reliant on the HTML code and tags that your website provides. It communicates to search engines what your page is about, what to rank it for, and how good of a user experience it is. Many sites fail to configure their HTML well and do not use important tags and use very inefficient means when structuring their code, which results in slow-loading sites and a lack of search engine rankings.

Limited Content

As discussed in Chapter 1, to rank for a search phrase, you almost always need to have content that speaks to that phrase. Many marketing teams want to rank for a particular search term but lack the content. If you want to rank for a large list of search terms, you need to have content and dedicated web pages that speak to those phrases. Figure 3.11 shows an example of local bank Wintrust in Chicago, versus Chase in terms of keyword coverage. As you can see, Chase trumps Wintrust in the number of keywords it ranks for, due to having a lot of content (89,000 web pages), among other factors, versus Wintrust's small page count (1,290 web pages).

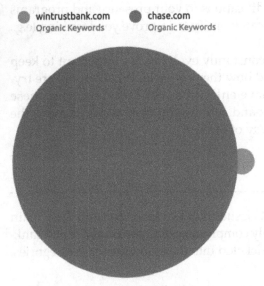

Figure 3.11: Chase bank versus Wintrust keyword coverage (source: SEM Rush)

Duplicate Content

Sometimes websites inadvertently create multiple URLs for the same page or content. This is considered duplicate content. Duplicate content was one of the early spam techniques that websites used to increase their search presence on Google and other search engines. Google instituted a penalty to discourage this practice. Unfortunately, many well-intentioned websites accidentally create multiple URLs and are flagged for duplicate content. This can result in search engine penalties and drop your search engine rankings.

Bad URL Structures

URLs and their structures carry a lot of weight in Google's ranking algorithm. As mentioned in Chapter 1, be sure to have a clean URL that's short and inclusive of the search term that you'd like the page to rank for. Do not use URLs that lack these characteristics. Here's an example of a bad URL: www.abc.com/axnlsiilihyihte/shahhd19999/1999.html.

Slow-Loading Web Pages

Slow-loading pages are extremely common. Google only recently started including them in their ranking algorithm, so brands seem to still be adjusting and optimizing load time.

Lack of Mobile Experience

It's incredible to believe, but despite living in a mobile device–centered world, there are still brands that lack a mobile experience. It's important to build user experiences centered around mobile devices, with simple layouts, fast-loading architecture, and strong calls to action.

Nonsecure Pages

We are living in a security-centric world these days, and it's important to have pages that use an HTTPS secure certificate, which verifies the page owner, encrypts valuable data, and makes users less vulnerable to identity theft and exposure of sensitive data. Google incorporates this into their ranking algorithm, but many brands fail to provide this.

Poor Calls to Action/Navigation

Extremely critical for ecommerce sites, it's important to have strong calls to action and highlight buttons and functions on a website so users see them strongly. Many sites bury these valuable features and fail to include them on top navigation and visible areas of a website.

Low Link Popularity

Many sites want to outrank competitors but are behind them in terms of link counts. They often fail to have active link-building strategies in place and are behind them in link counts. Using the previous example,

Wintrustbank.com has 48,600 links pointing to their domain versus Chase.com's 4 million links. This results in much higher authority scores and ultimately a better SEO value and performance.

Domain	Total Backlinks ⓘ	Referring Domains ⓘ	Referring IPs ⓘ	Authority Score
● chase.com	🏆 4M	🏆 26.7K	🏆 33K	🏆 74 ⌄
● wintrustbank.com	48.6K	355	482	38 ⌄

Figure 3.12: Chase bank versus Wintrust link coverage (source: SEM Rush)

Missing or Outdated Sitemap Files

Many websites fail to produce an updated sitemap file. This file communicates to search engines the current list of pages that you want indexed or crawled by the search engines. Be sure to keep your sitemap file updated and a full list of the URLs of the pages on your site.

Bonus: Interview with an Executive-Level Marketing Strategist

To get a look inside the ways brands can ensure effective marketing programs, I conducted an interview with John Doyle, who is currently executive director of brand experiences for a full-service, distinguished marketing agency. He's been in the marketing industry for 20 years and has worked in various executive-level roles helping brands ideate and execute marketing and content initiatives. I also worked with him over the years at a few agencies, on several SEO and content programs. The full interview is provided next, but here are the key takeaways of the interview:

- For brands to be successful, they need to have a clear understanding of what the problem is that they are trying to solve.
- Brands need to sober up and understand that consumers aren't thinking "brand-first" as much as brands believe they are or executing programs with the premise that they are.
- Brands need to do a better job of emotionally rounding out targets by going beyond the standard traits and should consider culturally trending topics in the world as well.

Here is the full interview:

Nick Papagiannis: Thanks for your time, John. So first of four questions: describe your role, your experience in the marketing world, and your helping brands.

John Doyle: I'll start with the experience as it culminates in the role that I'm performing now and the team that I'm with at my current agency. I was lucky enough to start as a copywriter and creative in a digital agency back in 2000, and basically worked in the digital agency space for about eight years, focusing on digital marketing. Before going to the agency where I am now, I helped to found the experience design capability at one of the larger, if not the largest, media networks in the world, under the pressure of needing to add creativity and go to market thinking with media programs centered on how they connect with humans and make them view or think about what the brand initiative was trying to do.

NP: That's great. Okay, so you mentioned you have 19 years, almost 20 years' experience in the marketing space. Over those years, what kinds of issues or areas do you find that marketers are neglecting during a marketing initiative that could compromise the success of a digital or even a traditional marketing program? What areas do they miss?

JD: There's probably a bunch of them, but given your questions, the two that I think are probably most valuable or often neglected are, number one, really getting sober about what problem it is you're trying to solve, or problems. Marketing communications oftentimes tries to reduce it down to the single most important thought. What is this takeaway? What is the message you take away? To me that's mission one. What are the problems that we're trying to solve and where do they exist? And obviously setting smart strategies to solve that is really critical.

The other thing is that marketers have a native, sort of like a built-in, bias towards the brand being valuable.. We're really good at believing what that company stands for and sort of following a line of that mission of that brand. Like, hey, this is pretty good. We believe in it. It's our job to try to stand it up and make it feel powerful and salient and meaningful in a very cluttered and competitive environment. . . . We have to be compassionate about our brands. We have to believe in their place in the world and their ability to make a difference in a consumer's life, whether that's super functional or emotional. However, I think the flip side of that is we can also sometimes forget the truth of culture and truth of consumer's lives and people's lives in that they are buried with options, buried with life needs, completely not thinking about brands as much as we tend to think that they are. We talk a lot about, just for example, storytelling, especially emotional storytelling.

I think we have to recognize we have to work really, really hard to make things matter to people who are loaded with options in our consumer culture. I think it's like marrying those two things can make you just work a little harder and recognize that, no, your ad isn't that cute when it's compared to the *Game of Thrones* finale.

NP: Are there other things, and you kind of answered it but, are there any other issues or areas that brands should be sure to look at when they're building out a marketing initiative?

JD: Obviously we're loaded with data, and right now we're living in the golden age of data availability. Sometimes the access to that data can mean a little lack of soul.

To really get into the head space of your consumer, you have the data of their passions or their behaviors or what they've done in terms of conversion and what dollars they've contributed to the company. But, you need to round them out as people, particularly on an emotional level. Ask yourself what other things are they? Try to figure out your audience as a more complete human, and then you might recognize how much harder you have to work, and then you might also find some opportunities to find the soul of your program by appealing to them emotionally.

The emotional quality of your audience is something that we don't think enough about. We think about them in terms of indices and sort of behaviors, cliff strings, contributions, cost to acquisition, lifetime value, but we don't think about them as humans with emotional needs. And I think this goes a lot harder than persona work.

It's a hard job to just try to really become empathetic to your audience. I think the downside to having so much data is that sometimes it can be really sort of overly scientific without thinking about the soul of things.

NP: What are the kinds of critical things brands must do to make sure SEO and even content marketing are successful?

JD: SEO describes a marketing technique that is about trying to search engine optimize. I think that the opportunity is to recognize that that's just one set of tools to help you get at understanding that there is a person searching for help, answers, inspiration, products, stores, reviews. I think the opportunity for search is forgetting the tool set and remembering the individual—and remembering that search is something that predates advertising by eons.

We've always wanted to search for information throughout history and we used tools to do it. Today though Google's obviously critical. What about Amazon? Or what about Yelp? They are search engines. They're search environments. They're search tools.

Here's another example of how SEO needs to be leveraged. Well, every time you as a marketer have questions, where you're not sure of the answer, obviously you can look at the data from in-store sales. You can look at third-party research. You can do a primary research study and bring people in and do a card sorting exercise. Like, how do you guys shop this category? We had done all of those things. To really objectify and ground ourselves in the truth of it, we used search data. We were trying to figure out, do people use the word *cable cutting, cutting the cord*? Do they understand OTT and streaming services? We were looking at things like search volume and then search kind of from having to figure out what is it that people have on their minds. What's the first question? What's the nesting question? What's this question? And that completely informed what we had to answer in different executions in how to chronologically structure a physical state.

So, we're redesigning their electronics section. How does it look? What are the fixtures? What are the signs next to the TVs? What's playing on the TVs when people are coming up? What's the lighting? What's the customer experience? All that kind of stuff, right? We're sitting there, and we're trying to figure out how to organize the TV aisle with streaming services like Roku and Sling box. What do we need to do to describe the television's features and functions? Do we need to talk about apps and streaming services that are on the TV? Do we need to talk about how many HDMI cords are in there? Do we need to describe the difference between OLED and high def and all that kind of stuff, right? We have all these questions.

So it's thinking about how you buy and how do you use, but then I think it's moving a couple things. It's moving concentric circles out from, like, the most objective, perfunctory terms of search to thinking about aspirational stuff.

How do we answer those questions as people come in recognizing that their search process that they would apply on Google or CNET does not stop the second they enter into a brick-and-mortar store? So, search as a tool to design interior architecture and interior design is something that we're doing.

Quiz

1. Marketers are _____.
   a. Overrated
   b. Business experts
   c. Not necessary
   d. Problem-solvers
   e. Problem identifiers

   Answer: d

2. Which of the following is not a reason stated in this book as to why brands fail?
   a. Lack of process
   b. Lack of data
   c. Inadequate skill sets
   d. Too aggressive timelines
   e. Unrealistic customers

   Answer: e

3. True or False: Stale skill sets are considered a business problem mentioned in this book.

   Answer: True

4. Which of these are not considered the mind-set a modern-day marketer should have?

   a. Process-driven

   b. Data-focused

   c. Open minded

   d. Eager to learning new things

   e. Social media enthusiast

   Answer: e

5. Which of the following is not considered a deliverable for website optimizations?

   a. Technical audits

   b. HTML tag optimizations

   c. Copy optimizations

   d. Landing page design consultation

   e. Social media plug-in strategies

   Answer: e

6. Which of the following are not common SEO issues?

   a. Bad HTML coding

   b. Minimal content

   c. Bad URL structures

   d. Nonsecure pages

   e. Too many links on a page

   Answer: e

7. Which of the following are nonwebsite optimization tactics?

   a. YouTube optimization

   b. Reputation management

   c. Social media optimization

   d. Mobile and app store optimization

   e. All the above

   Answer: e

8. True or False: Link detoxification, which disavows or tells search engines certain links are to be ignored, is a tactic that should be done often.

   Answer: True

9. Which of the following are not relatively new optimization areas in the SEO world?

   a. Amazon SEO

   b. Voice search optimization

   c. Link detoxification

   d. Title tag optimization

   Answer: d

10. Content marketing is a core piece of SEO, and the following deliverables are critical to it. (Choose all that apply.)

    a. Keyword research

    b. Content strategy

    c. Content calendars

    d. Copy or copywriting

    e. Meta descriptions

    Answer: a, b, c, d

CHAPTER

CHAPTER

4

Stakeholders for the Modern SEO and Organic Content Process

Now that we have walked through the modern organic process that can optimize free traffic levels to your brand, it's time to start thinking about the modern-day team structure that's needed to execute an effective organic program.

SEO and organic content are not a one-person show. It takes a diverse set of talents and expertise to execute a full-service, effective program. Traditional SEO was basically one expert and minimal support. The SEO expert was in charge of compiling consultative deliverables (primarily website audits and HTML recommendations).

As search engines have evolved and the process has gotten much more complicated, it's necessary to evolve that structure. There are several roles needed to fulfill a modern organic and SEO process. The dotted lines typically are not direct reports to the SEO expert but instead work closely with them to ensure program success and effectiveness. Oftentimes, it's not possible to have all these roles as part of the project team, but when possible, try to enlist the team members and structure shown in Figure 4.1.

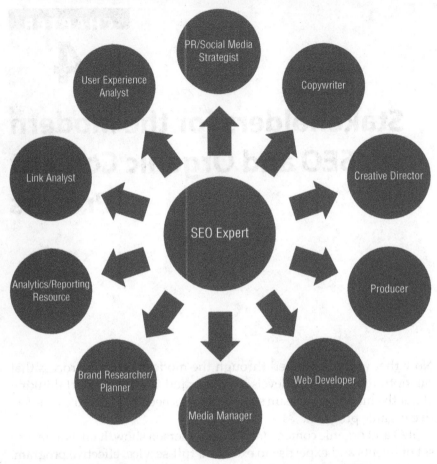

Figure 4.1: Ideal project team structure

This chapter details each person's role on an SEO and organic content project.

SEO Expert

As the quarterback, traffic cop, and ultimate owner of the project, the SEO expert is in charge of driving the strategy; pulling together technical audits, HTML code in relation to SEO, and link deliverables; enforcing best practices; and reporting insights.

Possible deliverables include technical audits, tag optimization, copy editing and optimization, landing page design consultation, Google Search Console monitoring, competitive analysis, website consulting, content calendar consulting, link strategies and execution, press release/article reviews, off-site optimization, reporting, and monitoring.

PR/Social Media Strategist

PR and social media content is a commonly missed SEO opportunity to grow organic traffic. It's important to be sure to collaborate all PR and social media initiatives, specifically the organic initiatives that drive content plans and content assets. SEO can provide search data to inform content creation and content calendars and identify influencers and blogs that have strong SEO that could benefit their brand or client's website. Press releases and YouTube videos and other social media content are great opportunities for integration as well. If SEO isn't pulled into this to help ideate and/or enforce best practices, brands are likely missing big opportunities (organic traffic, quality links, etc.) and are wasting budget. PR/social media managers should also be included on the content strategy deliverable and be provided with the list of keyword targets from the SEO expert.

Possible deliverables include content calendar consulting, link strategies and execution, press release/article reviews, and off-site optimization.

SEO Copywriter

Copywriting is an extremely critical role for a successful SEO program. Copywriters are the ones who create long-form content, edit existing copy on web pages, identify topics using search data, and identify links to embed in copy. Copywriters are almost as well versed in SEO as the SEO expert when it comes to content best practices.

Possible deliverables include tag optimization, copy editing and optimization, landing page design consultation, content calendar consulting, press release/article reviews, and off-site optimization.

Creative Director

Creative directors on brands provide the creative vision, lead ideation, and ultimately drive the ideas that are presented to brands. They are the creative force and understand brands better than anyone on the project. They can be in charge of anything digital or traditional

(TV, e-print, etc.). They are the keyholder to the advertising a client chooses to do. They ultimately own content ideas and their execution, whether organic or paid, traditional or digital. They are an extremely important stakeholder to an SEO program. It's important that they incorporate SEO data and best practices in their creative brief. Sometimes it makes sense to create a separate creative brief for SEO projects (example provided in Chapter 5) that creative directors and teams can use with the sole purpose of boosting SEO and free traffic. Creative directors should also be included on the content strategy deliverable and provided the list of keyword targets from the SEO expert.

Possible deliverables include content strategy and ideation, content asset development, copywriting, and optimization.

Producer

Producers are essentially the owners of timelines, vendor management, and project plans, and they keep the project on task and hold stakeholders accountable throughout the execution. They are a critical piece of the team since they keep the project within budget and help push the execution of tasks. Without them, tasks are inevitably missed, and the project runs at a high risk.

Possible deliverables include program or project plan, status reports, and vendor management.

Web Developer

Web developers are the technical experts and a sounding board for the SEO expert. Website technology is changing constantly, and they provide great insight on how web pages are built and other technical expertise when it comes to coding HTML and implementing fixes on the site to make the site and web pages in line with the latest search engine guidelines.

Possible deliverables include technical audits, tag optimization, copy editing and optimization, landing page design consultation, HTML code, and website consulting.

Media Manager

Media managers execute paid media programs, which oftentimes include content on a partner site or even on influencer sites. Sometimes this content is a simple article, but sometimes it's a robust custom content program. It's important that the media manager discusses any content programs they are planning on doing and includes the SEO expert in the project brief and proposal requests that go out to potential partners. The SEO expert can provide a review of the proposal/briefs and include SEO guidelines and search term targets, as well as auditing partner sites to determine which partner possesses the best SEO standing on the list. Media managers should also be included on the content strategy deliverable and provided the list of keyword targets from the SEO expert.

Possible deliverables include media plan optimization and cross-collaboration.

Brand Researcher/Planner

Brand planners offer a valuable perspective on brand positioning and the overall engagement strategies needed to connect a brand to their audience. They sometimes perform their own content strategy deliverable, but not down to the "search term" level. Oftentimes the SEO expert will take the planning insights and build the SEO content strategy deliverable from the brand research planner. Also, brand planners create and draft the creative assignment brief. There are opportunities to incorporate SEO search insights and strategies or merge the SEO creative brief together with the assignment brief the brand planning team pulls together.

Possible deliverables include brand strategy monitoring, persona development, project briefing, surveying, content strategies, and social listening studies.

Analytics/Reporting Resource

A strong and effective SEO program requires ongoing reporting. Reports can be pulled weekly, biweekly, monthly, or quarterly depending on what the teams would like and how scrutinized performance is. Therefore, an analytics expert should be on board with the SEO program team to help format and populate monthly reports with data. The SEO expert provides the insights that go into the report, based on the data the reporting analyst pulls.

Possible deliverables include Google Search Console monitoring, reporting, and monitoring.

Link Analyst

We already know that linking is one of the three pillars of good SEO. It's so important that it's necessary to have a dedicated link person to help acquire inbound links from relevant sites and content. Link analysts also look for existing links that aren't optimally structured and reach out to websites to see if they can edit the link to make it SEO friendly. They also present link strategy deliverables and help provide high-level options for acquiring links to boost the SEO program performance.

Possible deliverables include link strategies, link building, link disavowing, and press release and article reviews.

User Experience Analyst

Google says, "Our goal is always to provide you the most useful and relevant information." That alone explains why a good user experience resource is necessary to be on the SEO program team. At the end of the day Google wants users to keep coming back and using its search engine. Google's algorithm is designed to provide users with the best experience from a technical and content relevancy standpoint. They want to rank trustworthy websites that offer quality content and a great website user experience at the top. It's important that SEO user experience professionals are available on the project to help ideate content ideas and to design venues and website enhancements an SEO expert may end up recommending.

Possible deliverables include technical audits, tag optimization, copy editing and optimization, landing page design consultation, Google Search Console monitoring, competitive analysis, website consulting, content calendar consulting, link strategies and execution, press release/article reviews, and off-site optimization.

External Vendors

External vendors are a convenient way to offer temporary services that can help move a project along when resources are unavailable, especially with fixed and tight budgets. When it comes to the three pillars of good SEO, there are many vendors that can help, but it's the SEO expert's decision on when to pull in a vendor (with the help of the producer). The categories of vendors for each pillar of good SEO are shown in Figure 4.2.

Possible deliverables include content creation, content discovery and promotion, technical support, link building, and any other support.

Website Tech Environment	Content	Popularity
• Freelance Web Developers • Crawling and Auditing Tools	• Freelance Copywriters • Content Marketing Platforms • Video Producers • Keyword Research Tools	• Link Building Partners • Content Discovery and Promotion Vendors • Video Promotion Vendors • Newswire Services

Figure 4.2: Vendor deliverables and expertise

Project Goal and Mind-Sets

It's important that each team member understands the goal of the project and how success is measured, not just from a data perspective but from an overall execution perspective. If the project isn't executed to its fullest, the team won't be fulfilling the brand or the client's need in the best way possible.

You may have some goals already in mind, but it's important that they stay in the context of project execution and not just the client's key performance indicators. Here are a few goals every project should consider:

Work generates as much free or organic traffic as possible. The end goal is to capture as much free traffic for a brand, which will ideally yield a similar increase in sales and other conversions. Content shouldn't be created unless there's a team to ensure its optimization and positioning in the best way possible.

Free traffic coming to brand assets is engaged and active. It's important to capture an audience that's relevant and engaged. It's not a matter of just capturing any mass audience. When traffic is captured while seeking specific content, they'll likely be more apt to digest and engage with it. This can translate into repeat visits, liking and sharing content, and stronger brand awareness and trust.

Free traffic coming to brand translates into free sales at a solid rate. Free traffic that converts into a sale or some other conversion represents a sale that's not tied directly to paid media budget or investments. The return on investment when converting free traffic to a sale is significantly higher than a sale coming from a paid advertisement. It's important to think about this when the team is building the project brief, content assets, and overall marketing strategies.

Each channel and expert is being used in the best manner possible to promote free traffic to brand assets. Ultimately, the goal of SEO and content marketing is to capture and connect organic, qualified, and engaged traffic to brand assets. On a high level, that's the gist of it. The project team should understand their role and have a mind-set that's focused on that.

To ensure that each role has the right mind-set, I've compiled the following suggested questions for each role player to ask themselves at the beginning of and throughout an SEO program. This list is not exhaustive, so feel free to tailor it to your program and team structure.

SEO Expert

- Do I have the right team members in place to maximize free traffic and SEO benefits to brand assets (website and other assets)?
- Am I following the right, modern process to good SEO?
- Did I list each possible brand asset (on the website and off the website) to optimize for SEO?
- Did I map out and communicate the KPIs of the project?
- Am I up to speed on the latest SEO advancements and tactics? Am I including that in our plan?
- What SEO tool am I using to gather important search data that can indicate how to best reach our target audience?
- What data points can I pull together to help inform the content strategy of the program?

PR/Social Media Strategist

- Am I in tune with the current content strategy of the program?
- What social media tactics am I working on right now for this brand so the SEO program team knows?
- What social media assets is my PR team actively producing content on?
- Does the PR team have a content calendar in place?

- Are we actively blogging or producing other website content? What's the schedule?

- Do we work with other websites, influencers, and partner websites to create content?

- Do we create digital press releases and use a newswire service?

SEO Copywriter

- Am I in tune with the current content strategy of the program? Is there a content strategy available or does it need to be created? If not created, I need to work with the team to create one.

- Do I have any ideas from past projects on what kind of copy works well and generates traffic and user engagement?

- Am I familiar with SEO best practices when writing content?

- What kind of guidance do I need from the SEO expert to create SEO content? Am I including the SEO expert in reviews?

- Am I able to create long-form content, video scripts, white papers, blog articles, and other content asset types that can drive traffic? If not, how can I learn to do that?

- Am I familiar with how search optimized content can drive non-branded traffic to our brand assets? If not, let the SEO expert know and share case studies.

- Do I understand that highly searched topics require an advanced content response beyond basic web text?

Creative Director

- Am I in tune with the current content strategy of the entire program? Is there a content strategy available, or does it need to be created? The content strategy should inform all paid and nonpaid channels. If not created, I need to work with the team to create one.

- Am I familiar with how search optimized content can drive non-branded traffic to our brand assets? If not, I need to let the SEO expert know and share case studies.

- Do I understand that highly searched topics require an advanced content response beyond basic web text?

- Do I understand the full list of content types that can drive organic traffic?

- Do I understand how search algorithms work?
- Do I understand the target audience and at what points they use search to connect with content, to satisfy their needs?
- Do I understand the brand personality, guidelines, and what's going to be aligned with content assets and messaging?

Producer

- Do I have a project plan or timeline in mind?
- What technologies are we using to execute the SEO program?
- What deliverables do we need to compile along the way?
- Is the contract signed and do we have adequate staffing?
- How often am I creating status reports and meeting with the team to discuss tasks and the program?
- How can I track the project hours and budget?

Web Developer

- Am I familiar with the technical factors that affect SEO? If not, I need to work with the SEO expert to learn them.
- What technology is the brand website using?
- How can I implement basic SEO?
- Am I familiar with schema.org tags and the latest schema options?
- Do I understand voice search and the emerging conversation commerce technologies?
- Am I familiar with the most popular website systems and their available SEO capabilities and plug-ins?
- Do I understand how to build a fast-loading, user-friendly, device-agnostic website?

Media Manager

- Am I in tune with the current content strategy of the entire program? Is there a content strategy available or does it need to be created? The content strategy should inform all channels. If not created, I need to work with the team to create one.
- Am I familiar with the technical factors that affect SEO? If not, I need to work with the SEO expert to learn them.

- What paid media are in planning or execution stage that revolve around text content, influencer, or custom organic content?

- Is there a paid media proposal template, and can we integrate SEO considerations in it?

- Are there opportunities to embed organic or in-text links to our brand website, in our paid media initiatives?

- Are we using SEO keywords in our paid media content and proposals? If not, I need to work with the SEO expert on how to best use them.

- Are we measuring organic traffic and interactions in our paid media reporting?

- Are we working with third-party websites that are posting content or articles about our brand?

Brand Researcher/Planner

- Do I understand the target audience and the points at which they use a search to connect with content along the purchase funnel and/or to satisfy their need states?

- Am I in charge of creating the content strategy? Typically, this is true, but if not, who is and how can brand planning help? The content strategy should inform all channels (paid and nonpaid).

- Do I understand the brand personality, guidelines, and what's going to be aligned with content assets and messaging?

- Am I familiar with how search optimized content can drive non-branded traffic to our brand assets? If not, I need to let the SEO expert know and share case studies.

- Do I understand that highly searched topics require an advanced content response beyond basic web text?

- Do I understand the full list of content types that can drive organic traffic?

- Am I creating personas and journeys around our target audience? Do we have search terms in mind for them? If not, I need to work with the SEO expert on how to best use them.

- Am I writing the project brief?

- Am I conducting surveys and focus groups? If so, I need to include questions on how and when users search and what kind of content they seek along their journey.
- Are there other data points (e.g., social listening data, brand sentiment, focus group feedback) that I can provide the team during the project briefing meeting and stage?

Analytics/Reporting Resource

- What's the primary goal of the project?
- What data points can I pull together for the planning team, to provide a content strategy?
- Do I understand what SEO metrics can communicate organic traffic, engagement, and conversions? If not, I need to work with the SEO expert to learn them.
- Do I understand what reporting tools are available for the assets I work with (website measurement, YouTube, social channels, media partnerships)?
- Do I understand what's going to be included in the SEO report and how often we will be providing one? If not, I need to work with the SEO expert and producer to understand the scope and cadence.

Link Analyst

- Do I understand the search keyword targets that are critical to the project?
- Do I understand what content needs to be promoted across the project?
- Do I have a good understanding of what paid media and PR content is being created to optimize link building opportunities?
- Do I need to do a follow up meeting with the PR and paid media manager to discuss link building opportunities and processes?
- Am I aware of the different content types that can drive links to the brand assets?
- Do I understand what analytics and data I can provide in the SEO report? If not, I need to work with the SEO expert and analytics team to solidify data points.

User Experience Analyst

- Am I creating personas and journeys around our target audience? Do we have search terms and content venues in mind for them? If not, I need to work with the SEO expert on how to best use them.
- Am I in tune with the current content strategy of the entire program? Is there a content strategy available or does it need to be created? The content strategy should inform all channels. If not created, I need to work with the team to create one.
- Do I understand that highly searched topics require an advanced content response beyond basic web text?
- Do I understand the full list of content types that can drive organic traffic?
- Do I understand how to best incorporate user experience practices throughout the SEO program that can boost organic engagements and conversions?
- Am I included in the monthly reporting and have I provided what data points can inform user engagement and other useful user experience data points?

External Vendors

- Am I aware of the project goals and strategy?
- Am I aware of my role in the project? Have I been properly briefed on what I need to provide to ensure project success?
- Do I have an understanding of search engine algorithms and how to best support SEO programs? If not, I need to work with the SEO expert to understand them.

Recommended SEO Tools to Use

While not an exhaustive list, I've compiled the recommended SEO tools to use for your program. These are my favorite tools to use when I execute a program.

SEO Website Crawling/Auditing

Auditing your website technology environment for errors and factors that compromise SEO performance is the first of the SEO pillars to good

SEO. It's critical that you use a tool that's easy to use and provides prescriptive details on issues and an overall scoring summary of your technology standing. There are many SEO tools available for this. Here are my personal favorites:

Screaming Frog: This free tool is a great SEO crawling tool and provides a thorough crawling and reporting of your website technical areas. It's not the most user-friendly tool and non-SEO experts can get overwhelmed by the interface and data it outputs. Since it costs the least and yet still provides a great crawling and reporting of your technical standing, I've provided a walk-through on how to use this tool in Chapter 2.

Cost: Free

SEMrush: This tool is an end-to-end SEO solution that provides a comprehensive feature list to manage your SEO. It's my personal favorite for small businesses with limited budgets.

Cost: Low

BrightEdge: This is a great, user-friendly tool for large sites that require heavy SEO program management.

Cost: High

Keyword Discovery Tools

Keyword research is one of the most important tasks that brands do in their SEO program. It can fuel website content and all other kinds of creative areas. It's critical that you use a keyword tool that's easy to use and provides important data around search terms, their volume (number of searches happening), and the competition for those terms. Here are some great tools to consider:

AnswerThePublic: This is a great, user-friendly tool that provides common questions around a category. It uses Google's search suggest data (commonly seen as you type a search when it tries to autocomplete or suggest search phrases).

Cost: Free

Ubersuggest: This is also a user-friendly tool that provides common questions on a category, which also uses Google search suggest data.

Cost: Free

Google Ads: This is a free tool for users that have an Ads account set up. It's not the most user friendly, but it does provide valuable data directly from Google around all sorts of keyword terms (a use case is outlined in Chapter 2).

Cost: Free

SEMrush: SEMrush provides a great keyword tool called Keyword Magic. It provides common questions and general search terms. I find this to be the most user-friendly tool out there that provides a complete list of search phrases around search topics (versus just autocomplete or suggested search data).

Cost: Low

BrightEdge: BrightEdge provides standard keyword research data, but also provides great competitive data. You can get an idea of what keywords are driving traffic to competitor sites as well.

Cost: High

Content Production Tools

Producing content is extremely critical to SEO. If you don't have in-house copywriters or a freelance writer available, there are a few tools on the market that can help connect you with writers who are skilled in writing SEO content.

Textbroker: This is a great, user-friendly tool that allows you to set up requests to the Textbroker writer network. The writers accept your assignment after reading your brief, and they create the asset you are looking for. You have options to provide feedback as they're writing it. It also has plagiarism and SEO checking features. I've had a lot of success creating basic SEO text articles with this tool.

Cost: Low, depending on the assignment and expertise level required

Skyword: Skyword is a comprehensive service that offers self-service and managed service offerings. Unlike Textbroker, Skyword can create strategic deliverables and advanced content assets. For brands with a large content and marketing budget, this is the best service to use. They can help you create all sorts of content types (video scripts, infographics, etc.) around search volume. I've also seen a lot of success with this tool and recommend it.

Cost: Medium to high, depending on the assignment, content type, and expertise level required

Content Discovery

In addition to standard paid advertisements on social media (e.g., YouTube, LinkedIn, and Facebook Sponsored ads), partner websites, and other channels, there are some vendors that are strictly in the avenue of content discovery and promotion. My favorite partner is Outbrain.

Outbrain: I have had a lot of success with Outbrain, which is a content discovery service that can help align your content with similar content and boost traffic to it. Brands can run refined programs and can target on a local and demographic level as well.

Cost: Medium to high, depending on the assignment

Website Analytic Tools

There are many website analytics tools available, but in general I recommend Google Analytics and Google Search Console for tracking SEO performance. Both are free to use.

Link Building Tools

As discussed in Chapter 1, link building is one of the three pillars of good SEO and critical for ranking well and getting good SEO performance. There are multiple ways to build links (as outlined in Chapter 6), but if you have an opportunity to complement those link building tactics by supplementing it with link outreach activities or to contact sites using a platform, consider using the following tools:

Pitchbox: This is a great link outreach tool that allows you to send emails to relevant websites and influencers to see if they can add a link back to your content and website.

Cost: Low

SEMrush: SEMrush has a link building feature that allows you to set up keyword targets, an SEO competitor list, and an email widget that allows you to email key website contacts and ask them to add a link to your website. It's pretty user-friendly, and as with any SEMrush paid subscription, there are support teams available to help guide you through executing your program. If you are a small business, I recommend SEMrush as an all-in-one tool for link building, site crawling, and keyword discovery.

Cost: Low

Resource Checklist for SEO Program

Do you have the following stakeholders assigned to the SEO program?

- User experience
- Reporting/analytics
- Media manager
- PR/social team member
- Web developer
- Producer
- Copywriter
- Creative director
- Link analyst
- Brand planner

If not, do you have resources to do the following?

- Write copy for articles, long-form content, scripts
- Pull reporting data
- Reach out to partner sites
- Build press releases and other PR content
- Manage timelines, budgets, and vendor contracts
- Conduct brand and engagement research
- Direct videos or work with video directors
- Seek out and/or edit links from relevant sites and put strategies together for long-term link acquisition

Questions to Ask When Hiring an SEO Expert or Consultant

- How long have you been doing SEO?
- What makes a successful SEO program in your opinion?
- What is your most successful program and why was it successful? Please provide KPIs.
- What is your least successful program and why was it not successful?
- Do you practice SEO practices that are 100 percent white hat and in line with Google's guidelines?
- What resources do you have for producing content? Do you have copywriters, video producers, photographers, etc.?
- How do you stay up to speed with the latest SEO news and algorithm updates? Will you provide me with point of views?
- Do you provide SEO nonwebsite venues like Amazon, YouTube, blogs, news releases, and partner content?
- Do you have any references or past clients I can speak to?
- Why do SEO programs fail in your opinion?
- How often will you provide a report and walk-through on performance?
- Will you provide a link strategy and provide link building services?

Quiz

1. Which of the following roles are needed in the organic contact process? (Choose all that apply.)

    a. SEO expert

    b. PR/social media strategist

    c. SEO copywriter

    d. Creative director

    e. Producer

    f. Web developer

    g. Media manager

    h. Brand research and planner

i.   Data analytics resource

j.   Link analyst

k.   User experience

l.   All the above

Answer: l

2. The SEO expert is the _____ of the organic content process.

a.   General

b.   Quarterback

c.   Pitcher

d.   Expert

e.   None of the above

Answer: b

3. True or False: PR and social media content is not a commonly missed, high-impact opportunity to grow organic traffic.

Answer: False

4. True or False: Creative directors ultimately own the creative ideas and strategy on an organic contact process/project.

Answer: True

5. Which of the following is not an organic content project goal or mind-set?

a.   Generate as much free organic traffic as possible.

b.   Capture traffic to brand assets that is engaged and active.

c.   Leverage each channel expert assigned to the team by asking them how their channels can drive free traffic.

d.   Try to use as few paid advertisements as possible.

Answer: d

6. True or False: It's important to think that the investment required to build free organic traffic can sometimes be higher in the short-term than getting a sale from a paid advertisement.

Answer: True

7. _____ is a free tool to use when conducting SEO website crawls and audits.

   Answer: Screaming Frog

8. Which of the following tools does not offer keyword research or discovery capabilities?
   a. AnswerThePublic
   b. UberSuggest
   c. SEM Rush
   d. Pitchbox
   e. Brightedge

   Answer: d

9. True or False: Content discovery platforms can bring an enormous amount of traffic to content you are trying to promote, which can in turn lead to more link popularity, social media shares and likes, and general awareness of your content.

   Answer: True

10. True or False: External vendors can be used to *fully* execute the organic content process from the initial stages to the end stages.

    Answer: False

CHAPTER

5

Data-Informed Creative

It's a struggle to get a straight definition of *content* from marketers. If you ask someone working in paid media, they may say that content is a sponsored article on a partner website. If you ask someone working on the creative side of marketing, they may say that content is a video that's posted on a brand website. In public relations departments, content may mean a press release or blog article. Most marketers are short-sighted when it comes to defining what content means, which can result in less than optimal results. The benefit of SEO experts is that they are in charge of getting "content" indexed by search engines. Google is our ball, and content search engine indexing is our sport. Being part of the organic search engine universe exposes us to all kinds of content. We have a broad perspective when it comes to defining content, developing content, and creating engaging content that works as hard as possible and enables brands to perform better.

Dictionary.com defines *content* as "something that is to be expressed through some medium, as speech, writing, or any of various arts." I believe that marketers need to think of content using a definition as broad as this. Content to me is a brand utilizing some kind of asset to connect with their audience and/or express themselves. When you start to think of content like that, you will start to see the vast opportunities there are to reach your consumer. Oftentimes, search engines are the top layer of that connection. Remember Google's mission from Chapter 1: "Google's mission is to **organize** all the world's information so users can universally **access** it and are provided with the most **useful** information." *Information* is Google's way of saying *content*. Google has a daunting task to maintain its vision since content types are quickly evolving. For it to stay relevant to users and their lives, it has to constantly evolve to include all types of content. SEO experts have to stay in tune with the latest search engine changes to ensure that a brand's content (regardless of where it sits) gets indexed and ranks as well as possible on search engines. Otherwise, the number of people consuming and connecting with that content will be compromised.

Fighting Inertia and Navigating Personalities in the Content Space

I would be doing you a disservice if I didn't have a part of this book that spoke about the truths of the marketing industry. When implementing the process that I'm speaking to in this book, one must be mindful of the blow-back and ego-land mines you will come across. It can be extremely difficult to tell someone who traditionally led brand strategy, creative strategies, and IT strategies that they are now held to a process and to a team with equal stakeholder equity. This can be an extremely difficult mind-set to change. There a few ways to provide a push to change:

- **Get executive mandate:** Work with your company's C-level or executive department to have them mandate a changed process.

- **Test it:** To be in marketing is to be testing new ideas and concepts. Consider the testing processes like the ones mentioned in this book to see if they work for you and your organization. Once a project works, the results can speak for themselves.

- **Work in an SEO silo:** Many SEO agencies use this content process under their "SEO scope" and mask content projects as "SEO tactics" when they are basically just content projects under the disguise of SEO. This can help ease the level of change for creative and those who typically controlled the creative process 100 percent.

- **Do nothing:** This is the worst thing you can do. Marketing changes with the times. Marketing was much different as little as 20 years ago. The brands and teams that changed are thriving today. The ones that didn't are no longer around. Do not do nothing.

Why Search Engines Are Important for Consuming Content

From a brand perspective, the stats are staggering.

- "89 percent of consumers turn to Google, Bing, or another search engine to find information on products, services, or businesses prior to making purchases," according to Fleishman Hillard.

- According to Nielsen, nearly half an adult's day is dedicated to consuming content (http://www.nielsen.com/us/en/insights/ reports/2018/q1-2018-total-audience-report.html).

- 51 percent of website traffic is still coming from organic search traffic.

- Google is responsible for 94 percent of total organic traffic, according to HubSpot.

Content consumption is by far the top online behavior, and search is a critical driver in the content consumption experience. Brands that create content that's not indexed by search engines and search vehicles risk wasting resources and getting poor performance.

Journey Writing and Persona Development

When determining what type of content to create, it's important to take a step back and put together a more strategic view of your consumer and target audience. There are two higher-level approaches that a marketer should compile prior to moving ahead with creating content: journey identification and personas.

Journey Identification

Journey identification is the process of conducting research to determine the path or paths that users follow when making a purchase or re-purchase and the influences on that purchase. The output of journey identification are a journey or a determined pathway and the items that influence users while researching a product category and ultimately making a purchase or re-purchasing a product to satisfy a need. The journey can help identify the different types of content, channels, and behavior a user relies on to ultimately make that purchase. A journey can typically be formalized by answering the following questions about your target:

- What triggers the need for a person to purchase a product or service like mine? Some of the common purchase triggers include the following:
  - **Life events:** Having a baby, retiring, buying a home, etc.
  - **Replacement:** Having a product that breaks down, for which fixing is not an option.
  - **Convenience:** Needing to purchase a product to save time and money.
  - **Lifestyle enhancement:** A product will enhance a user's lifestyle in certain areas (e.g., entertainment, health).
  - **Safety:** A solution can help provide safety and reduce risk.
  - **Competition**: A solution or product can put you ahead of your peers.
- Does that person already have a product brand in mind?
  - If not, what, who, or what content influences the person in their choice of brand of the product?
  - If yes, how did that consumer choose that brand? What factors influence the person?
- What does the research process look like prior to them making a purchase?
  - Do they go online?
  - What channels and content do they use?
  - What are the search phrases that they use?
  - Are they looking at reviews?
  - Are they asking their friends for input?
  - What are the key service attributes or product attributes that stimulate a decision to purchase?

- What does the purchase or checkout process look like? Are there important actions to take note of?

- What does the user need after making a purchase, or what did they do?

- What kind of content or communication does your purchaser look for after making a purchase?

- What triggers them to re-purchase the product or seek out a replacement? What does that process look like?

Persona Development

Persona development is the process of creating a profile of your target audience and/or typical customer. This can include key demographics such as gender, household size, income, leisure activities, interests, and other personality traits and distinct behaviors.

Here are some basic questions to ask about your target consumer when creating a persona:

- What is the age range of this person?

- What is the income range of this person?

- What is the race and gender of this person?

- What tools do they use to research our product before making a purchase? Do they go online? If so, what types of websites and channels do they use?

- If they have a brand in mind already, how did they hear about it? Why did they choose that brand?

- What other types of behavior does this type of person typically enjoy doing?

- Do they have a family, or are they the head of the household?

- How long does it typically take to make a purchase decision in your product category? Are they constrained by time and in a rush to satisfy a purchase need?

- What does their day-to-day life look like?

If there are multiple persona or audience types you are targeting, be sure to formalize a persona deliverable for each one and run through the questions above.

Once these deliverables are identified and formalized, it's important to understand your audience's need states throughout their purchase process. Once that is done, the next step is to create content to satisfy those need states.

Need States at the Core of Content Strategies

Oftentimes, there is so much data available, it's hard to figure out where to begin when determining your content categories. After determining your audience's journey and persona, employing a need-states approach can help you craft user need states that can help inform content ideas. I define *need states* as what your audience is seeking out or emotionally craving at a moment in time and during each phase of the entire purchase process.

Figure 5.1 shows the typical purchase process in term of need states.

Figure 5.1: Typical need states

Recognize a Need

This can happen repeatedly throughout a consumer's lifetime. When you are selling a product or solution, it's important to understand how a need is triggered. This isn't supposed to be a guessing game; it should be determined as part of your research process either through digital data or preferably through survey data (by simply asking, what made you think you needed X product?). Use search data to verify those triggers and understand exactly how people search around them or ask questions around them. Be sure to use content to fill this gap.

NOTE Sometimes products with great advertising or marketing trigger needs before a consumer realizes they may need or want one. We will refrain from factoring things like that into this process and keep things linear and simpler. In my opinion, it's important to keep things simple when it comes to marketing and marketing process because long processes tend to overwhelm an already complicated subject.

Determine How to Fill That Need

Once a consumer realizes they need something, they are likely quickly going to think of a product or products. Understanding if they have a product in mind and how to break that or how to be the first product that they come across in the need state should be your priority at this stage. Look to data to see how people search for a product category or what prior websites they visit. Use content will fill this gap.

Research into Products or Brands That Can Fill the Need

Once a consumer realizes the type of product that can fill their need, they will typically conduct some research into which product is the best quality, is the best reviewed, and has the best value. Determine through surveying or even other digital data what sways users to decide on a product in your category. Then using this, create content and be sure to use *traditional sales and marketing principles* (outlined later) within your content to explain why your solution is the best.

Make a Purchase Decision

Consumers purchase your specific product at this stage. Consider confirming with them why they made the decision to purchase your product and what attributes of other products they liked of your competitors. You can do this via purchase surveys and collecting other feedback data. Be sure to use that data to optimize your offering and provide content that highlights and brings key benefits of your product front and center of that content. Work with your SEO expert to ensure that content ranks well for comparison searches and figure out content promotion strategies to boost the visibility of that content.

Use the Product to Fill That Need

At this stage, consumers are using your product. It's important to provide content on your site that explains how they should use the product (directions, set up, maintenance, etc.) and any feedback widgets that they can provide feedback on (reviews, surveys, etc.).

Express Satisfaction or Dissatisfaction

You want the user to express their satisfaction or dissatisfaction so you can alter your marketing strategies accordingly. Provide product directions and use content on your website; also embed surveys and any other widgets that can collect feedback for you. Circle back with them via email or other kinds of quick surveys to gather their feedback.

Depending on your product and the type of product it is, this could be an ongoing process. It's important to think about your target audience, the consumer journey, and need states. This will help you craft content on your site for each of the stages and to rank for important searches along the way.

Content Production Process Principles

The ideal content creation process should involve many areas of expertise. To get the most out of content, brands need to embrace the following principles:

- Ideas, need states, and pillars should be data-informed.
- Content should be optimized for search engine indexing.
- Content needs a distribution and promotion strategy.
- Results should be measured and referenced into the next round of content.

Data-Informed Content

When I first got into the space, I couldn't believe the resources that were put toward content without any strong data points justifying their creation. It seemed like content assets were created by gut instinct to support a broader campaign idea, which was typically created by focus groups or surveys. Nowadays there are many data sources available to provide insight into whether a piece of content is warranted. Here are some of the data sources (in order of priority) you should consider including in your content ideation process:

1. **Search keyword data:** As discussed in detail in Chapter 2, there are many tools available that provide marketers with insight into

what topics users are searching for and what exact phrases they are using. Searching keyword data provides a simple way to help ideate and provide a case (in the way of demand) for topics. Identify the categories of topics you'd like to consider, and then have your search engine expert (or do it yourself) input these topics into a keyword tool that will provide how often a term is searched per month and how competitive it is to rank for that topic. Highly searched topics with low competition offer the most ROI opportunity but are hard to come by. Highly searched topics with medium competition usually are good bets. Try to avoid topics that have less-than 1,000 searches with high competition.

2. **Social media listening tools:** Social media monitoring tools crawl the Internet and index discussions happening on social media channels, discussion forums, and other venues that house user-generated content. They provide reports that summarize comments and common discussion points happening within a category. These points can help provide insights into what users concerns or needs are. They can help identify disconnects between a brand or category and their audience. Content can help bridge that disconnect. Consider pulling reports about a category before ideation and briefing teams on a content initiative.

3. **Website analytics from your site or a partner (third-party) site:** Most websites use website analytics tools, like Google Analytics and Google Search Console. These tools provide useful data around what current content on your site users are frequenting the most, are engaged with the most, and use prior to converting. Try to discern what they find useful and why they find it the most engaging. If you are running a program with a partner site, consider asking them for these data points in your request for proposal or before working with them. Use any website engagement and traffic learnings as best practices as you ideate and brief on a content initiative.

4. **Internal website search widgets and website search data:** From my experience, one of the most under-utilized reports on a website seems to be the website search report. If you have a search box on your website that allows users to search for something, it's important to set up report tracking on that feature (most website analytics

tools allow for that) and monitor the report for that feature closely. The report provides the topics and items that users are looking for and oftentimes not easily finding on your website. If there are any interesting topics or items, note them in your ideation and content briefing.

5. **Online surveys:** Most websites are able to provide surveys to website users. Consider adding an open-ended question or listing topics for users to provide feedback on. While most users may decline it, there may be some users who respond and provide you with insights that can steer the content ideas. It's important to keep surveys running long enough to have statistically significant data collected. Obviously, the more popular topics or user patterns should be notated in your content briefing and ideation.

6. **Google research:** Google provides a dedicated website called Think with Google, which provides a library of great studies and research for most industries. Additionally, it just released a free research tool called Find My Audience that provides brands with insights on what kind of YouTube content your target audience is looking at, including when they are in a purchase phase. While it doesn't cover all business categories, it may inform your content creation strategies and audience profiling. The tool is available at `https:// www.thinkwithgoogle.com/feature/findmyaudience/`.

Using this tool can help you come up with YouTube content and media strategies and even inform content outside of YouTube. Figure 5.2 shows some output of the Find My Audience report for coffee shop regulars and their interests.

These are just *some* of the data points available, which should be used to feed content initiatives. There are others, particularly from paid media programs, that can offer insight too. Since this book is focused on SEO and organic content marketing, we will refrain from delving into paid media data sources.

Table 5.1 shows a content framework for you to reference when considering content projects.

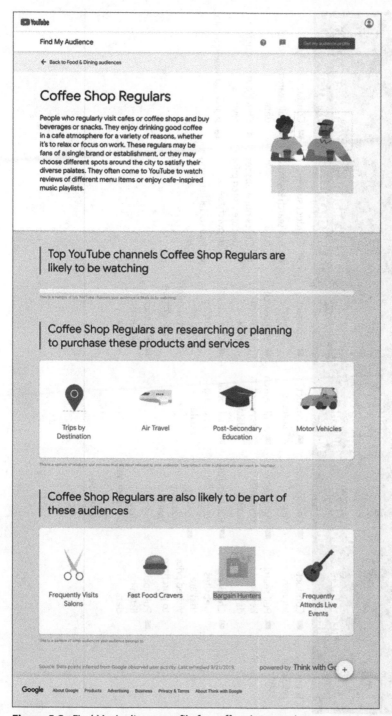

Figure 5.2: Find My Audience profile for coffee shop regulars

Table 5.1: Content creation framework around need states

	RECOGNIZE A NEED	DETERMINE HOW TO FILL THE NEED	RESEARCH INTO PRODUCTS OR BRANDS THAT CAN FILL THE NEED	MAKE A PURCHASE DECISION	USE THE PRODUCT TO FILL THAT NEED	EXPRESS SATISFACTION OR DISSATISFACTION
Brand research action	■ Conduct surveys ■ Pull search keyword data ■ Check out websites that are visited prior to purchase ■ Pull social listening data	■ Conduct surveys ■ Pull search keyword data ■ Pull social listening data ■ Look at websites that rank high for those searches and are authorities	■ Conduct surveys ■ Pull search keyword data ■ Pull social listening data	■ Conduct surveys ■ Pull search keyword data ■ Check out websites that are visited prior to purchase ■ Pull social listening data	■ Conduct surveys ■ Pull search keyword data ■ Check out websites that are visited prior to purchase ■ Pull social listening data	■ Conduct surveys ■ Pull search keyword data ■ Check out product reviews ■ Pull social listening data

	RECOGNIZE A NEED	DETERMINE HOW TO FILL THE NEED	RESEARCH INTO PRODUCTS OR BRANDS THAT CAN FILL THE NEED	MAKE A PURCHASE DECISION	USE THE PRODUCT TO FILL THAT NEED	EXPRESS SATISFACTION OR DISSATISFACTION
Data points	▪ Survey data ▪ Search keyword data ▪ Website tracking data ▪ Social listening data	▪ Survey data ▪ Search keyword data ▪ Website tracking data ▪ Social listening data	▪ Survey data ▪ Search keyword data ▪ Website tracking data ▪ Social listening data	▪ Survey data ▪ Search keyword data ▪ Website tracking data ▪ Social listening data	▪ Survey data ▪ Search keyword data ▪ Website tracking data ▪ Social listening data	▪ Survey data ▪ Search keyword data ▪ Website tracking data ▪ Social listening data ▪ Product review data
Brand questions to answer	▪ What are users thinking when they realize they may need a product to fill a void? ▪ What mediums affect them or do they use?	▪ How can my brand answer those questions or intercept them during the user's research phase?	▪ Why is my brand/product the best solution for the need? ▪ What avenues are they using to research possible need solutions?	▪ Where did the user buy a solution? ▪ What influenced their decision?	▪ What did the user like about my product? ▪ What did the user dislike about my product? ▪ Did the user look at my website for guidance?	▪ Were there any good results and/or surprises in using the product? ▪ Will the user share their experience? ▪ Do they have a platform to share their experience? ▪ Will they buy again?

The Content Production Process

An integrated content process that upholds the aforementioned content principles is key to having a strong content that performs well in the way of organic traffic, engagement, and conversions (sales, etc.); see Figure 5.3.

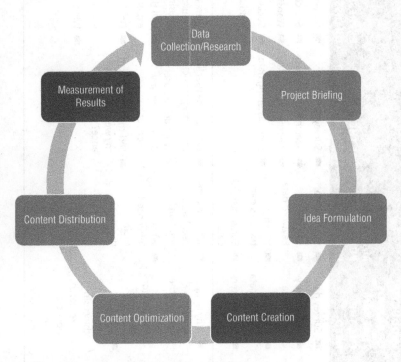

Note: Shaded boxes are tasks requiring heavy SEO support

Figure 5.3: Content process

Data Collection

The first part of the process should begin with data collection and research. Marketers should leverage the data outlined previously to identify demand and engagement patterns, which provide ideas on what content should be created and what it should look like. Things should not move along to the next process until data has been reviewed and findings have been summarized.

Doing a thorough review and identification of demand metrics around topics is a key step that most ineffective marketing ideas fail at. Ideas that aren't supported by data are often rudderless and can morph into pointless content and bad results, wasting resources and budget. The SEO and analytic resources should pull together a content gap analysis and suggested response strategy during this stage to also be presented in the briefing (discussed in Chapter 4). The task owners are the SEO expert, analytics, PR/social teams, brand planners, and media team members.

Project Briefing

Once data is solidified, a project brief should be created. This document is meant to provide copywriters, creative directors, and other stakeholders with insight into the parameters and guidelines for the project. The format of this should always be evolving, should answer some basic questions about the project and provide best-practice guidelines, and outline the goals (performance data) for the project. Since a good project brief is so critical, I've provided a sample at the end of this chapter.

Required attendees for the project briefing include the creative director, copywriter, SEO, producer, media manager, web developer, user experience, and brand strategist.

Idea Formation

Once the brief is solidified and presented, an ideation or brainstorm session should be held with key stakeholders to identify what kind of assets should be created and what kind of form they should take. This could be as simple as a copywriter, creative director, or the entire stakeholder teams.

The best ideas should be outlined and presented to the brand team along with the potential traffic numbers that can be quantified based on the data presented in the first step. Adding the SEO expert will allow for a more refined traffic expectation, as there are many studies available that show what percent of traffic an asset can expect based on the average search ranking of the asset. Once the idea is presented, it's time to begin.

Task owners include creative directors, copywriters, and the SEO expert.

Content Creation

Depending on the type of asset (article, video, white paper, study, tool, etc.) that's being created, this step can take some time and require some approvals and many different meetings and check-ins. It's important to keep the SEO expert in tune with the creation process because they can help enforce guidelines and best practices. Oftentimes, the SEO expert can proofread and ensure the guidelines in the brief are being met.

Task owners include creative directors, copywriters, and SEO experts.

Content Optimization

The content optimization process is done just as the content creation process is finalized. There's a fine line as far as timing; the intent is to provide a dedicated phase for final, minor revisions (if possible) and for the SEO expert to add any SEO indexing elements as part of the deliverable (tags, URL recommendations, meta tags). These elements are dependent on the venue where this asset will reside (website, partner site, YouTube, etc.).

The task owner for this step is the SEO expert.

Content Distribution

Content should always have an organic distribution strategy, especially if paid media content promotion isn't being utilized. There are many organic ways to promote content that SEO teams should provide guidance on. Assuming the content is search engine friendly and the first two of three pillars of good SEO are optimal, then a content distribution strategy is the last critical stage that can make or break a content asset's search engine ranking. Depending on what the content asset is, some organic distribution tactics include syndicating links to the content via partner websites, social media shares and bookmarking, e-newsletters, influencer initiatives, and online press releases.

Task owners include the SEO expert, media managers, and PR/social.

Measurement of Results

Measuring results is an extremely important, final part of the content process. It can take some time to build statistically meaningful performance data. Once the data is sufficient, an analytics resource should pull together the data points in a formal or informal report. Then a post-mortem meeting should be held to discuss the success or results of the project. Learnings should be rolled into the next content idea and project brief.

The content process is ever-evolving, with new data points and guidelines available coming into play. This overall framework is meant to provide guidance on how to execute an effective content idea.

Task owners include the SEO and analytics experts, and the entire team should attend the post-mortem meeting.

Bonus: Content Marketer Interview

To get a look inside the fast-moving science of content marketing and how brands are using it, O conducted an interview with Caleb Gonsalvez, who formerly the content director at Skyword, a popular content management platform. The full interview is provided next, but here are the key takeaways of the interview:

- Brands and marketers have a difficult time defining what content is in their world.

- Content should deliver value, and brands need to find a balance between quality and quantity.

- From a nonbrand side, marketers should "test the waters" around content topics by first trying lower-fi content (text articles, social media posts, blogs, etc.) for a significant amount of time (e.g., six months) to get an idea of what the market wants and needs before spending time and budget on larger-scale content initiatives.

- Content categories have evolved to focus on providing audiences with educational, informational, entertainment, and purpose-driven experiences.

Here is the full interview:

Nick Papagiannis: Can you describe your role, and how you support businesses' and brands' content needs?

Caleb Gonsalvez: I'm the director of brand strategy for Skyword. Skyword is a content marketing platform, but we have layers of managed services where we actually do a lot of content creation and content strategy for clients. I have a thorough understanding of what best-in-class content marketing is, because obviously *content marketing* can be a pretty broad term. It means a lot of different things to a lot of different people.

NP: How does that translate tactically?

CG: I tend to go into larger enterprise organizations, find out what their business goals are, find out what audiences they're trying to reach, and essentially provide my version of a content strategy that bridges that gap. It's not just a matter of asking what type of content influences or engages the target customer that you're going after but how do you string that thread and tie it back to business objectives? We're in marketing for a reason, and you have to use content to drive revenue or other forms of conversion. You can't just do it for fun. So what does that look like?

NP: That's great, and then what are the big content challenges you're seeing clients dealing with these days?

CG: The one that drives me the craziest, and I think it's like an epidemic within the industry, is when *content marketing* became a formal buzzword. I feel like everybody just rushed in and was like, "Oh, we do content!" and they basically relabeled traditional marketing as content, and I think it polluted the term in a way.

I always make the joke that you can walk into a room full of 100 marketers and ask them, "What is content?" and you get 99 different answers. Why I think that's an issue is it's everybody saying that they're doing one thing, and they're all doing different things. That's not to say that content marketing can't take many different forms, but don't try to put lipstick on a pig.

First and foremost, I think content should always just deliver value. I always say deliver value to your customers before you ever ask for value in return, and if you don't, you're bragging and promising and sort of yelling at them like we've always traditionally done. So I think that's a challenge. Everyone's trying to justify their jobs and look at the numbers, and how are they delivering value to the company? They're using the term *content* too broadly, and I do think that has polluted the industry in a way, because for my experience—and I've learned just as much from our wins as I have our failures—when you do "content marketing" right, it can be amazing. But if you're just trying to do the same thing that you've always done and slap the term *content* on it, you're not going to get anything out of it, and it's ultimately going to end in failure.

The other challenge I hear often is the quality of content versus quantity of content pieces debate, and which is more important to achieving your goals. I often have to change people's perception on it, that it doesn't have to be one or the other, too. It's hard to do.

NP: Do you feel that you're seeing clients create content without any real data behind it?

CG: The expectations on marketers today is almost unfair, because some folks are coming from a creative background—you know, more traditional advertising, like coming up with the copy and making it interesting and captivating—but everything now, especially with marketing automation systems and even CMPs [content management platforms], is measurable now. So some people are really comfortable with the analytics side of things, and in that respect, they're good with doing data-backed research on social listening, consumer behavior, search behavior, but then if you tend to be good at that aspect, when you actually go in to create the copy or you create the content, it's not as compelling; it's not as visually appealing or all these different things. But if you're on the creative side of things and you don't want to limit yourself, using data can feel restrictive.

So that's what I think is challenging, and the best marketers have a little bit of both, but at the same time, if you're a jack-of-all-trades, master of none, that's a challenge too, so again, it is a little unfair. So finding that balance between using data without compromising the integrity of the content can be a challenge.

NP: Do you find different types of content assets are required in this day and age? So, instead of writing an article about car insurance, maybe there's something much more creative that brands should be doing. Do you find that for specifically competitive topics or categories, brands need to think a little bit bigger and think about different types of content assets instead of just basic assets?

CG: Since content marketing is getting a lot more visibility and it's not a proof of concept anymore, it has more visibility on the senior leadership level, and while that's great because you can get larger budgets or you have more access or people are more receptive to your ideas, it's a double-edged sword because everybody suddenly is a marketer. Content becomes reactionary where somebody goes, "We need a video on this," and then they push it down to the content marketing team or whoever. Obviously, however, that organization is structured; they might not even have a content marketing team, but it falls under a certain system.

That's neither here nor there, but it's like they just feel like they need a video, so they produce a video, and videos take a lot of time, and they're very expensive, and then they put it out there and it gets a thousand views, and they're like, "Well, that was a failure. Video doesn't work," and that's a backward way of thinking.

What I always try to encourage clients to do is test the waters with lower-touch content types like text-based content—either social media posts, a blog post, or a micro site or something. We then feel out what the market wants and what the market needs, but we don't think about it as a channel strategy or an asset-level strategy. We think about it as a topical-level strategy. What is it that your audience cares about? What is it that they find interesting? What would they want to engage with? Come up with those ideas, and that's where you can use data, a ton of search data, a ton of social data that you could basically use as a barometer out of the gate, and then think about what the right medium is to tell that story or create content around it.

Advanced content types take a lot of time and budget, for example, even creating a white paper. Everybody loves white papers. If you're a B2B organization, they're like, "Oh, we need a white paper. Oh, we need an e-book," and I'm like, "Well, do you?" which is great, totally, but white papers are not easy to do, and half the time, especially on a B2B side, you've got to interview a bunch of subject-matter experts, some of them externally, some of them internal. You've got to have a writer who is not only adept in the subject matter, but they also have to be good at interviewing and then stringing everything together. That's hard to do sometimes, so it can take six months. I've seen companies take six months to a year to put out one white paper, and they hope it sticks; they hope it works.

So one thing that we've started doing—and a lot of this is even through our own technology—but we'll put feelers out there. We'll create, let's say 50 assets, like lighter touch, maybe 400- to 600-word blog posts accompanying social media posts, even maybe some lighter designed assets, like micrographics. Nothing too intense, but we'll put that out there. We'll do it for six months, and then we'll go back and we'll look at the data and we'll see if there are broader seas that have really resonated.

So let's say if you have 10 categories that you've created content around, and you can create subcategories if you want to get really granular, if you're a pretty adept marketer, but then look at the trends. Are there two or three categories that knock it out of the park where every time you write a blog post the traffic just skyrockets because it's from an organic perspective, or every time you put a subject on social, on an X topic, it gets the most engagement? Then look at that data that you didn't spend too much time or too much money on and find the overlap. Create essentially a Venn diagram of all the interest, but where the concentrated piece is, and then use that information to go create a white paper, and then what we do is we'll take that white paper or another gated asset, and we had that as the call to action on the original posts. We'll go back and do a little refresh of the content. So you're maximizing the use of assets that you've already created. You're doing your due diligence to make sure that you understand which pieces of content.

To the best of your knowledge, you know it's going to perform because your audience told you this is what they want, as opposed to you assuming what they want, and then you still get that white paper, but it's saved you so much effort in the long run, and the likelihood that it's going to perform is that much higher, because you used your own proprietary data, which you got through creating content, to inform that strategy.

NP: You mentioned utility. What other attributes about content do brands need to think about that content needs to have in order to capture as much organic traffic? Are there any others outside of utility?

CG: I think why it was so hard for me to answer that initially is I instantly delineate in my head between B2C [business to consumer] and B2B [business to business]. Whenever I go into a strategy session or I'm thinking about a strategy that I'm about to build, I always put the audience first and just think about exactly what they would find interesting. Then I just try to employ as much empathy as I can, and I put myself in their position. What does this person care about? What do they deal with from the time they wake up to the time they go to bed? What are all the touchpoints? Where do they spend their time, and what are they reading? What are they interested in?

From there, that's when I try to come up with the topic or themes, what the content should employ, what attributes it should have, and then and only then do I think about how I can tie it back to the brand and the business objective, because I think consumers in general—again, B2B or B2C—have gotten smart enough to smell through the fluff.

Any marketer who doesn't think that way is not a good marketer and is not doing their job. So when I think about the different attributes it might have, I think about the audience and I think about the potential channel, social versus digital versus paid, etc., but I do think that content does fall under at least four camps. There's the educational, informational content. That kind has to work really, really well on the B2B side. There's the entertainment piece, which is more B2C. The one that I think has become its own category in the last couple years, and probably the one that I'm the most excited about, and the one that I watch the most, is purpose-driven content.

I'm talking about brands that align themselves with social issues or economic issues and go all in. There are a few banks that have been doing this really well. If you think about the banking industry, especially retail banking, it's a commoditized industry. There's no differentiation whatsoever, except branch locations, which really doesn't even matter anymore, because everybody's moving towards digital.

They're aligning themselves with LGBTQ issues or trans issues or minority-owned businesses, and they're just creating content and they're creating experiences on focus. They're putting their money where their mouth is, and they're supporting events and hosting community events. It's incredible and I love watching it. There's so much you can do with content there, but as long as you're authentic and the brand has to live those values too, it makes a huge difference.

I think there's been a lot more attention on that. It's not about entertainment; it's not about education. The last one that I would put in there is like the true product-focused content. You still have to have that sometimes, right?

NP: Right.

CG: "Here are the features and benefits. This is why you might use it." That's not going away, but again, that other category of the corporate social responsibility, but really, it's more of a purpose-driven marketing. I think brand strategy, content strategy, and purpose are going to blend so closely that you won't be able to tell them apart in the next ten years. That's my assumption.

NP: You mentioned, kind of, where things are going. Are there any technology advances that you feel are affecting content production or content reading? Any tech areas that you think are going to significantly enhance the content experience in the next 10 years or so?

CG: This is probably not a popular opinion, but this is my opinion. I'm looking forward to the consolidation of platforms.

I'm thinking about the era of 2008 to 2012, where the proliferation of social media platforms just exploded, and now obviously it's whittled down mostly to Facebook, Twitter, Instagram, and LinkedIn, but even those platforms are. . .Facebook is getting a lot of crap, LinkedIn is getting a lot of crap, Twitter's getting a lot of crap. The only one that's really booming is Instagram in my opinion. Even Snapchat is falling down.

At the time, everybody saw all of these channels pop up, and they were like, "We need to be everywhere! We just need a social strategy!" and nobody ever thought to say, "Okay, what does that actually mean?" Now I think we're seeing the residual effects of that, where those platforms are plateauing in a way. Again, this is a little controversial, which is why I'm trying to find the right words. I think people are going to rebel against the thought that "everybody needs to be on every platform." I think people are just going to get overwhelmed. I think that's what we're seeing now. So on the platform side of things, the technology, the digital side of things, I do think it'll consolidate, and I think people will find their own little pockets, more than they ever have. But on the brand side, sort of the marketing side, the business side of things, I don't think the integration of platforms is going away, and I think any system that can come up with a really strong attribution model.

I always make the running joke that the marketer who figures out the perfect attribution model will be a god among marketers. They would be a very rich individual, because attribution models are hard, and I think we're getting better at it, especially with CMPs and marketing automation and CRMs. They're all getting tied closer and closer together, which in some ways complicates it and in some ways makes it more effective.

So, how that shakes out, I'm not entirely sure. I think we're in the middle of it. Obviously, we're in the CMP space. Even within our own space, we saw the explosion in 2010, and it's getting whittled down now, and that's just one segment of the industry. Did that answer your question?

NP: Yes, it does, and I agree. The consolidation of platforms is going to be a lot easier for folks, but it could be more competition for brands resulting in higher costs.

CG: Marketers have more visibility than they've ever had. They have more direct attribution to revenue than they ever had, but their budgets are not getting bigger, so they have to be smarter about where they spend their budget and which platforms they're on. While that is very hard to do, because there's so many options, you don't have to be everywhere. So I think for folks, they need to pick. Again, I will sound like a broken record, but I truly believe that everything should be audience first, and I say audience instead of just customer, because it can be people who could be future customers. It's just people who you think that you can influence or who you can add value in their lives. That's your audience, in my opinion. You need to take a look at the channels that you're on, and you need to look at the content you're creating, and you need to think about the audience.

If you find that LinkedIn isn't good for a B2C brand, then cut it out. You don't need to have it. Nobody's making you have it. But again, this is what I was saying earlier. When there was that boom, everybody just jumped on it, and they were like, "We need a Facebook strategy!" I used to work at TripAdvisor prior to joining Skyword; we were launching our Facebook pages, and everything was about getting folks to "like" the page. We designed all of this imagery, put that arrow up to the "Like" button, and spent so much time and so much effort designing it and trying to up our conversions. Then a couple years later, Google . . . . Well, Google pulled back too. Facebook cut back the algorithm and organic search for brands, and all of the social media marketers who spent all of this time developing these channel strategies lost so much value.

So, you have to be careful on where you head your best, and how much time you spend on each channel, and if you think it's a good channel for your audience, dedicate the time, but you will get stretched thin if you try to do too many things.

Sample Project Brief

A sample project brief for an article or long-form content project is provided here. This is meant to serve as an example to one of the most common forms of SEO and content projects. The brief is designed to offer direction on what the project output should be.

Brief

- What business problem are we solving for?
- What target audience problem are we solving for?
- What data points support this initiative?
- What search terms are we targeting to rank for?
- What is our target audience?
- What is our voice (first-person/third-person, singular/plural)?
  - I, we, us, you, they, etc.
- Are there any key formatting requirements? Bullets, call to action, etc.
- Is there content online and/or on our website that this should link to?
- Are there examples of content from other sites that meet a similar need?
- What does our content demand diversity analysis indicate?
  - What is the suggested content response?
  - Will this project follow that framework?
  - If not, why?

Guidelines

- Be original. Is this content unique?
- Aim for 1,000 words or more:
- Include a certain term in the article headline.
  - Term will be provided by search team or mentioned earlier.
- Include a targeted search term at least 1 time per 100 words, especially above the fold.
- Answer the question or solve the problem.
- Include images and other visuals if possible.

Quiz

1. True or False: A key question when determining a persona is what is the age range of the person?

   Answer: True

2. Which of the following are questions to ask when formalizing a journey?
   a. What triggers the need for a person to purchase a product?
   b. What does the research process look like prior to them making a decision?
   c. What kind of content does the user look for when making a purchase?
   d. All the above.
   e. None of the above.

   Answer: d

3. True or False: Content should be defined as "something that is to be expressed through some medium: speech, writing, or of any various arts."

   Answer: True

4. Which of the following is not a phase in the content process?
   a. Project briefing
   b. Idea formation
   c. Content creation
   d. Content optimization
   e. Delete old content
   f. Measure results

   Answer: e

5. True or False: Content consumption is *not* the #1 behavior online.

   Answer: False

6. True or False: The following are all content principles:

   - Ideas, need states, and pillars should be data-informed.

   - Content should be optimized for search engine indexing.

   - Contact needs a distribution and promotion strategy.

   - Performance results should be measured and referenced into the next round of content.

   Answer: True

7. True or False: Online surveys are great data source to leverage during the content ideation process.

   Answer: True

8. True or False: The more competitive and higher frequency search phrases should be avoided.

   Answer: True

9. Content should always have a _____ strategy.

   a. Distribution

   b. Amplification

   c. Diversity

   d. Localization

   Answer: a

10. Who is the ultimate task owner of content optimization?

   a. SEO expert

   b. Social media expert

   c. User experience expert

   d. Creative director

   Answer: A

The Best Content That Can Drive Traffic

The main goal of this book is to educate you on how to utilize content and SEO to maximize the free or organic traffic levels to your website and nonwebsite content.

The best way to do that is to utilize both together by using search volume or demand and competition metrics of your topics to dictate the level of content response and by using a diverse set of topics to capture several topics and their respective users. There are many benefits of this approach, including the following:

- Builds your brand to be an authority on a diverse set of topics
- Gives brands ideas about what type of content to create
- Helps your website and content rank for many different types of searches
- Ensures resources and dollars are being utilized in the most cost efficient and impactful manner
- Builds long-term traffic
- Builds awareness and consideration

- Elevates a brand to where it needs to be, regardless of competitive environment
- Requires relatively low cost and gives outstanding long-term return on investment

Missed Opportunities

Content marketing is not easy, so it's pretty obvious that brands often miss the mark from a process and science standpoint. We've outlined many things as far as process and the overall science of content marketing, but there are some important execution steps that should be outlined to prevent any mishaps and missed opportunities.

Oftentimes, brands neglect these key areas of content marketing; using demand metrics to inform the level of content response, having a content diversity approach, and having a formal content discovery program.

It's not a matter of just collecting data and using that data to create a basic content initiative; it's important to look at certain metrics to identify the necessary level of sophistication required to have a successful content program. In general, high-demand, highly competitive topics require a much more well thought out deliverable than low-demand, low-competition topics.

It's also important to think about the different types of content that exist. Content can range from very basic to very complicated and rich in form. Many brands often fail to understand the different types of content and forms that exist on the Web as well as off the Web. Brands tend to put a basic content response together because they stay in their comfort zone with what they know. A well-versed content marketer should know all the current forms the content comes in as well as new and emerging forms the content will be coming in. Some examples of emerging content include conversational commerce, augmented reality, immersive experiences, and 3-D content. These are not typical of brand content; they are just some of the examples that are on the horizon or already exist.

Content discovery is extremely critical to having successful content. It helps improve the traffic to your content and can help make your content successful by bringing a meaningful amount of readers to it.

Content Discovery

We discussed the idea of content promotion in Chapter 4, "Stakeholders for the Modern SEO and Organic Content Process," but it's important to also discuss the idea of content discovery, which is quite similar but requires a more strategic mind-set. *Content discovery* means connecting users with your content while they are already consuming content. It can be an effective means to capturing a significant amount of traffic to your website.

Brands often fail to put together journeys along the content consumption process. Using journey mentality can help brands also understand the ways they can improve discovery of their content via content discovery vehicles. There are paid vendors that could help with your content discovery initiatives. There are also organic and unpaid methods that require a brand to identify themselves, i.e., not through a vendor.

Oftentimes, brands fail to formulate content discovery strategies and tactics. There are multiple steps when determining how to ensure your content will be discovered as well as possible.

Step 1: Identify a customer's journey.

Step 2: Identify the persona or personas that you are going after.

Step 3: Identify the websites and different venues that are online or offline, which your persona may use to consume broad content.

Step 4: Identify how to intersect your users with your content. This might require paid tactics or an analysis that delves into the different ways you can intercept your audience. For instance, you may conduct an audit that identifies that you are sending an email newsletter to your audience. This may be a simple method to use to connect your users with new content you were trying to promote.

There are many content discovery methods available to leverage as a marketer. Here are some standard content discovery methods to consider:

- **Email newsletters:** Newsletters are frequently used to communicate news and new content to audiences already in your database. Be sure to leverage newsletters to highlight links to new content.

- **Social media updates:** Social media updates are also frequently used to update new content. Make sure to build up your social media presence and use updates to link and promote new content or important content.

- **Search engines:** Search engines (Google, Bing, even YouTube) are an obvious content discovery engine. Be sure to work with an SEO expert to ensure your new content gets crawled and ranks as highly as possible, or consider using paid search ads to boost traffic to new content.

- **Partner sites and other partner assets:** Whether a vendor of yours or even an influencer, partners offer a great opportunity to boost content discovery. An example may be a car brand working with dealerships to post or share content on their website or emails or social media.

- **Local directories:** Oftentimes, local directories that list your business allow for website links to be included in your profile. Be sure to leverage this feature to link to content hubs and priority content.

- **In-store tactics:** If you have brick-and-mortar stores, the in-store experience offers an opportunity to promote content and showcase content to users who are already aware of your brand. Consider adding posters or adding links to takeaways like receipts, flyers, bags, or other assets to promote content hubs and important content.

- **Events:** If you hold events, be sure to leverage things like take-home materials or announcements to promote content hubs and priority content.

- **Catalogs:** Catalogs offer a great opportunity to attach content or include URLs or links to priority content on your website.

- **Print ads:** Ads offer broad exposure for your brand, and many allow for URLs to be embedded in them. Consider adding a link to your content hub or priority content.

- **Video or TV ads:** Video ads offer an opportunity to promote a URL to your website or content hub. Consider adding language at the end encouraging views to visit your content hub URL or priority webpage, as this can bring broad awareness of your priority content.

- **Paid tactics:** Content discovery engines are available from the very basic offerings to broad offerings such as paid agreements on high-profile websites or sponsored content. Consider adding content discovery to your media planning, which can increase views significantly.

Use Demand to Dictate Your Content Response

When I mention content in the SEO world, many folks think it means text articles or website landing pages. As we said before, Google's goal is to index all the world's content. That content can come in many shapes and types. Its algorithm is evolving to rank all types of content.

Per our discussion of data collection, it's important to understand how competitive a topic is. The more competitive a topic is, the louder a brand has to essentially "shout" to be heard or seen.

Think about a crowded New York City street, with hundreds of people walking. It's hard to be noticed and to get ahead of the pack. You may have to shout loudly or dress differently to get noticed. There are typically millions of pieces of content in a high-traffic category or in a general search. For example, *car insurance* has 2.8 million rankings in organic Google Search Results. It's a tough place to crack into. There's not a simple text article or landing that will rank or leapfrog content that's secured a high position.

If you are facing a similar issue, it's important to think beyond text articles. Competition in the organic search or content space is your worst enemy. You have to think about providing something different and more comprehensive. The demand is there, but you have to shout louder and look different by offering more advanced content. Lower-competition topics allow for an easier way to rank into Google's top results. For instance, *state farm auto insurance bodily injury limits* is much less competitive and easier to rank. An SEO-optimized landing page with long-form text and good linking will likely rank higher if done right. It's much easier to rank for this term than, say, *car insurance* because there's less competition for that term and less exactly phrased content. Assuming your tech environment is SEO friendly, there are three tiers of content response that I recommend based on how competitive and highly searched a topic is.

1. **Standard content response** is for low to medium competitive topics with lower search volume of less than 5,000 average searches

per month. This is more typical of SEO onsite practices, including the following:

- Long-form article creation
- Basic link building and content promotion

2. **Advanced content response** is for medium to highly competitive topics that have a medium search volume of 5,000 to 100,000 average searches per month.

- Long-form article creation
- Video (one-off or series)
- Tools (e.g., calculators, quizzes, listicles, guides)
- White papers
- Images (e.g., infographics, decision trees, checklists)

3. **Advanced Plus content response** is for high to *extremely* highly competitive topics that have a search volume of 100,000 average searches per month or more. The goal should be to use search data and guidelines to inform other marketing tactics and brand experiences.

- Ongoing video (TV, online)
- Podcasts
- Films
- Events
- Products and services
- Dedicated advertising campaigns
- Games
- Dedicated websites
- Editorials and "feature" or custom content on partner sites
- Digital magazines or books
- Experiential marketing tactics

Table 6.1 shows an example of a content response strategy that's based on search volume for a credit brand.

Table 6.1: Content Response Strategy Based on Search Volume

CONTENT TOPIC	SEARCH VOLUME	COMPET-ITIVENESS	SUGGESTED CONTENT RESPONSE	CONTENT EXAMPLES
How to buy a home with bad credit	1,200	Low	Standard	Long-form for article/web page on website
Identity theft	60,500	Medium	Advanced	∎ Video ∎ White papers ∎ Dedicated content/ section on website
Debt consolidation	100,000	High	Advanced Plus	∎ Dedicated website ∎ Products ∎ Dedicated video channel

The Importance of Content Diversity

The more relevant content is, the better it is in the case of SEO. It's important to realize that sites that publish a lot of content often, even daily (whether website writers or user-generated content), typically get the most online traffic.

If online marketing were fishing, the content library would be your net. The more content you have, the more traffic you will catch. Furthermore, having a diversified content portfolio, similar to a diversified investment portfolio, benefits a brand's presence in a few other tactical ways. It promotes multiple means of attracting clicks, it offsets competition risk by spreading a brand's traffic footprint across more topics, and it allows the brand to become an "authority" on multiple topics. All these benefits sum up to more traffic and better performance.

Many sites belong to a specific industry and often fail to explore building content that speaks beyond their immediate product category. It's important to consider other high-demand content topics in your broader category. In fact, it's fairly simple to figure out what content topics are driving traffic to your site and what topics your site is exposed to. If your site has Google Search Console installed, which all sites should have, there's a performance report that outlines the search terms and topics that are driving traffic to your site. Consider pulling the report and identifying what topics are driving traffic to your website.

CASE EXAMPLE

Here's an example of a content diversification analysis for a brand in the credit category:

Using Google's Keyword Planner tool, we can see from Figure 6.1 the relevant subcategories Google assigns to the credit category (most other keyword tools do as well). In fact, the percent of the pie indicates how much search demand/volume of the total credit pie these subcategories get.

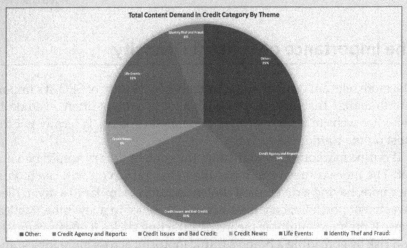

Figure 6.1: Total content diversification opportunity

Digging into the performance data that Google Search Console offers for the credit brand's website, we can see in Figure 6.2 what terms are currently driving traffic to the brand. In fact, we see they are only currently getting most of their traffic from *credit agency* searches and other brands (marked "other" searches).

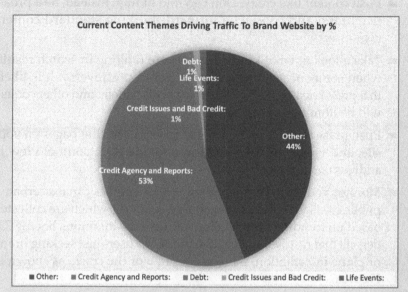

Figure 6.2: Current level of content diversification

The disconnect between the two pies is significant, and building content around the subcategory framework that Google's keyword tool offers can yield much more traffic. In fact, our initial analysis estimates that brands can earn millions of new, relevant website visits each month.

Thus, it's important to have a diverse yet relevant content strategy and content response.

The SEO expert and analytic resource should pull together this analysis, also called *content demand gap analysis*, during the research phase of the content process. This analysis should also be shared during the briefing stage and within the brief itself.

Reputation Management: Content Responses When Your Brand Is in Trouble

Oftentimes, brands can find themselves with negative PR or controversies. Search engines are likely one of the first tools an inquiring customer may use to learn details about the issue. There are some things you can do as a marketer to break through the noise and negative press to tell your story.

- Push content like crazy. Don't go into hiding; instead, be a proactive brand and conduct a forward-thinking standard content response.

- Take a look at what kinds of assets are ranking in search results when someone searches for your brand controversy. It is likely that press releases, testimonies, blog posts, videos, and other content will be dominating the results.

- Push press releases on newswire services, landing pages on your site, and videos on YouTube that provide your point of view to address consumers.

- Monitor your trending searches. Search engines can exacerbate a public crisis via their autosuggested searches, which are collected based on trending search behavior. Take the infamous Boeing 737 defects that resulted in negative press. For users just seeking brand or plane information, there are results for the crash, as shown in Figure 6.3.

boeing 737

boeing 737-**800**
boeing 737
boeing 737 **max**
boeing 737-**900**
boeing 737-**700**
boeing 737-**900 united**
boeing 737-**800 passenger**
boeing 737 **max crash**
boeing 737-**900er**
boeing 737 **max 8 crash**

Figure 6.3: Suggested searches for *Boeing 737* include *crash*

Many brands are armed and ready to address negative press and provide an arsenal of content to rank and dominate search results. One of my favorite examples involves a Taco Bell controversy from several years ago, when they were sued for having poor-quality meat. They provided a robust content response that allowed them to get ahead of controversial searches by developing multiple content assets to help rank for these negative, autosuggested searches. Taco Bell successfully used YouTube videos, landing pages (with embedded YouTube videos), press releases through online wire services, blog entries, and social media updates to tell their side of the story and outrank negative headlines (Figure 6.4).

Figure 6.4: Taco Bell's content response to controversy

In case you are faced with negative press, be sure to have a defensive SEO content plan and infrastructure in place. At the end of the day, Taco Bell was lauded for its response, and it's a great example of how a strong content response can provide brand benefits, especially during times of crisis (Figure 6.5).

Figure 6.5: Taco Bell rebounds

Bonus: Starter List of Potential Content Types

The list of content types is vast and continuously expanding. We've provided a list for you to get started. It provides some basic types for you to incorporate into your strategy.

BONUS: STARTER LIST OF POTENTIAL CONTENT TYPES	
Standard	**Advanced Plus**
■ Long-form article/web page	■ Event footage
■ Infographics	■ Podcasts
■ Decision trees	■ Ebooks/emagazines
■ Checklists	■ Classes
■ Webinars	■ Custom content on part-
■ Photos/images	nered website
■ Website video	■ Dedicated video channels
■ Tools such as calculators,	■ Websites
apps	■ Products
■ Whitepapers	■ TV spots
■ Listicles	■ Charities
■ Blogs	■ Radio shows
■ Quizzes	■ Video, including animated,
■ Recipes and help content	educational, documentary,
■ Online press releases	scripted shows

Content Principles

Since content is extremely critical to brand performance in the way of traffic, which can translate into stronger brand awareness and consideration, content should be created with the following principles in mind:

- **Uniqueness:** Content should be unique for a search phrase. Brands should provide a unique point of view on a topic and avoid creating similar content that's already on the Web. In fact, reducing content duplication was one of the original features of Google's spam algorithm and is still part of the algorithm to this day. Content duplication can result in low rankings and negative SEO performance.

- **Search engine friendliness:** As we've been saying all along in this book, content that's invisible or ranking poorly on search engines is going to perform poorly. Be sure to follow search engine guidelines and/or work with your search engine expert to make sure your content is optimized for search engines.

- **Utility:** It's important that content offer value to readers, whether through statistics or expert answers. The more utility a piece of content offers, the more likely it will be shared. It's also likely that readers will link to it. Assuming your content is search-friendly, links and shares will increase the SEO ranking of your page.

- **Visual appeal:** While long-form text articles tend to perform well, it's important to also include images and basic visuals to enhance the reading experience. Images such as charts, graphs, infographics, art, and decision trees create an enhanced experience visually and can increase important engagement metrics like time on a page, so be sure to keep things visual. Additionally, images can rank for Google Image results, the tab option on the search engine results page. Be sure to tag your images using the best practices outlined in the previous chapters.

- **Longer length:** As we mentioned in previous chapters, most top-ranking pages these days tend to have a significant amount of text. Be sure to have longer-form content.

- **Freshness:** Content should be fresh and regularly edited. Keep the content on the same URL, since it likely has built up SEO value, but be sure to always revisit content and make edits to include the latest statistics, studies, and any other updates needed to keep things fresh.

- **In demand:** Most importantly, content needs to be in demand. As mentioned in Chapter 5, "Data-Informed Creative," be sure to build content that people are looking for. You don't want to go through the effort of building content if it's not something that you know that people are looking for.

Link Building

As we've said before, popularity is one of the three SEO pillars. The main way that search engines determine popularity is by the number of links pointing to a piece of content from other websites. Link building is a tricky subject when it comes to SEO. Over the years, SEO teams and link vendors have found ways to artificially add inbound links to websites, making them look popular and essentially manipulating the Google algorithm into ranking for them. As a result, many of Google's spam updates have targeted artificial link building. It's a difficult subject to talk about in some ways because even if proper inbound linking is done incorrectly, your site can be penalized and even de-indexed from Google on rare occasions. It's important to think of links as "content promoters" and essentially anchors that link to valuable content that users find useful. They are essentially endorsements and votes for your content. The more "votes" you have, the more trust and SEO value search engines place on your website, which help it rank for more searches.

Google has a list of quality guidelines that it expects sites to follow, available at https://support.google.com/webmasters/answer/35769.

One key rule in the quality guidelines is for sites not to participate in artificial link building or link schemes. Some examples that Google lays out for link schemes include the following:

- Buying or selling links that pass PageRank or link value to your site

- Excessive link partnering or reciprocal linking, e.g., you have a partner site that offers to link to your site if you link to them

- Large-scale article marketing or guest posting campaigns that have keyword-rich anchor text links

- Text advertisements that pass link value

- Buying advertorials or native advertising and adding links that pass link value to your site

- Links that have exact match anchor text in press releases or articles distributed on other sites

- Links from low-quality directory sites

- Adding links to sites in forum or article comment sections of another website

Google's algorithm is smart enough now to identify artificial link building tactics like these. Violating their quality guidelines will likely bring penalties and compromised SEO performance of your site. Thus, it's important to promote healthy, organic link building.

In fact, Google outlines the following in its quality guidelines:

The best way to get other sites to create high-quality, relevant links to yours is to create unique, relevant content that can naturally gain popularity in the Internet community. Creating good content pays off: Links are usually editorial votes given by choice, and the more useful content you have, the greater the chances someone else will find that content valuable to their readers and link to it.

It's important that link strategies are smart, Google-friendly, and organic (not paid). Consider working with an SEO expert to establish a formal link building process for your site that uses the following principles.

1. **Build a link strategy:** This can be a PowerPoint or even a standard document that outlines the following:

   a. The goal of your link-building program.

   b. Key content on your website that's valuable and "voteworthy."

   c. A competitive analysis of your competitors using a link analysis tool like SEMrush, Ahrefs, or Majestic SEO. This can provide insight into their tactics and relevant sites that they have targeted that may be worth replicating.

   d. Work with media or social media/PR teams to determine if they have any tactics in place that can be used to promote content assets and other potential methods to help bring awareness of your voteworthy content.

   e. Consider an email newsletter. If you have a lot of contacts available in a contact database or the potential to build one, an email newsletter can provide a lot of views to your content and build awareness of your voteworthy content.

   f. Make sure your web page template and content have social sharing features. Consider working with your web page design teams to add features that add social sharing or other widgets to encourage sharing of your pages to bring more organic views to your content.

g. Consider link cleanup. Use the link analysis tools (mentioned earlier) to identify any high-quality websites that are linking to your website already but whose links aren't pointing to any valuable pages. Consider reaching out to the sites to determine whether they can change or edit the link to point to your vote-worthy content. Be sure that anchor text links are not more than 25 percent exact as you encourage new links or try edits to make different anchor texts.

2. **Begin outreach strategies:**

   a. Begin reaching out via email or phone to the sites identified in step 1.

   b. Send out a weekly email newsletter that includes a few links (up to three) of your top-priority voteworthy articles or content.

   c. Leverage your social networks: Use your social media assets to share voteworthy content.

3. **Report and analyze:**

   a. Be sure to include a link building and link quality summary in your SEO reporting. This report should outline how many links you have pointing to the site and their quality (if you are able, use a link analysis tool, where this is readily available).

The Benefits of Social Media

The brand benefits that social media has offered have been exponential. Users also have seen brands adapt and use social media data to help create content that users are demanding. If there's a silver lining to social media, it's been that brands have received important factual data to help increase their responses and address consumer needs. From an SEO and content marketing side, social media has provided significant benefits to help brands reach their goals, including the following:

■ **Brand communities:** Brands have the ability to build up followers and forums now, where users can exchange questions, share positive experiences, provide feedback, and stay in tune with the latest brand news.

■ **Customer relationship management:** Brands have the ability to better address user concerns and provide users with more positive experiences (Figure 6.6). Additionally, they can provide promotions and other incentives to brand advocates and loyalists. Better product reviews can improve your SEO listings and improve click-through rates (Figure 6.7).

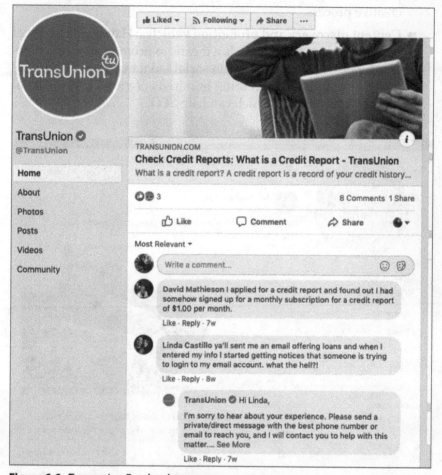

Figure 6.6: Transunion Facebook response to a user post

Figure 6.7: Air Jordan product review

- **Data-informed content creation:** This is one of the key data points outlined earlier. There are many tools that provide insight into popular discussions and concerns around a brand and a given product category that can help fuel content marketing and the creative process.

- **Content discovery and promotion vehicles:** Having a long list of brand followers offers brands a means to promote new and vote-worthy content fairly easily via social media updates (Figure 6.8 and Figure 6.9). This can bring hundreds of views and potential links to new content, which can help SEO.

Figure 6.8: TransUnion content promotion tactic via Facebook Share

Figure 6.9: TransUnion article "What Is a Credit Report?" that was promoted on Facebook

- **Brand search coverage:** Social media assets offer additional web domains that can rank for your brand searches, which can crowd out or knock down potentially negative search results. For example, the Walmart example in Figure 6.10 has zero negative organic links on the first page and is dominated by Walmart social media listings.

Figure 6.10: Walmart brand search results pulling in social media assets

Interview with Content Discovery Expert

Content discovery is a bit of a quiet science. There is not a lot of content, and there are not many best practices available. It's also more of a try-by-learning exercise that brands need to implement strategies around themselves. There are paid content discovery vehicles that can provide end-to-end solutions, with my favorite being Outbrain. I was able to get some insight into the science and Outbrain by interviewing the head of Outbrain's North America division, Andrew Furman. Andrew has helped me over the years with regard to content discovery, and he's a great friend of mine. Here's an interview I did with him recently that reveals his take on things.

Nick Papagiannis: What is your role in supporting businesses and brands?

Andrew Furman: I serve as a senior vice president at Outbrain overseeing revenue for all of North America. As the largest discovery platform in the world, Outbrain enables people to discover the most interesting and exciting content from a wide range of premium websites, apps, and news feeds that are personalized to them based on their interests. For the past eight years, I have been consulting our brands and agencies on how to successfully execute digital native strategies and initiatives to increase brand awareness and drive sales more efficiently.

NP: What are the big content challenges you are seeing your clients dealing with?

AF: Earning the audience's attention. We now live in a world where the transaction between brand and customer is occurring more and more online and not in a physical location, placing the brand at a deficit. As such, it's more important than ever for brands to connect with their consumers online, start a conversation, and build a relationship. This is a big challenge because people not only have more access to content, but they are bombarded with more disruptive advertising than before. As it's often difficult for advertisers to break through the copious amounts of available content and engage with their target audience, brands need to provide value in order to command the attention of their customers.

NP: What kind of solutions do you recommend to your clients to solve those challenges?

AF: I recommend that clients change their strategy from "push" to "pull." The only way a brand can establish a relationship with a consumer is to provide value. Brands need to be more thoughtful about both types of engagements they have with their consumers, as well as how they engage. There are many platforms that can help brands develop quality content assets at scale. We enable brands to get their creative assets in front of their target audience in a way that lets their consumers choose to engage as opposed to force-feeding it to them. The quality of the engagement will always be significantly higher if the consumer is able to self-select. In addition, it is very important that the user experience is simple and easy to navigate once the user engages with the brand.

NP: What can brands do to improve their use of content discovery?

AF: With the rise of online advertising, many brands are trying to reposition their standard display ads as native. Unfortunately, this does not work, as display ads are designed for disruption, while native ads are designed to evoke engagement and trust. Thus, brands need to invest more in their creative strategies to develop assets that are engaging, provide value, and are a positive experience for their target audience.

NP: What are tech advances and areas around content promotion that businesses should look ahead to and prepare for in the coming years?

AF: There is going to be greater personalization of all digital user experiences. Brands will be able to personalize their messages to consumers wherever they are and whatever platform they are on. As there will only be more content and more platforms for users to engage with, brands will need to get better at getting their message to stand out and resonate with their target audience, so personalization will be the key driver. The next generation of consumers will require a more sophisticated user experience to engage with a brand's content. Content used to be all about written articles. Now it is all about videos. We have to assume brands will continue to evolve the way in which they engage with consumers, especially since it continues to get harder and harder to command the attention of today's younger consumers. In the next decade, brands will focus their efforts to provide a more interactive or immersive experience for their target audience to fully engage with their products directly from their desktops or mobile devices. One future technology that will enable this capability is mixed reality (MR). Imagine the potential if someone could stand in an immersive dressing room as if they were in a physical location. A customer could swipe through a digital inventory of outfits that they can then "try on" and, through MR, appear as if they are actually wearing the outfit. In seconds, they could make any necessary product selections—size, color, fabric—with the click of a menu all while immersed in a virtual environment that appears to be real.

I anticipate mixed reality to become the standard way of engaging with consumers not only on desktops/mobile devices, but it will transcend in some form to outdoor advertising like digital billboards or in transit bus shelters where you have the customer's captive attention. In this new world, brands are going to have to learn how to create content that will closely mirror the experience of actually touching the product in a store.

Quiz

1. Using search keyword or demand metrics to inform content response provides which of the following benefits? (Choose all that apply.)

    a. Builds brand authority

    b. Helps you rank for many different types of searches

    c. Ensures resources and dollars are being spent in a cost-efficient way

    d. Builds long-term traffic

    e. Keeps brands active

    f. Helps users find what they are looking for

    g. Builds awareness and consideration

    h. Elevates brand to where it needs to be, regardless of competitive environment

    i. Relatively low-cost and outstanding long-term ROI

    Answer: a, b, c, d, g, h, i

2. According to this book, when it comes to content marketing, what do brands often miss the mark on?

    a. Content discovery

    b. Content response

    c. Content diversity

    d. All the above

    e. None of the above

    Answer: d

3. Identify which of the following are steps needed to compile a content discovery strategy.

    a. Identify a customer's journey

    b. Identify the person you are targeting

    c. Ask an SEO expert

    d. Identify the websites and venues (online and offline) that your persons frequent to consume content

    e. Identify how you can intersect with websites and venues that your people frequent

    Answer: a, b, d, e

4. Which of the following is NOT a content discovery method that brands may leverage?

    a. Email newsletters

    b. Social media updates

    c. Search engines

    d. Partner sites

    e. Events

    f. All the above

    Answer: f

5. True or False: The more competitive or popular a search phrase or content topic is, the more a brand should think about providing comprehensive and creative content to capture traffic.

    Answer: True

6. Which of the following are the three content responses outlined in this book that brands should consider?

    a. Standard content response

    b. Advanced content response

    c. Advanced Plus content response

    d. Hyper content response

    Answer: a, b, c

7. True or False: Brands that provide an array and diverse set of content tend to get more traffic and search rankings.

    Answer: True

8. Which of the following choices represents a benefit to strong content diversity?

    a. More traffic

    b. Promotes multiple means to capture clicks

    c. Offsets competition risk by spreading a brands traffic footprint across more topics

    d. Allows a brand to build authority around multiple topics or content categories

    e. All the above

    Answer: e

9. Which of the following represents content responses for reputation management or in a time of crisis?

    a. Prepare to push positive content like crazy

    b. Take a look at what kinds of content assets are ranking when someone searches for your controversial topic

    c. Discuss with partners what you should do

    d. Produce a diverse set of content that crowds search results including press releases, website landing pages, and YouTube videos.

    e. Monitor your trending searches to see what other content you should create

    f. a, b, d, e

    Answer: f

10. Identify all the content principles that content should be created with.

    a. Uniqueness

    b. Search engine friendliness

c. Utility

d. Visually appealing

e. Enviable

f. Ambiguous

g. Longer-length

h. Freshness

i. In-demand

Answer: a, b, c, d, g, h, i

Thinking Beyond Traditional Search: Looking at Other Critical Search Venues

One key takeaway from this book is that SEO is not limited to your website. We've emphasized that earlier in this book, and it's time to start getting specific on how to optimize your presence on other channels. Still, today I get client requests and proposal requests for SEO optimization for the brand website only. It's pretty frustrating as an SEO expert to see brands continuing to put SEO in solely a website optimization bucket.

As I've been saying all along in this book, SEO is not just a brand website thing. It's an optimization tactic across all your organic assets. SEO experts are tasked with figuring out how to best optimize a brand presence regardless of the platform they are on. For example, the other day, I had to figure out ways a brand could optimize its presence on Walmart.com. This should be the standard from an SEO side of things. If anyone calls themselves an SEO expert and purely focuses on your website, find a different expert who provides a broad perspective on your organic presence that is inclusive of your website, other websites, and popular content venues. The list of content and venues is constantly expanding. From my perspective, there are currently many big ones that must be part of your SEO strategy. These include Amazon.com, YouTube.com, press release or news websites, blogs, influencer content or partner content, Facebook, app stores that may offer your mobile app, and podcasts.

Email and Customer Relationship Management

Customer relationship management (CRM) has become a core part of marketing. One of the most basic forms of CRM is the use of emails or email marketing. Email marketing is often overlooked from an SEO perspective. Brand teams should always leverage emails to connect with users, promote offers, and promote content. Emails allow brand teams to stay in front of users, which in turn keeps the brand top of mind with consumers when it's time for them to make a purchase decision.

From an SEO perspective, emails are often overlooked, and they can provide several benefits to your SEO and/or organic initiatives, including the following:

- Driving traffic to your site and new content
- Promoting off-site assets like Amazon pages and social media pages
- Provoking social sharing and link popularity to content outside of the email
- Understanding and insight as to what content users care about
- Understanding what kind of offers and promotions resonate with consumers
- Boosting subscriptions and views of YouTube channels and video content
- Encouraging the use and download of your smartphone apps and other assets
- Promoting podcasts, white papers, webinars, and other utility-based content

While traditionally a CRM tactic, there are SEO best practices that brands can leverage to help boost the performance of the email newsletters. These include the following:

- **Use text-based copy with popular search phrases in it:** Search data provides insight into what types of phrases resonate with consumers. Using highly searched phrases can help capture the attention of your email subscribers, since they likely use that language in search engines or when seeking content.
- **Use emails to promote content on your website:** Typically email newsletters are comprised of short summaries of content that is

housed on brands' websites, in particular their content hubs. Be sure to use emails this way and offer three to five article summaries and have the user click to your website to read and digest the rest of the content. This type of action encourages engagement and traffic to your website.

- **Include links to important nonwebsite assets:** This includes YouTube, social media pages, press releases, or other high-profile content. Doing so can help boost the views of this content significantly.

- **Use headlines throughout your email and use popular search phrases in them:** Headlines offer consumers a valuable summary of what content is about. When readers are in email consumption mode, they tend to scan through and prioritize what they read based on headlines. Consider using the headlines that get the most clicks in the other content hub, such as your website content.

- **Make sure your emails are mobile friendly:** This is a basic optimization that any content you produce should have. A non-mobile-friendly email template will likely result in less engagement, fewer views, and fewer subscriptions.

- **Have a strong call to action for users:** Whether it's encouraging them to view their content on your site, subscribing to your YouTube channel, or other recommendations, calls to action can help monetize your email marketing.

Amazon Optimization

Brands have now shifted focus toward Amazon since it has become the number-one product search engine on the market (Jumpshot Study). Users go to Amazon to search for products and reviews and the best deals. Amazon's search algorithm is called A9, and it differs from traditional search engines like Google or Bing because it requires a more comprehensive approach to ranking better for product searches. A9 uses traditional search engine relevance factors, but it also uses performance and review metrics to determine which listing to rank. It seems like Amazon shares the same goal as traditional search engines, which is to provide the best user experience and results, but A9 uses additional, different layers as a product search engine.

Brands should optimize on four key areas to boost their rankings on Amazon; these are relevance, performance, experience, and inbound traffic channels.

Relevance

Having the right terms in your product fields is critical for most search engines, but particularly for Amazon. There are several keyword tools on the market that provide keyword or search term details specifically for Amazon. Use these tools to determine what search phrases related to your products are being used on Amazon and what you need to target in your Amazon product copy and other page areas.

Product Title and Page Copy

There are a few key sections of product copy that need to be inputted when creating a product page on Amazon. The product title seems to carry the most clout when it comes to A9 assigning search relevance to a page, followed by description copy on the product page. Be sure to include the right phrases in your title and product descriptions, to help build relevance around the right keyword terms.

It's likely best to include your brand name and descriptive terms that users search with such as color, size, quantities, and other product attributes.

Figure 7.1: Amazon.com New Balance running shoes example

For example, the page shown in Figure 7.1 has the term *running shoes* in the product page title and the description and throughout the page. In fact, it has about 25 instances of the word *running shoe* throughout the page and 11 instances of the plural *running shoes*. This enables the page to rank more relevant for running shoes searches. You don't want to get carried away, and you want to have about 1 to 2 percent of the total words on the page be the term you target at most.

Brand Seller Name and Page

Your seller page and storefront seem to be highly valued by the A9 algorithm and user experience. When naming your Amazon store page, make sure to include your product category in your brand store name (e.g., *Adidas Shoes*).

Amazon Search Terms Field

Amazon and A9 will use the Search Terms field, as well as other product description copy and headers, to define relevance and to understand which searches you'd like to have your product pages rank for.

Performance

There are certain performance-oriented metrics that help drive A9's ranking choices. Unfortunately, this can make it even more difficult to impact. Consider optimizing the following:

- **Product reviews.** Amazon wants to rank the most satisfying product and search results first, so it makes sense that product reviews are a performance-related factor that's part of Amazon's algorithm. You can test this yourself by conducting a search for a product. You'll likely see that products ranking at the top for a broad product search have more reviews than those lower down on the list. Push reviews wherever possible.

- **Sales and pricing.** The price of your product is a major factor when it comes to acquiring sales within Amazon. This is mainly because of users being able to sort and filter product seller options by it. The more sales you have, typically the better search ranking you'll get. Since customers typically favor lower prices, it's important to offer the best price possible to win users and increase your search ranking.

Experience

It's important that you consider and provide the best user experience possible for your Amazon store page. Similar to traditional web pages outside the Amazon web, Amazon pages that provide a good user experience tend to result in higher click-through rates and sales. Both sales rate and click-through rate seem to be big factors in Amazon rankings. Consider doing the following to provide the best experience possible for users, which can help increase sales and clicks.

Custom Brand Seller Pages

Consider building a customer storefront, like the Adidas Store example shown in Figure 7.2.

How to set up a Custom Seller page:

Amazon offers two categories of selling plans, based on volume: Professional and Individual.

The Professional plan is $39.99 per month and offers many benefits that include bulk listing of products, selling outside the United States (Canada, Mexico), and customized shipping rates. Amazon also offers business optimization tools that come with automated pricing, a selling coach, and access to Amazon's MWS ad network.

The Individual plan offers fewer benefits but costs significantly less if you aren't selling many products. The cost is $0.99 per item, per sale. Both types of accounts require a closing fee that's determined at the point of sale based on the sale amount.

Fulfillment by Amazon (FBA) is available for both. Fees for this service are based on product size and weight. There is also a monthly storage fee based on how many square feet of space your inventory takes up.

To create a custom seller page, you have to be on the professional plan and have a registered trademarked brand. You also have to provide tax details for income purposes (i.e., you need the taxpayer ID of whoever will be receiving income). Once you get verified as a trademarked brand, you can assign registry rights to sellers or assign a user in your Seller Central Account. You can create a custom store by using high-quality content.

Figure 7.2: Adidas Amazon brand seller page

Product Images, Videos, and Details

According to GoodUI, offering high-quality images drives conversions and provides buyers a thorough view of the product, which keeps buyers satisfied and can reduce the risk of a product getting returned. A good sales rate and positive reviews will help you on Amazon, so be sure to provide good images for each page.

Be descriptive to increase sales and buyer satisfaction. Amazon provides a great walk-through at https://sellercentral.amazon.com/gp/help/external/G27381 on what product page details should look like. Be sure to have robust product descriptions and highlight key benefits using bullet points to help users complete a sale.

Inbound Traffic Channels

The more traffic and links to your seller page, the better it will perform. Links from other websites can increase visits to your product and store, and they can also help your page rank higher on Google and other search engines (particularly for the nonbrand terms included in your seller page name). Consider your seller page to be a big part of your owned media strategy, and always be on the lookout to increase links to it. Here are some other ways to boost organic inbound traffic:

- Share seller page and highlight listings on social media (Pinterest, Facebook).
- Include links to your seller page in blog posts.
- Partner with influencers to talk about you and your seller page.
- Include links to your seller page in announcements and other off-site content (press releases, blogs, paid media content).
- Be sure to include a strong navigation link and consider having a landing page from your website to drive to your seller page and be sure to include the landing page in your paid media programs (Figure 7.3).

Consider building an Amazon Skill, which is a custom program users can set up for their Alexa voice search device. Though they won't necessarily boost your SEO ranking for product searches, Skills can complement your seller page and can provide a voice-enabled experience for your customers, among other benefits.

Figure 7.3: Where to buy Cetaphil

Here's how to configure your Amazon store page:

1. Log into Seller Central and Select Storefront ➪ Manage Stores.

2. Add a logo and page description (for the storefront).

3. Choose the template option/design. You can preview how users will see your template by viewing the preview canvas.

4. Choose the content title designs. You can use Tile Manager to add, edit, move, and delete tiles from the Amazon Store; it is the little side page on the right side of your editing page.

5. Input your product information and complete the setup. You can use Page Manager to create, select, move, and delete pages from the Amazon Store; it is the little side page on the left side of your editing page.

6. Submit your store for approval. Once your store is approved, you are ready to sell products.

7. Be sure to create a custom URL for your page, with your target search phrase in it, e.g., amazon.com/adidas-running-shoes.

YouTube Optimization

YouTube has become the second most popular search engine, according to the *New York Times*. Since Google owns YouTube, videos have a direct feed into Google search results. When building video content, it's important you think about how to boost your exposure on YouTube and Google.

Here are a few key tasks that brands should do as part of the YouTube process to gain as much search exposure as possible for their videos:

- **Structure your video title for search:** The video title element is the most important element for ranking well in search results. It's one of the first places search engines look at when they rank a video. They look for phrases in the video title to determine which search phrases to rank the video for. Be sure to use popular search terms that are relevant to the video's content. You can even use a keyword tool as a proxy when trying to identify popular search phrases to include in your title.

- **Have a strong video description:** Make your video description at least 150 words and include the terms you'd like it to rank for. Also, include a link to your website, specifically to the web page with content that corresponds to your video topic. So, if your video is about improving your financial situation and you have a relevant article on your website about the same topic, make sure your description includes that. Place the link at the top of the description so users see it first.

- **Use hashtags:** Similar to other social media channels, YouTube offers the ability to input Hashtags in your description. Be sure to include several, relevant hashtags, which can encourage discovery and promote relevancy.

- **Optimize your script:** Since YouTube can transcribe videos into text scripts, it uses the script as another area to determine what to rank the video for. Be sure to include the search phrase you are targeting throughout your script. Strive to have the keyword term that you're targeting in the script once for every 100 words. Here are some script suggestions for creating YouTube video scripts (Figure 7.4):

    - **Script title:** Include the targeted search term in the title. Make it an obvious answer to a likely question.

- **Content:** Answer the question first in a direct, understandable manner. Make the value of the content immediately clear.

- **Your brand difference:** Once the question has been answered, briefly mention how you can provide further assistance.

- **Call to action:** Close with a call to visit your website for more information.

- **Length:** Provide enough detail to clearly answer the question but not so much as to seem daunting. Generally, this is one to three minutes.

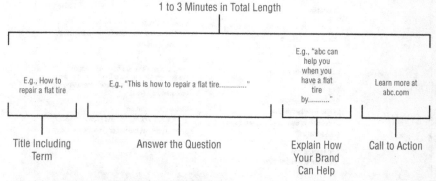

Figure 7.4: Video script format framework

- **Always include a call to action to your site:** With YouTube garnering so much traffic, brands have an opportunity to tap into and monetize it by getting users to visit their website or to make a purchase or convert in some other way. Make sure to end your description with a call to action that promotes a product or relevant service.

- **Choose video tags:** When uploading a video, YouTube offers a box for you to enter tags that give YouTube an idea of what to rank the video for. Be sure to input search terms you use in your title text and description, including names and branding.

- **Choose the right category:** Since YouTube allows users to drill down and find videos based on categories, always select an appropriate category (Figure 7.5).

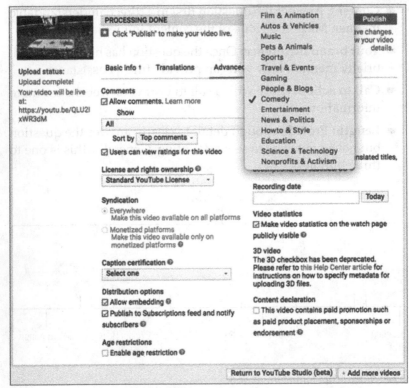

Figure 7.5: YouTube categories selection options

- **Allow embedding:** Having a number of sites embed your video can help increase your ranking, similar to how links help traditional websites rank. Be sure to check the allow embedding on the Advanced Settings tab.

- **Assign each video to a relevant playlist:** Make sure to assign an appropriate playlist after a video is uploaded (Figure 7.6). When you create a playlist category, include a relevant word that has a lot of search volume behind it. So, for a credit-oriented channel, choose *credit education* instead of just *education*.

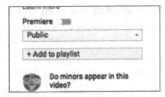

Figure 7.6: YouTube's "Add to playlist" option

Leverage Paid and Nonpaid Video Promotion Tactics

This is often the most neglected phase in the YouTube video upload process. Getting a lot of views of a video can be extremely critical for placing well in search results since YouTube's search ranking algorithm tends to favor videos with a lot of views. There are a variety of ways to help bring awareness and traffic to your new video. Some you have to pay for, and some you can do on your own for free.

From a paid side of things, there are several vendors that will help bring traffic to your video by embedding your video across the Web. Additionally, consider running a PPC program on YouTube to garner views. The more views and embeddings your video has, the better it will rank in YouTube and Google video results.

From a nonpaid side of things, there are several tactics you can do to bring more visits to your video. The first thing that you should always do is to share the video with your network whether through a status update or through a communication vehicle like your email newsletter. Additionally, embed the video across similar themed web pages on your website.

Digital News Releases

A press release is often a typical part of any PR campaign. Press releases can also help provide important links to your website and content assets. Additionally, there are a few things you can do to make sure your release ranks well on Google and gets picked up by news websites, which can result in SEO linking benefits and more views. These factors have a major impact on how well a press release will rank from a search perspective.

- **Distribution:** Using a major distribution service (e.g., PR Newswire or Business Wire) will typically give each release a direct feed into Google news results. This is an important place to appear *in addition* to general web search results. Even without the help of a distribution service, the following guidelines are best practices for helping releases become as SEO-friendly as possible.

- **Find the right relevant keywords for your release:** Use a keyword tool to identify brand-relevant keyword phrases with high search demand. Finding a nonbrand phrase with high search volume (such as a product category or broad topic) can help significantly.

■ **Have a search-friendly release headline:** Include the keyword phrase in the headline, which is the most heavily weighted element in the release for search. Try to keep it short and sweet, ideally no more than 100 characters, if possible. Figure 7.7 shows an example of how including *marketing services* in the news release title allows it to rank at the top for *marketing services* searches.

Figure 7.7: Google News search results for *marketing services*

■ **Include keyword search phrases in summary:** Whenever your release will have summary text when appearing online, be sure to include the keyword search phrase you identified in bullet 2 "Find the right relevant keywords for your release". If possible, the summary should be no more than 240 characters.

■ **Include keyword search phrases in the body text:** To continue to build up the relevance factor for the release, try to include keywords or phrases once in every 100 words throughout the body text. This gives a consistent theme for search engines to identify. See the example in Figure 7.8, which shows the frequency of the term *marketing services* that help it rank.

■ **Include relevant links:** Where appropriate, include hyperlinks to your own branded content, press releases, or company website in the press release. Though this practice won't likely factor in the search ranking of the press release, embedded links are good opportunities to leverage your release for link building opportunities. Be careful, as discussed earlier, don't use "exact match" links around the terms you are targeting for your website pages. If you're able to embed links, keep the ratio small and don't use more than one link in every 100 words.

Figure 7.8: Finn Partners marketing services news release

- **Use an optimized boilerplate/footer:** This standard language can rarely be changed, but it can be crafted to include language that's beneficial for search and website rankings. Key product categories or service offerings should be mentioned along with the company name and, if possible, include links.

Blogs

Blogs offer several SEO benefits. They are a great way to boost links back to your site, they offer an additional URL or domain to rank for important searches, and they can provide an easy way to publish content regularly around your brand or category. It's important to consider the following best practices when utilizing a blog platform or using a third-party blog service (e.g., influencer) to write content:

- Be sure to use an SEO plugin. Many blog platforms offer SEO plugins that can be activated and installed on your blog. Be sure to look for the highest-rated plugin such as the Yoast SEO plugin for WordPress, activate it, and configure it correctly to create unique SEO tags, good URL structures, sitemap files, and `robots.txt` files. Additionally, there are plugins available that can help improve page load times, which is a key driver of SEO rankings.

- Use the search phrase you'd like to rank for in the article title, URL, title tag, description tags, and H1 (header tag). Oftentimes, you can configure your blog plugin to automatically populate your title, description, and H1 tag with the article title. The plugin will then allow you to put in and overwrite the automatically generated tags with any custom tag copy you'd rather have. Be sure to utilize this setting when you have many pages to help save time and resources, then you can choose to overwrite the tags with your own copy when they don't make sense for individual pages. Figure 7.9 shows a blog page that's done a great job of incorporating the term *how to fix a flat tire* both in the URL (`https://www.toyotaofseattle.com/blogs/2066/maintenance/how-to-fix-a-flat-tire/`) and in the blog itself so that it ranks very high for it.

- Be sure the blog offers a mobile template for mobile websites and loads fast. Use Google's free PageSpeed tool to determine whether the load time is adequate. A score above 90 is fast, 50 to 90 is average, and below 50 is slow. The tool is available at `https://developers.google.com/speed/pagespeed/insights/`.

- Be sure the blog has a dynamic `sitemap.xml` file that's updated every time you add a new page.

- Include links in the body copy of your blog article to important pages on your site. Try to keep it to one link per 100 words of body copy.

Figure 7.9: How to fix a flat tire

Influencer Content or Partnered Content on Another Website

Many marketing programs leverage influencers or other websites to promote brands or products. These sites typically have clout and a lot of traffic, and their websites and content typically have strong SEO value. That's a great thing to leverage when you are engaging them to help with your marketing. If you are using influencers, there are usually a few SEO considerations and requirements to include in your proposal or project briefs that you use in the influencer briefs.

- Your influencer should allow you to provide keywords to use in any copy or video content.
- You should be able to provide SEO copy guidelines for content being created.
- You should be able to provide a list of pages you'd like the influencer to link to on your site (where to buy page, product page, etc.).
- You should be able to require the influencer to use "follow" links versus "no follow" links to your site from the influencer sites. This allows for SEO benefits to be passed to your content. To check whether your influencer uses no follow links, simply use your browser to visit a web page and view the HTML code for the page. Perform a search or scroll down and see if you see any links that say "no follow" in the HTML string for the URL. Here's an example of a no follow link (the no follow tag is bolded):

```
<a href="http://www.abc.com/" rel="nofollow">
```

Facebook Optimization

According to Statista, as of 2019, Facebook has more than 2.3 billion users. Brands have a great opportunity to engage these users, so it's no wonder why Facebook is such a priority. As is the case for many social media venues, the problem with Facebook is that brands have to spend money on ads to ultimately gain traction organically. There are a few considerations you can do organically to ensure you spend those dollars optimally.

- **Name your page and vanity URL correctly:** Be sure you name your page with your full brand name, and include it in your URL as well. If possible, include your product category in it as well. Be sure to set up a vanity URL that includes your name and service in the URL. Separate words in your URL with hyphens (-). This will help make your page relevant for searches for your brand and product category. It will also help it rank better in general Google or other search engine results.

adidas Running - Home | Facebook
https://www.facebook.com/adidasRunning/ ▼
adidas Running. 8.2M likes. Welcome to the Official adidas Running page. ... adidas Running updated their cover photo. ... Image may contain: shoes and text.

Figure 7.10: Adidas vanity URL

- **Be thorough when completing your About page:** The About page offers a great area to load with relevant content about your brand and to include searches or product phrases that will make the page rank well in search results for those phrases (Figure 7.11). Other areas to include those phrases include the description, story, and Notes tabs.

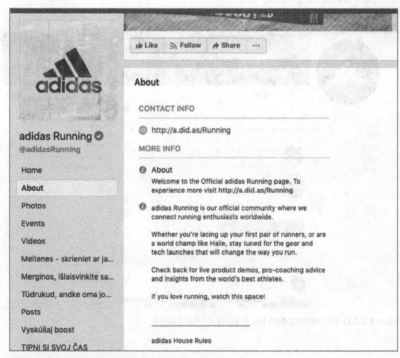

Figure 7.11: About page for Adidas on Facebook

- **Drive users to your Facebook page:** Be sure to include links to your page from your website and other important assets. It's important you link all your web assets together where possible to enhance discovery of them. These kinds of links will also provide traditional SEO benefits for search engine rankings and can help your page rank on general search engine results for your brand on Google and the other search engines.

- **Drive traffic to them via sponsored ads:** Since Facebook tends to rank popular content and pages (evaluated by likes) higher than nonpopular content, consider spending on paid advertising to increase traffic and likes of your page.

- **Be active on Facebook:** Drive discussion and comments on Facebook so users visit your page. Once users visit your page, it stays in their history, and it ranks higher in search results on Facebook.

- **Be sure to have location pages set up:** If you have multiple locations, be sure to set up location pages to broaden your reach and to rank for local searches happening on Facebook (Figure 7.12). Consider including your product or service category as discussed in the first point.

Figure 7.12: Location page for Adidas on Facebook

- **Use status updates to link to new and interesting content on your website:** Use Facebook as an asset that can promote traffic to your website. Always share new content on your website on your Facebook page.

- **Keep audience optimization open and unrestricted:** Facebook offers you the ability to limit your newsfeed posts, so be sure to leave this box unchecked (Figure 7.13).

Figure 7.13: Facebook audience optimization

App Store Optimization

If you have a mobile app available on the App Store or Google Play, app store optimization (ASO) is another critical nonwebsite tactic to have in place as part of your search engine optimization plan. ASO can help brands ensure the success of their mobile applications. There are many levers of ASO, but following some of these best practices can help increase your chances of having a successful app strategy in place by increasing your app's ranking in store results and general search engine results (app pages are also pulled into search engine results):

- **App name:** To capture the most searches for your app name and general category (music apps), be sure to include a few terms in your app description and title if possible (e.g., Pandora Radio, Trip Advisor Hotels, Flights Restaurants). Be sure to keep your app name less than 30 characters to avoid being cut off in your results listing.

- **App description:** Make sure to have a description of your mobile app that outlines the unique features and benefits and a strong call to action (Figure 7.14). Similar to the app name, be sure to include some of your important terms that you want the app to rank for here as well.

Figure 7.14: App Store description for the Adidas app

- **Keywords:** If you're focused on ranking well in Apple's App Store, be sure to include as many keywords as possible. Use data from your Amazon keyword tool to determine which categories people search for and include them.

- **Screenshots and videos:** Make sure to offer high-quality screenshots of your app and tout special features and benefits in those screenshots. Adding visuals is a great way to communicate app benefits for your audience.

- **Ratings and reviews:** Ratings and reviews are key drivers of how an app gets ranked, so be sure to ask for reviews and ratings for your app.

- **Downloads:** The number of times your app has been downloaded is another metric that app stores look at when ranking your app. Make sure to have a "download strategy" in place to build awareness of your app and encourage users to download it. At a minimum, consider building a landing page on your website that links to your listings on the App Store and Google Play and share that landing page via social, email, and paid media channels.

- **Link to the app itself:** Be sure to link directly to your app listing on the app store to build SEO value for the actual listing as well, since visits and links are rumored to be part of the ranking equation.

- **Make sure the app and your landing pages show in search engines:** Make sure your app shows up in Google search results for when users search for your brand on their mobile device.

Optimizing Podcasts

Podcasts are a great way to establish authority around your business or product category. They establish an ongoing connection with your target audience by offering valuable information and entertainment. With users increasingly listening to podcasts, brands are looking to employ them more in their marketing strategy. In fact, a recent HubSpot study says, "17 percent of marketers plan to add podcasting to their marketing efforts in the next 12 months. "

There are other benefits to podcasts as well, including the following:

- **Alternative to videos:** Podcasts allow you to create valuable content to connect with your audience, without the need of visual equipment and shoot requirements that video content brings.

- **Building traffic to your website and owned properties:** Assuming you post your podcast on listening channels (YouTube, Google Play Music), you can leverage podcasts to capture more traffic to your website by embedding website links.

- **Low budget:** A podcast can be as simple as a quality recording within a quality sound environment.

- **Enhancing the brand experience and building trust:** Having a quality podcast with a sufficient following can earn respect and trust from users. In fact, 78 percent of consumers believe that providing custom content (like podcasts) can build trust, according to Crowdspring.

- **Convenient to users:** Podcasts are a convenient and popular way for users to consume information that interests them. In fact, 32 percent of Americans listen to a podcast at least once a month.

If you choose to conduct a podcast, consider these SEO and user best practices to help improve traffic and listenership.

From a general podcast perspective, be sure to do the following:

- **Write out the script beforehand:** It doesn't have to be the exact script of the actual podcast, but be sure to have a rough script and a list of talking points already written out so your content moves along well and addresses each goal of the podcast. Be sure to call out the following items in your podcast:

  - Summarize what you will be discussing today (in a short sentence)
  - Consider mentioning the date
  - Introduce your guest
  - Plug your or the guest's latest publication or product
  - Be sure to speak slowly and highlight the questions (if there's an interview) when entering a new topic or section
  - Have a call to action for your podcast
  - Highlight your sponsor, if you have a sponsor

- **Solicit feedback from users:** Set up feedback mechanisms via surveys, social media updates and comments, video comments, or other means to see if users are enjoying your podcast, if they find it useful, like your topic or have ideas for new topics, and if they have anything they'd like to see improved.

- **Time your podcast:** Try to stay within a set time for each podcast so users have an idea of when the content is wrapping up. Additionally, it helps you avoid endless conversation and keep things concise for the users. The Audacity to Podcast recommends the lengths listed in Table 7.1, which I agree with, depending on how often you publish content.

Table 7.1: Recommended Podcast Lengths

PODCAST FREQUENCY	EPISODE LENGTH
Semidaily	1–5 minutes
Daily	1–15 minutes (sometimes 30)
Weekly	15–60 minutes (with exceptions)
Biweekly	60 minutes
Monthly	60–90 minutes

- **Consider the format:** There are different types of podcasts available. Consider doing one of the following popular formats:

  - Interviews
  - Cohosts
  - Call-in
  - Solo commentary

From an SEO side, there are several best practices you should consider since they can help increase subscribers, traffic, and ultimately the findability of your podcast.

- **Name your podcast well:** The name of your podcast can make or break it in terms of search relevance, and it carries the most weight. As discussed in previous chapters, include a high-demand search phrase in your podcast. Perhaps it's a service or product category. For example, if you're a bank with a focus on money management or if that's your keyword target or relevant category phrase, name the podcast "Bank ABC's *Money Management* podcast."

- **Add a section for your podcast on your website:** It's important that your podcast ranks in Google search results to maximize the exposure of it. Be sure to have a section of your website that highlights your overall podcast and have a separate page for each episode with a summary. Also, be sure to cover the standard SEO website and web page best practices mentioned in earlier chapters (from HTML tagging to website structure) on your podcast page and episode pages and include your target search terms on each of those pages in the way of webpage copy, metadata, URLs, page headers (h1, h2), and other tags. Also be sure to list episodes in an RSS feed.

■ **Have a dedicated page for each podcast episode:** Having a dedicated page for each podcast topic allows you to market the podcast via paid advertisements, organic search listings, social updates, and other content promotion tactics. Additionally, it helps drive traffic to your website. Be sure to include popular search phrases in each episode title. Include the episode title in the page copy, metadata, URL, and other important SEO page areas. Make sure each episode web page is uploaded into your `sitemap.xml` file immediately after it's published.

■ **Be sure to use popular search phrases or topics in your script:** If you are writing about a specific topic, be sure to see what the popular questions or search phrases are underneath that topic and include that in your script. This will help your podcast page rank for those searches.

■ **Consider adding a transcript of your episode:** Though not required, consider working with your web development team to include a transcript of each episode on the page so search engines can crawl it (it can be through a scroll feature or "scroll box" as long as the script is included in the web page HTML). This helps increase the web page copy, which as we've discussed is great for search rankings.

■ **Share out your podcast and each episode page:** As we have discussed, links from other websites to pages are critical to help them rank for searches. Consider content promotion strategies to help improve traffic and links to your podcast pages.

■ **Upload your podcast to popular listening venues indexed by search engines:** Consider uploading your podcast to Google Podcasts or Apple Podcasts to make it easier for download and listening. If successful in doing that, be sure to add a link from your website encouraging people to subscribe to your podcast via these channels.

Leverage Sales and Marketing Best-Practice Principles

Regardless of whether your content is on your website or other channels, it's important to always remember to highlight and cover the traditional sales and marketing principles in your content regardless of channels or subject matter.

Once your content addresses the need state, it's important to spend a small amount of time highlighting some of the traditional marketing principles that have stood the test of time. Typically, this can be at the bottom or last section of the content piece.

Here's a reminder of the important highlights your content should strive to provide after answering a user's need state:

- **Product:** Figure out what your profile of your product is. How does it satisfy a need or want? What are its key features? What benefits does it offer? How does it work? Your content should highlight what your product is in some capacity, while keeping it relevant to the content theme.

- **Price:** Price can be a tricky thing to insert into your content piece, but be sure to highlight the value of your product or service. If your product solves a problem or provides efficiencies or cost savings, be sure to call that out in some way. Highlight any special promotions or discounts if you have any.

- **Place:** Highlight how your potential customer can get your product. Maybe it's through free shipping in the mail, maybe it's through setting an appointment by a toll-free phone number or via your website, or maybe it's by visiting your office. Be sure your content calls that out.

- **Promotion:** Be sure to highlight any messaging or taglines, and be sure your content fits within your overall promotional and creative strategy.

Those are the standard four principles of marketing that brands should consider whenever they're creating content regardless of the venue. I believe there are even more, and if you look online, many thought leaders discuss that there may be up to seven different types of principles that should apply to marketing. Here are a few others to think about:

- **Packaging:** Packaging can be interpreted in many different ways. In general, I would say that the definition of packaging from a marketing principles standpoint is essentially the way you package your product, website, or even content to users. This essentially is the visual side of marketing. Ideally, a brand will focus on how it packages its products and content to users as one of its core principles of marketing. This can range from the way they actually package a product to visual displays of pages and content, even including fonts, logos, and color choices. Whenever creating anything as a brand, present your offering in a way that is visually superior from your competitors and appealing to your audience. Luxury brands generally do a great job of packaging, and brands that provide an experience tend to do more visually and yield better results and catch users more often than a basic packaging approach.

- **Reputation:** Having a strong and well-respected reputation should be viewed as a principle of marketing. Particularly in the digital world, where users tend to post reviews and word-of-mouth content is logged in public, it's important to have an outstanding reputation. It's critical from my perspective that brands focus on providing a quality offering that meets or exceeds consumer expectations, as well as excellent customer support and policies, so that users are happy with the brand and provide positive reviews and feedback online. When creating a product, service, or other utility for consumers, be sure to emphasize your consumer-friendly policies, reviews, and the quality behind your products. This will help influence your reputation scores online and satisfy your audience.

- **Personnel:** Hiring the right personnel provides many benefits and should be considered one of the principles of marketing in my opinion because it offers a brand so many benefits. First and foremost, quality personnel provide your audience with quality personal interactions. Internally, hiring the right person can help you provide higher-quality products and execution of your offerings and content to your audience. In general, good personnel can yield better products, smarter marketing, better customer service, and more effective business outcomes. Personnel is a critical principle of marketing because at the end of the day, it can provide a better return on investment and overall performance for your business. It's important that you focus on hiring high-quality personnel because at the end of the day it will affect the way your audience views your business, buys your product, and helps sell your company to other noncustomers.

Following these principles will help you focus on providing the best marketing that you can and can help provide the best business outcomes. Whenever creating content, products, or other commercial offerings, be sure to keep these principles in mind regardless of the venue or platform you use in your brand design.

Quiz

1. True or False: Brands often fail to recognize that SEO is not just a website thing, and it should include optimizations around outside platforms such as Amazon, YouTube, social media sites, press releases, blogs, and partner websites.

   Answer: True

2. According to this book, when it comes to Amazon, brands should focus on optimizing which key high-level areas? (Identify all that apply.)

   a. Relevance

   b. Performance

   c. User experience

   d. Optimizing inbound channels

   e. Bounce rates

   Answer: a, b, c, d, e

3. Which of the following is not a key area for Amazon when it comes to establishing relevance around a search phrase?

   a. Product title

   b. Product page copy

   c. Popularity

   d. Brand seller name and page

   e. Amazon search term fields

   Answer: c

4. True or False: The two key performance factors that affect Amazon rankings are product reviews and sales and pricing.

    Answer: True

5. True or False: YouTube is the second most popular search engine.

    Answer: True

6. Which of the following tactics can help you perform better on YouTube? (Choose all that apply.)

    a. Structure video title for search

    b. Have a strong video description

    c. Use hashtags

    d. Include a call to action to your site

    e. Choose video tags

    f. Change the title frequently

    g. Choose the right category

    h. Post several videos around the same topic

    i. Allow embedding

    j. Assign each video to a playlist

    Answer: a, b, c, d, e, g, i, j

7. True or False: To get the most out of your press releases, it is best to use a distribution service like PR newswire, since they have a direct feed into Google news and can help get your release posted on publisher sites.

    Answer: True

8. Which of the following are not best practices for optimizing your Facebook presence?

    a. Name your page correctly

    b. Drive users to your Facebook page

    c. Be active on Facebook

    d. Link up your account with Instagram and post Instagram pictures

    e. Set up location pages if you have multiple locations

    f. Keep audience optimization open and unrestricted

    g. Watch the amount of comments you get regularly

Answer: d, g

8. True or False: App store optimization (ASO) is a critical nonwebsite tactic to have in place as part of your search engine optimization plan.

Answer: True

9. Which of the following are not best practices for optimizing podcasts? (Choose all that apply.)

    a. Write out the script beforehand and use popular search phrases

    b. Keep your podcast to local topics

    c. Time your podcast

    d. Use a popular format

    e. Look for similar podcasts and use similar scripting techniques

    f. Name your podcast well

    g. Add a section on your website promoting your podcast

    h. Consider adding a transcript of your podcast

    i. Share out your podcast on each episode page

    j. Upload your podcast to popular listening venues indexed by search engines

Answer: b, e

10. Which of the traditional sales and marketing principles continue to apply even in today's digital world? (Choose all that apply.)

    a. Product

    b. Price

    c. Pictures

    d. Place

    e. Promotion

    f. Purchasing

    g. Productivity

Answer: a, b, d, e

Optimizing for the Future

Every day, we see evidence that our world is hyper-evolving, from artificial intelligence to driverless cars and from voice searching to augmented reality. Because of these constant changes, it's important to have a search strategy that can adapt to user behaviors and technological advancements. The brands that are most ready to adapt to these changes will thrive, leaving behind the ones that are not able to adapt. It's important that brands possess the right mind-set, process, and culture to withstand and excel with the changes that inevitably come. In particular, brands and their cultures should strive to have the following attributes:

- **Flexibility:** It's important that brands are flexible and have an open mind to position themselves for upcoming changes in the commerce and shopping experience world. Flexibility is critical to ensure that the brand is quick to identify and understand what technology changes apply to their way of doing business and how technological advancements can help their business and the way they interact with customers.

- **Employees who are change enthusiasts:** The technology world is changing at a hyper pace and will go even faster in the next few years. It's important for brands to invest in dedicated resources that can evaluate their brand process, consumer processes and trends, and the ways to effectively optimize both for the best outcomes. This may require having stronger project or process management leaders in place who focus on optimizing processes with the latest technology and implementing processes that optimize the brand to consumer experience.

- **Thin and agile teams:** Since frequent changes are inevitable, it's important that teams remain agile. Since size has a big effect on implementing change, this could mean brands need to look at reducing the size of a team or structure of a team, while effectively maintaining their team's outputs.

- **Technology enthusiasts across the board:** Not only should brands have dedicated research and innovation experts, but the brand and marketing teams as a whole should have an enthusiasm toward technology and stay in tune with the latest technologies and focus on how other brands are best using technology to connect with users.

- **Experts yet generalists:** Currently, brands tend to house those who have traditional skill sets and new or emerging skill sets separately. As time evolves, skill sets may eventually merge. Until that happens, it's important that brand teams own their specialty but are well-versed enough in other skill sets to know when to pull other experts in and even speak to other skill sets on a high level. This ensures that brands are able to best optimize resources and ensure outputs are as effective as possible.

- **Internal education:** Internal education across team members is becoming more critical as technology changes faster and faster. It's almost impossible for individuals to keep up with the changes by themselves. For brands to capitalize on the latest technology advancements, having an internal education program will be critical to having teams that are well versed with the best ways to market and connect with consumers in tomorrow's age.

While these are the traits and practices that brands and marketing teams should adapt in their everyday place to embrace change, there are some immediate trends happening particularly in the SEO and content world that should be on your radar.

Voice Search and Conversational Commerce

Google reports that 55 percent of teens and 40 percent of adults use voice search regularly. Gartner is forecasting that 30 percent of searches will be purely voice by 2022. Voice search has become a critical part of the user experience and purchase process, but brands and websites still seem to lack a voice search strategy, mainly because the ins and outs of voice search are still being learned. Additionally, there isn't a clear way to measure voice search presence, so it can be tough to create, optimize, and refine a voice search strategy.

There isn't a voice search paid advertising opportunity today. Brands must solely take an organic and content approach to grow their presence in the space, but long-term there may soon be paid search opportunities.

Siri, Cortana, Bixby, Google Now, Alexa, and Google Home are the names of some of the most well-known digital assistants. In general, voice assistants work the same in some ways. Depending on what the user is asking for, assistants typically pull personal information from the user's device (phone numbers, history, etc.), along with general search engine databases, the same ones that provide standard search engine results, and display it using their core SEO algorithm (Google, Amazon, etc.).

According to eMarketer, people primarily utilize voice search to conduct general online searches, find product information, ask general questions, and find local information. These days there is so much demand and hype around voice search that technology is evolving the science to a newer, broader term called *conversational commerce*. Conversational commerce is a more comprehensive voice strategy and view that encompasses the entire customer interaction process from sale to post-purchase. It encompasses chatbot technology, dialogue management technology (like Google's free DialogFlow tool), and brand and product content to respond to customers' voice searches on all sorts of devices and platforms, from the pre-purchase to use stages. The result is a solution that provides users with an automated yet sophisticated brand response to any questions or needs.

Long-term it's important for you to start thinking about how to leverage conversational commerce to enhance your customer experience, but short-term you can start by optimizing your search engine presence by doing the following:

1. **Refine your customer journey to focus on voice interactions:** Conduct an audit or working session with your project teams to gather all the possible touchpoints where a customer or prospect can use voice devices. Once you figure out all the areas of the funnel and the consumer need states, determine which need states are likely to provoke a search on the major search engines and assistants.

2. **Consider building comprehensive applications that go beyond standard search engines:** You might be thinking too small when

it comes to expanding your voice search presence. Voice search is not just a search engine tactic. Consider mobile apps, chatbots, your website, and other assets that can connect users via voice with the content they are seeking.

3. **Analyze your current voice search results standing:** Use an SEO tool like SEMrush or BrightEdge to determine where you stand on Google quick answers and Alexa.

   ▪ **Google quick answers:** Google quick answers are results that appear on the top search engine results page, with the response already provided on the results page. For instance, if you do a search for *what time is it?* Google will provide the time on the results page. This is called a *quick answer*. Quick answers are typically pulled into Google Home device responses.

      ▪ Additionally, if you are using an SEO program management tool, look to see whether the tool reports on how many "quick answer" results your site ranks for. While not a complete tactic, because no tool currently reports on all voice search results, this is an indicator of how many voice searches you are ranking for specifically on Google Home since it tends to also pull them into voice search results. Figure 8.1 shows an example of a quick answer result.

Figure 8.1: Quick answer example

   ▪ **Ask basic questions about your brand or products on your devices:** If you have a Google Home device or have the Google Assistant installed on your phone, run some tests. Ask questions about your brand, product, and category "information" searches to determine how/if you rank and what ranks. If your site content doesn't rank for these, this indicates you need improvement on your voice search presence.

- Work with your SEO expert or use a keyword tool (discussed in Chapter 2) to identify what popular searches are happening around your brand or category.

- **Alexa:** If you have an Amazon presence or sell your product on Amazon, do a search using an Alexa device to see where you stand for important searches. Also do a search for Alexa Skills on Amazon.com to see what skills are available in your business or product category. From this, you can figure out if there's an opportunity to create a skill for your category or if you can partner with an existing skill to promote your product or content in any way.

4. **Verify and claim your location pages:** Take a look at popular directories, particularly Google My Business, which Google pulls into voice search responses for location questions. Verify the location and amenity details for your listings to make sure they're accurate. Claimed pages are looked at as trustworthy and more commonly pulled into Google Home results.

5. **Take a look at your website analytics reports:** While there isn't a voice search report available yet, you can look at your Google Analytics report for Audience ➪ Mobile ➪ Devices to determine which type of operating systems are driving traffic (Figure 8.2). Determine if any operating systems are from mobile operating systems that are Amazon or Google oriented. Look at the operating systems at the top and bottom of the list and consider running manual tests to see if you are ranking for your most important terms or searches.

6. **Optimize your website and content for SEO:**

- **Focus on mainstream website SEO (outlined in Chapter 2):** Continued focus on a traditional SEO is still a core area for a successful voice search program. Best practices that remain critical include optimized HTML tags, URL structures, longer-form content, spider-readable text, use of HTTPS, fast-loading pages, and providing a sitemap and robots.txt files to ensure proper page indexing.

Figure 8.2: Device report

- **Optimize your mobile site experience:** The SEO space has been warning brands for years about loading speed on mobile websites. It's important you have a fast-loading, mobile-friendly site so you can get the top ranking for mobile searches, which leads to better voice search results as well.

- **Optimize snippets through** `Schema.org`: Structured snippets are richer search results populated by advanced HTML (Schema tags) that offer additional ways to convey to Google what your content is about and how to display a search result. This will help search engines and assistants determine which result information to include in voice search results. Consider working with your SEO expert or conducting an audit of all the `Schema.org` tags available that correspond to content available on your website. Teams should conduct an audit of all the possible tags; you can find a full list of `schema.org` tag options at `https://schema` `.org/docs/schemas.html`.

- **Create content that fits along the voice search journey and conversational keyword searches:** Voice search seems to be a great avenue for asking questions in a conversational kind of way. Consider creating content around common user inquiries that might come up in a typical conversation. Figure 8.3 shows the results of a Google survey about the type of conversational information users want to get information on when using their voice search devices. Consider creating content around these items and work with your SEO expert to make sure they are optimized for voice search. You should further refine your content strategy by looking at keyword data to identify what types of questions people are asking for your brand or store locations. Be sure to identify nonbranded keyword terms or general questions about your category. Voice search results are extremely competitive in that they typically produce only one ranking, so it's important you have a comprehensive list of keyword terms to capture as much traffic as possible.

What voice-activated speaker owners would like to receive from brands	
Information about deals, sales, and promotions	52%
Personalized tip and infromation to make life easier	48%
Information about comoming events or activities	42%
Options to find business information	39%
Access to customer service or support	38%
*Source: Google/Peerless Insights	

Figure 8.3: Google survey results: what voice searches want from brands

Machine Learning

Artificial intelligence (AI) and machine learning (ML) are the most popular marketing terms these days and often are often used simultaneously. They are used so often together that people often think they are the same thing, but they are not the same thing at all.

Artificial intelligence is based around tasks and productivity. Artificial intelligence is the idea that machines or computers are able to carry out tasks in a much more intelligent way. Oftentimes these tasks are repetitive and have some kind of pattern associated with them.

Machine learning, on the other hand, is the idea that given basic data and information, machines are able to establish learnings or insights that allow them to draw conclusions. Conclusions are a form of intelligence, and from there these machines can evolve their actions.

In the simplest form, machine learning is more about pattern recognition and gathering insights. Artificial intelligence, on the other hand, is about executing tasks. Because the topics are so complex, it's much easier to think of them in a basic way.

Applying Machine Learning Across Broader Brand Initiatives

Machine learning can be an exciting thing for brands to leverage across marketing and in general business. Machine learning can help automate the learning process when it comes to ascertaining data. For years brands have been collecting valuable data about their audiences, but the volume can sometimes be extremely large and difficult to interpret. With machine learning, data of all sizes can be quickly summarized and interpreted. Additionally, business operations in general can be optimized by combining machine learning and artificial intelligence. Essentially repetitive and arduous tasks can be automated and quickly conducted then with traditional methods. If you are wondering whether machine learning can be of use to you as a marketer, consider these questions:

- Am I collecting data?
- How was that data stored?
- Is the data stored electronically or in a database?
- How am I using that data?
- What questions do I need answered in order to execute my marketing initiatives more effectively?
- Do I have the capabilities to build programs that can identify patterns, aggregate data, and take insights from that data and patterns?
- What kinds of actions can help me run my marketing initiatives more effectively?
- Can the programs produce some kind of output or action?

These questions are just scratching the surface and provide a basic foundation for when you are assessing whether machine learning can help your marketing initiatives. Ultimately, machine learning can help optimize your marketing initiatives and process.

SEO and Machine Learning

Machine learning is already used by search engines, according to some speculation. In my opinion, when it comes to SEO and ranking well, machine learning has a lot of potential to help search engines efficiently evaluate website content and other areas pertaining to their algorithm. Machine learning will allow search engines to quickly provide an assessment of which websites should rank in which positions. We mentioned the big three pillars of good SEO in earlier chapters, and machine learning can provide insight to search engines around each of these in their own way (Table 8.1). Machine learning can answer questions for search engines around these, in a much more efficient and less labor-intensive manner. As machine learning takes hold, especially in search engines, it's critical that brands practice quality SEO and focus on good SEO tactics that optimize the three pillars of good SEO.

Table 8.1: The Three Pillars of Good SEO and Questions That Machine Learning Can Help Answer

TECHNICAL	CONTENT	POPULARITY
Is this site in line with our technical guidelines? ▪ Loads fast ▪ Mobile friendly ▪ URLs	Is content high quality? ▪ Is it unique, not duplicated or plagiarized? ▪ Will users find it useful?	Do users like this content? ▪ Does the site have links coming from poor-quality sites or spam sites that are already flagged? ▪ Does the site have a huge increase in links in a short time?

Artificial Intelligence

Artificial intelligence has quickly become one of the most popular buzzwords in the business world. From chatbots for customer service to making optimization recommendations, marketers and businesses in general are beginning to view it as a core technology in their toolset, as the following statistics from Forrester (https://www.datamation.com/artificial-intelligence/artificial-intelligence-in-business.html) show:

- 57 percent of businesses expect it to help improve customer experience and support.

- 20 percent of major retailers will use an item to personalize the brand experience throughout the purchase process.

- 20 percent of all workers will use automated assistance technologies to make decisions and get work done.

- 80 percent of executives say artificial intelligence boosts productivity and creates new positions.

- There's been a 300 percent year over year increase in artificial intelligence investment.

The statistics are showing a big investment in business and brands, and marketers should be thinking how and if artificial intelligence can help their processes and outputs. Artificial intelligence can be a great thing for brands and the world, and I believe they can help elevate our quality of life and brand experiences.

From a business perspective, if you are not thinking about how artificial intelligence can improve your output, efficiency, customer service, intelligence, process, and product quality, you are running behind the industry. Incorporating artificial intelligence can be a difficult and costly task. It's important brands and businesses do self-reflection, by asking themselves these questions:

Customer Service

- Are there repetitive questions that we are seeing from our consumers?

- Is it expensive or costly to manage our customer service responses?

- Do we have very little time to dedicate to customer service?

- Do we offer a product catalog, product instructions, and other company documentation that can be repurposed into chatbots or other forms of artificial intelligence?

Process

- Is our business or operational process repetitive?

- Is there an opportunity to automate arduous or costly tasks in our process? Will this help our bottom line?

- Are there difficult personnel limitations that hinder or limit our process outputs?

- Are our outputs inconsistent at times?

- What are their critical inputs to our process? Can they be automated?

Intelligence/Decision-Making

- What are the important decisions that we have to make day to day to execute our business or marketing programs?

- Do we feel like we have accurate and thorough consumer intelligence that can help inform our business decisions? Is it consistent?

- Internally or operationally, are there critical yet repetitive decisions that happen on a day-to-day basis?
- Is there a significant amount or high volume of critical decisions that happen day to day?

Output/Productivity

- Is our business or operational process human driven and prone to flawed outputs?
- Is our process or output limited to a set schedule because it's human driven?
- Is human capital making for high costs in our process?

Artificial intelligence is continuing to evolve, and many thought leaders are saying it's going to become the biggest change in our day-to-day experiences since electricity. I believe we still have a long way to go before it significantly changes the way we do business and marketing programs.

For now, in my opinion, at the very least brands should begin asking themselves how artificial intelligence can help them produce the best products, marketing programs, and outputs and consider applying it to their business processes.

Artificial Intelligence in Search Engine Algorithms

Artificial intelligence in the digital world can mean many, many things. It's still evolving and still has a lot of room to grow in the search engine world. It's important to discuss the current ways AI is moving toward affecting your SEO presence.

Google has been public about its use of AI (called RankBrain) in its algorithm for certain search results. Google's ranking algorithm or system for ranking websites has been a rule-based system that's centered around popularity, web page content, and HTML tags. According to Wired, Google's AI system, RankBrain, is used in about 15 percent of search queries that are first-time searches on Google. There is some speculation that AI's role may continue to grow and one day become the primary driver for organic search results. If it does, it will significantly alter search engine optimization practices and strategies.

It's important that you stay ahead of the curve and position content to perform in the best way possible for the potential influence of AI in SEO. Follow these steps to optimally position yourself for the growing presence of artificial intelligence:

1. **Make sure content is crawlable and user friendly according to Google:** Stay up to speed on Google's Webmaster Blog, which

provides an avenue for its announcements, algorithm changes, best practices, and any potential forthcoming instructions around AI. Additionally, make sure to employ structured data markup or `Schema.org` tags where possible to provide users with the most optimized search result. I believe these tags are the future for communicating the necessary detail about what your content is about to Google's algorithm.

2. **Make content promotion a top priority:** Google has always looked at user signals or popularity of content to sift out spam and elevate quality. As we said in Chapter 1, it's one of the pillars of good SEO. Popularity has been a core part of the algorithm since the inception of Google. I don't expect that to change, even if RankBrain controls all search results in the future. Since popular content will likely continue to be rewarded, brands should formalize a strategy that promotes content as much and as often as possible to drive links and shares of content.

Content Production and AI

Since content production and creation are becoming more data informed, long-term I see a potential for an opportunity to automate much of it. There are already tools out there that can create content based on user demand—just look at chatbots. While likely a long time away from becoming a fully driven AI process, content production is becoming more predictable with the rise of data. Copywriting can be costly and potentially time-consuming. It's only a matter of time that the entire process becomes fully automated via AI. Be prepared and stay in tune with the latest tools coming to market.

Bonus: Interview with Artificial Intelligence Expert

AI is the most radical change happening right now in the technology world, and I want to emphasize the need for businesses to examine how AI can help them. The changes happening in the next few years will make or break businesses. I view AI as an existential threat to companies and marketers that aren't on board with it. I interviewed Max Cheprasov, the chief automation officer at Dentsu Aegis Network, one of the largest marketing and tech holding companies in the world. I worked with Max while at iCrossing, and we are still friends today. Max is a visionary and is extremely intelligent and very disciplined in the marketing operations world as well, and I'm thankful he gave me the opportunity to speak with him. Max offers a valuable take on what businesses and marketers should be preparing for. The full interview is provided next, but the key takeaways of the interview are as follows:

- There is no limit to what can be automated via AI right now. Brands are still in the trial or experimental phase of AI, but expect 80 percent of today's tasks to be potentially automated very soon.

- There is a lack of talent and skill sets in the AI space, since many of the big technology companies (Amazon, Alphabet, IBM, and Microsoft) have acquired the few experts in the field for their own use.

- All brands and companies need to form a strategy and leadership (chief automation officer) around AI and automation if they want to remain competitive in business within the next three years.

- Research indicates a job drop-off of 16 percent due to AI. Future jobs that won't be automated will be jobs that require a high degree of emotional intelligence, creativity, and morals/ethics.

Here is the full interview:

Nick Papagiannis: Why don't we start with a description of your role right now and how you support businesses and brands or even your agency?

Max Cheprasov: I work for Dentsu Aegis Network, a global advertising, digital marketing, communications company with almost 65,000 people globally. I lead the automation or Robotic Operations Center, essentially leading business efficiencies and operational excellence with AI and robotic automation in mind.

So, what we do is we find opportunities within business units where there's a lot of repetitive routine activities and processes that are done manually, and then we look to optimize that process through Lean Six Sigma. We basically go through traditional business process management first, and then we try to blend in latest AI technologies and robotic automation technologies into the process to take out as much manual effort and manual steps of the process as possible using the latest technology.

NP: Are there some broad questions brands should ask themselves when they're looking at integrating AI or taking on AI initiatives? You mentioned repetitive tasks. Are there other things that brands should think about?

MC: Well, there is no limit right now to what can be automated because this technology is so new. For the longest time in our history we've been doing so many things manually, and some legacy systems and solutions could benefit from automation. And I think a lot of brands—or the way we began identifying potential use cases are experimenting with the latest AI technologies to see where it fits in the best, and where it can scale. There is no blueprint or specific bulletproof advice that I could give any given brand. You need to identify areas, and you can find them in back-office functions; business functions like HR, finance, and IT; as well as the middle-office and front-office operations. But anything that people do today, I would say 80 percent of it could be qualified for an automation exercise.

NP: Wow, that's pretty amazing.

MC: Yeah, the statistics out there say that in the knowledge worker space and specifically in the digital economy organizations and businesses like Dentsu, especially within the entry-level positions, 60 to 70 percent of what people do every single day can be fully automated using today's technology. So, the opportunities are huge, and most businesses don't even realize it yet because the technology is so new. Some of these things have been emerging only in the past 24 months, and they don't have the leadership or the experience to go through the experimentation, the research and development, and the scaling basically. A lot of people are just still not in the early adopter stage. If you look at the innovation curve, I would say a lot of people are placed still in that first step of being innovators who are just trying to experiment and see where this fits in.

NP: That kind of leads into my next question: the big challenges with your clients in implementing AI. You mentioned leadership, people, just lack of awareness.

MC: Definitely lack of talent. The companies like Amazon, Alphabet, IBM, and Microsoft—they have acquired pretty much every single data scientist out there and those who are really good at automation. So it's hard to find the right people who have not only the AI and automation domain expertise, but you also need to find talent that understands your business and your pain points. And then another challenge is managing the internal structural and process changes that come with implementing AI.

So the AI expertise, the business domain expertise, and change management—those three things are very rare out there. What we tried to do is to scale our team by using internal hires. We bring in people who raise their hands and they say, "Well, I've always wanted to learn more about this latest technology. How do I upskill in order for me to become, let's say, an automation AI solution designer?" So they already have the business background; they understand our business. All I have to do is train them up in AI and automation to give them the basics, and then obviously I would have to look for their potential when it comes to change management, because that's where most companies today fail. Once brands have a product or solution that's automated, they have to roll it out and track and measure the benefits and impact.

So everything starts with a solid business case of how you're going to, in your success criteria, make sure that when you do deploy and go for change management, that all those things have been properly evaluated and reported back to the sponsors to ensure that, hey, everything we've promised to you has been delivered.

NP: So at the end of the day, the solutions you deliver are essentially doing a custom analysis and figuring out what automation opportunities there are and then using change management skill set to help implement those changes. Is that kind of how you bucket them, I guess you could say?

MC: Yeah, I even say something as simple as automation is a catalyst for change management. Automation is also a catalyst for innovation because before you can automate anything with AI, you need to go through business process management exercises. You need to make sure you've got a well-documented and accepted recipe for success. Once you have your lean process, then you can layer on top of that AI or automation technologies and take out the manual steps of that process.

NP: So at the end of the day, everything is custom.

MC: Well, some things are custom, but some things are out of the box. So, for example, the speech to text. Voicea is an AI agent that's available out of the box, and it's able to dial into meetings, take meeting notes, and action items. And that can be leveraged by any business out there. But what it is that you do with that data is going to be custom.

For example, for us, we can take those meeting notes, we can take those action items and understand which voice, which person, on the call they belong to and automatically connect that information to our project management solutions, assign those tasks automatically to those people, and send notifications automatically. So things that a project manager typically would do on a call like record meeting notes, create tasks in the project manager platform, assign them, follow up—most of it, if not all of it, can be fully automated.

NP: That's amazing. You mentioned it's evolved quickly in the last even 24 months. Looking out in the next three to five years, what do brands need to think about outside of the standard automation questions? Are there emerging technologies? You mentioned like some of your tools, voice-to-text, stuff like that—are there other things that they should really think about and brace for?

MC: Every single brand needs to form a strategy around AI and automation if they want to remain in business in the next three years. It's as simple as trying to ignore AI as some companies have ignored the Internet in the .com era because, today, it's not about .com anymore. It's about AI. So if you don't know what's going on in the AI and automation world and you don't have an expert sitting in your CTO or COO office mapping out the strategy and already experimenting with those technologies in one way or another, you're already behind. So make sure you've got a chief automation officer or CTO or COO, somebody forming a strategy and a team around how to identify opportunities within your business or for your clients, what you could do with automation and AI, and start experimenting. Identify small use cases; see where it can scale. Like I said, there is no blueprint to follow, so you need to start experimenting and then learn from that.

NP: So, the skill set that experts should have is obviously being technically savvy. They understand the tool sets and the tools that are out there. Anything else?

MC: I would recommend looking for people who are digital natives who have operational excellence background. They've been in the operations role or project management role because then they're used to working in the cross-functional environments. They are disciplined when it comes to process, and they're disciplined when it comes to change management.

So, people with project management, program management backgrounds, and, like I said, digital natives who are willing to upskill their technology skills when it comes to AI and robotic automation. Those are the three things that I'm seeing as the most important things in the success formula.

I've been following McKinsey Institute's white papers since it began issuing reports on automation technology about three years ago and suggesting based on their research and their surveys how much knowledge-based work can be automated using today's technology. That number has been climbing every year by about 5–10 percent, meaning that as AI continues to evolve, and it's not about just the mechanical automation, but also even going into the creative world. So we're talking about how to do copywriting. How do we do design using AI? So I would say that in the next three to five years, AI is going to be affecting brands in a creative sense.

On that topic, also what we've been watching out for is what kind of skills people need to have when it comes to future jobs. And the three things that keep coming up over and over again are that people need to have a high degree of emotional intelligence (EQ) but also creativity, and morals and ethics. And you can look this up on LinkedIn. This is what they've been suggesting in terms of their research. So because other stuff outside of empathy, creativity, and morals and ethics, most of it we'll be able to automate.

NP: So, you think today's workforce will be 80–90 percent automated. What do you think will happen with all those displaced workers?

MC: Well, first of all, I think in three to five years we're going to have a very augmented workforce. We're already talking about an HR that's no longer just HR. It's also supplemented by a digital workforce. So, there's going to be a huge displacement. And we're already seeing this in the self-driving cars. As part of this, there's also going to be new jobs created. For my team, for example, take the automation solution architect or the automation product manager. Those jobs and job descriptions that I created recently in the past six months have never existed. And I'm sure other businesses and brands or technology companies that are involved with AI and automation are developing or creating new jobs as well and new job descriptions. But I've also seen research from IBM in Forrester about a couple months ago where Forrester has made the prognosis that the net job gain, the ones that are going to be displaced plus the ones that are going to be created, it's actually going to be a substantial negative, about a 16 percent drop.

NP: So, there's going to be a risk of high unemployment then?

MC: That's why a lot of people, including—who's the candidate for the Democratic Party?—Andrew Yang, are talking about the concept of universal basic income. What he's talking about is automation and the need for universal basic income. And even Bill Gates I think a couple of years ago said we need to think about potentially creating Social Security numbers for robots so that we could tax corporations on those little workers because they're displacing too many workers. So, who's going to create the income that will be required to pay out the universal basic income for the displaced workforce?

It's hard to say what's the right thing to do because it's a global transformational wave—I would say a tsunami that's coming at all of us. That's why it's important for large corporations now to really get ahead of this game.

Customer Relationship Management Interview

Customer relationship management (CRM) has been a core marketing tactic for many years now. From email to sophisticated rewards programs to targeted offers, it's important to realize that CRM is evolving very quickly even beyond these tactics.

Customer relationship management is a broad data science that begins at the prospecting stage and ends with the lifetime of the customer. The science is evolving at an incredibly fast rate, and to get a better idea of how brands are leveraging it and the future of it, I interviewed Gary Opp, a CRM expert at of one of the top technology companies in the world.

Nick Papagiannis: Can you talk about what your role is and how you support business and brands?

Gary Opp: I've been in the CRM space for 11 years now in different capacities, and I'm a customer success manager for enterprise accounts, specializing in business applications. That includes CRM as well as a related suite of technologies.

NP: Why do you think CRM is critical to business?

GO: There's actually much more money to be had in maintaining existing streams of revenue and trying to expand business within your existing customer base than just focusing your entire budget on always going after netting new business.

NP: What do you see when you get into clients? What are their big CRM challenges these days?

GO: The same problems have always been challenging for CRM deployments. CRM needs continual attention and buy-in, starting from executive leadership on down. There needs to be a strategic direction for the tool that's constantly revisited and tweaked as needed, to reinforce the importance of using the system. So without quality, consistent data going into the tool, CRM becomes worthless.

NP: How will you guys use that data, and how do you market to users? Is it a content strategy, a contact strategy? I mean, what is the output that you see clients doing with the CRM software?

GO: Your CRM system should be a central hub for pulling in information about your customers and contacts from a variety of different sources. So at the end of the day, like I said, a CRM system should just be that centralized hub for data. And we live in a data-driven world. People like to talk about the challenger sale. It's a methodology that's kind of recognized as a best practice. But that's all based on knowing as much as you can about their customers, their industry, and then layering in how your product or services can benefit them in a way that perhaps they're not even thinking about.

NP: Do you have any clients that are more retail, kind of B2C [business to consumer]?

GO: When you're talking about B2C, it's a little bit different because a lot of times companies try to do CRM in order to really know who their end customers are. You've got obviously your real name and probably have three different emails or more, right? You've got a work email, you've got a personal email, you've got an Instagram handle, you've got a Facebook name, and it can be really hard for companies to know that all of these different end points are actually the same person.

The way that a lot of companies try to get around that is by leveraging some type of a loyalty program. So that then your consumers want to be logging in and interacting with you in a known way so that they receive benefits. Again, this is tariff miles or points at a restaurant that you go to. That's where the app-driven world we have comes into play. Each time you go into Starbucks, you want to check in, and then after nine coffees, you get your 10th one free.

All of that is enabled by the consumer sharing or logging in in a consistent way for the company, but in return, the company is collecting data—collecting data about you, depending on how much is shared in the sign-up process, but more importantly, how often, when, where you're buying their products or interacting with the company. And then marketers can take all that data and try to segment it as best they can, based on whatever demographics or geographically or by gender or by age or whatever it is, and then start to tailor campaigns around those things.

NP: When you talk about tailoring campaigns for those things, are you able to provide two or three best practices that businesses should consider when they're doing the kind of marketing campaigns that are tailored to that data?

GO: A lot depends on what your product or service is to begin with. So, again, Starbucks might interact differently than, for example, McDonalds, right? Most people that go through the drive-through or go through the checkout line at McDonalds don't log in in any way. Out of necessity, they have a different marketing approach than companies do that, maybe, you are buying their clothing through a portal or an app.

NP: Are there top CRM solutions that are in the market that businesses should be aware of?

GO: If you look at any Gartner or Forrester study, there's no secret on who the top players are in the industry. Generally, the top two are Salesforce and Microsoft with its Dynamics product. And then there's a lot of kind of more niche players. Oracle is still there. Siebel is kind of the older CRM system but yet still has a very large market share.

NP: Are there small ones tailored for really smaller budgets and small businesses?

GO: Ones like Sugar come to mind. It's been out there for a long time. And then even a lot of those systems have kind of different tiers as well that people can take advantage of.

NP: Obviously, marketing is advancing really quickly right now. Are there any things in the CRM world that businesses should look ahead to?

GO: Well, privacy is a big thing. Essentially we now live in a world with GDPR [General Data Protection Regulation], and there are regulations in different countries. Depending if you're an enterprise-level firm, you're already aware of these things, but it still takes a lot of thought and careful planning to make sure that you are not in violation, especially if you're a global company, in how you're conducting business and how you're retaining personal information about your customers. And then how you're obviously letting them know if you are collecting their information and getting permission to do so.

As far as advances from a technology standpoint, the two big areas that are huge right now are anything related to artificial intelligence and anything related to machine learning. The one thing that companies aren't lacking in is data. They have their own historical data, product data, people data about their own employees and their customers, industry data . . . it goes on and on. But they struggle with pulling it all together in meaningful ways, and that's where the power of AI and ML will be coming into play and is already starting to come into play.

Companies that can tap into all of those sources of data and then layer in things on top of it, like weather signals or real-time news updates, will be able to leverage AI and ML to benefit and create intelligent systems or systems of intelligence—systems that proactively bring things to the end user's attention, recognizing buying signals, suggesting next best actions, identifying new opportunities or under-penetrated markets.

Businesses that can quickly come to the forefront in those areas will have a serious advantage over their competitors.

Other Future Content Discovery Vehicles

Smart TVs, appliances, homes, and all the other next-generation technologies offer varying ways to provide users what they're looking for and when they are looking for it. Every time there's an advancement there's a big reaction from the marketing space on how to best position brands to take advantage of it. Case in point: when augmented reality came to the forefront of the search marketing world in Yelp, everyone thought it was going to be the new way to search. When I looked in depth, I realized that brands just needed to be connected to the platform correctly. I believe as time moves ahead and new content discovery vehicles manifest, this will also be the case. In some ways, I believe the big FANG companies (Facebook, Amazon, Netflix, and Google) and other top tech companies like Microsoft will retain their dominance through acquisition, and their current rigorous innovation strategies will be leading the charge on next-generation content discovery. The best approach to position a brand is to make sure they are positioned well on these platforms to begin with. What will likely happen is that these platforms will repurpose existing content and brands on these platforms to their new content vehicles, rather than create a whole new database of information (which is not practical or cost effective). So, my recommendation is to be sure to be optimized on all owned properties and continue to work with SEO experts and read next-generation books (like this) to stay ahead of the curve.

Quiz

1. Fill in the blanks: With all the technology changes on the horizon, it's important that brands possess the right _____, _____, and culture to withstand and excel with the changes coming ahead.

   a. Personality, process

   b. People, process

   c. People, mind-set

   d. Mind-set, process

   Answer: d

2. Fill in the blanks: It's important that brands have an _____ and _____ mind to position themselves for upcoming changes in the commerce and shopping experience world.

   a. Open, flexible

   b. Flexible, enthusiastic

   c. Enthusiastic, Practical

   d. Open, enthusiastic

   Answer: a

3. Which of the following important tech advances should brands prepare for and optimize their presence on?

   a. Conversational commerce

   b. Artificial intelligence

   c. Next-generation CRM

   d. All the above

   Answer: d

4. True or False: Optimizing your voice search presence begins with refining your customer journey to focus on voice interactions.

   Answer: True

5. Fill in the blank: It is possible to get a sense of a brand's voice search standing by looking at how many _____ it has.

   a. Images

   b. Quick answers

   c. Search volume

   d. Links

   Answer: b

6. To have an accurate and strong local result for when someone uses voice search to search for your brand location, it's best to _____.

   a. Build an Alexa skill

   b. Build local content via your blog

   c. Offer a chat feature on your website

   d. Verify and claim your location pages

   Answer: d

7. True or False: Google already uses artificial intelligence in its ranking algorithm.

   Answer: True

8. To optimize for AI within Google, it's best to conduct traditional SEO optimization but also to _____.

   a. Make sure content is mobile friendly

   b. Make sure social sharing widgets are available on web content

   c. Focus on load time and content length

   d. Make sure content is crawlable, user friendly, and popular

   Answer: d

9. The future of CRM will be enhanced with which of the following?

   a. Artificial intelligence and machine learning

   b. Content and unique consumer specific promotions

    c. Dynamic messaging and static content

    d. Email and targeted offers

Answer: a

10. True or False: To best prepare for the future, at a bare minimum, it's best that brands continue to optimize their presence and activity on the top technology and content platforms.

Answer: True

CHAPTER

9

SEO and Content Marketing for Your Small Business

The aforementioned SEO and content marketing tactics are geared more toward national companies with national or global brands. A small business must use the tactics that I mentioned earlier, as well as a few additional tactics. Being a small business competing in a big business category against large national brands can be an extremely difficult position online. It's important to understand and take advantage of all the local search opportunities available for your business to make sure you get as many customers as possible.

I have to preface this section by saying that I have a soft spot for small businesses because my father had several small restaurant businesses while I was growing up. I saw him have his good years and bad years. I saw the amount of effort he had to put into making the business run. I know how difficult it can be to get a business thriving. If you follow the SEO and content rules that I outlined in previous chapters and that I outline in this one, I believe you will be ahead of the curve.

The Small Business Mind-Set Needed to Win Online

As I mentioned, my father had his own small businesses that ranged from restaurants to produce delivery. Each of these businesses was in a hyper-competitive category, and each of them had their hardships. I learned a lot from my father during those times, especially when I saw him struggle. Additionally, as an adult, I have consulted many small businesses from a digital marketing standpoint. I've seen businesses that are extremely successful, as well as businesses that weren't successful and even ended up closing.

In my experience, I would say that the businesses doing the best overall tend to embrace a different mentality than the ones that are not doing well. That being said, it's important to have the proper small business mind-set when it comes to marketing online, and marketing in general. There are several traits that small business owners should consider developing to get the best performance from their online channel and to drive more business into their stores or locations. These include the following:

- **An eagerness to learn:** The marketing landscape is always changing. Competitors are always changing. Technology is always changing. The things that influence consumers are always changing. It's important as a business owner that you stay in tune with the newest and emerging technology and competitive changes by adopting an ever-learning mind-set.

- **An open mind:** Having your own business does require a little bit of ego; however, that doesn't mean you can't have an open mind. You may be doing things the way you think are correct, but they might not be. Plus, with all the technology advances and changes in your industry, you might be working in an obsolete manner, which gives competitors an opportunity to beat you.

- **A thorough understanding of your competitors and competitive landscape:** You'd be surprised at how many small businesses don't understand who their direct competitors are. Whether you're a retail store or just an online store, the competitive set that you are dealing with can quickly change. Be sure to solidify your true competitors by working with a marketing consultant or by staying in tune with your market to identify who your top competitors are. Learn about your competitors' tactics and product offerings by using online research as well.

- **An understanding of the four pieces of marketing or principles of marketing:** We discussed the principles of marketing in earlier chapters, but it's important that even small business owners evaluate their product offerings, pricing, place, and promotions.

- **Enthusiasm about your business category and product:** Being a longtime small business owner can wear down your enthusiasm. It's important that you are enthusiastic about your business and your product category, because enthusiasm provides an energy and excitement that can translate into stronger execution. Additionally, there are always new competitors entering your space with strong enthusiasm at the onset. Be sure to always choose a business or product category that you are enthusiastic about and will maintain enthusiasm about.

- **Time:** One of the most treasured and rare aspects of starting your own business is time. Free time and time for free thinking are extremely important when having your own business. It provides an opportunity to evaluate performance, brainstorm improvement ideas, and adjust your marketing strategies.

- **A strong work ethic:** Having a strong work ethic is typically a core characteristic of a small business owner. Managing your own business requires a lot of energy and a lot of time, so it's important that you possess a strong work ethic to stay ahead of your competitors, effectively manage employees, and provide the best product offering to your customers.

- **An ever-changing menu:** While not necessary to run a small business, it's important to constantly evaluate your product offering and product menus. Take the time to evaluate which products are providing a strong ROI and which ones aren't. You want to get to the point where you're offering products that provide strong profits to you and value to your customers.

- **A dedicated marketing budget:** I can't tell you the number of times I worked with small business owners who tried to do everything themselves from a marketing perspective to save on costs and to minimize their marketing budgets. In this day and age, businesses live and die by their online presence and reputation. It's extremely important that you have a dedicated marketing budget to spend online and offline to bring in new customers and to remarket existing customers. It's also important not to look at marketing as an expense, but as an investment. A small business owner should ultimately work to identify a return on investment with their marketing budget. When done correctly, it should always be positive. Make adjustments and optimizations to turn negative ROI into positive ROI by working with a marketing consultant who has an expertise in your industry or with someone skilled in marketing.

▪ **Feedback mechanisms:** Reviews, surveys, social media comments, and chatter provide an ongoing feedback mechanism for your business. Be sure to monitor reviews and solicit input from your customers and prospects to further optimize your product and business.

As a small business owner, it's important to incorporate these traits and mind-set into your marketing and overall business approach. I believe without these it will be difficult to maintain your business performance and overall customer satisfaction.

Common SEO Problems for a Local Business

Small business is a hypercompetitive segment in the SEO world. There are likely many similar businesses that are competing for the same search rankings that a small business is. It can be extremely difficult to deal with the following issues, so a good SEO strategy is critical:

▪ Not ranking for a search phrase
▪ No reviews or negative reviews
▪ Low traffic and sales

In my opinion, a small business must do what a national business does to gain traction in search engine results, but even more to also rank for localized searches. If you are a small business, consider doing the following to improve your presence for localized searches.

Steps to Improve SEO for a Local Business

Let's assume you have a small business or service that you offer in a city or small, localized area. Let's summarize the key areas and steps that you need to maximize your SEO performance.

1. **Create an SEO-friendly website:** Every business should have a website these days. Be sure to build a simple website that outlines your company, services or menu, reviews, location, and contact

information. The customer experience practically depends on it, so be sure to have one. You can use a simple website management system like Wix, Weebly, or GoDaddy to easily build a website that's SEO optimized, as they provide SEO widgets and packages. These website systems offer free website templates that look great and make setup easy, in that you likely only have to implement copy or text about your business. Figure 9.1 shows an example of a `Wix.com` restaurant template that's free to use.

2. **Install website analytics:** Install Google Analytics and Google Search Console. These free tools will provide valuable insights and traffic data. You can see how often people come to your site, what content they are looking for, what pages they spend the most on, how often they call you, and many other things. Google Search Console will show whether there are any crawling issues with your website and what your average ranking position is.

3. **Start a content program, geared toward local content or your local market:** As I have said throughout this book, if you want to rank for a search term, you need to have a dedicated web page that speaks to that term. See previous chapters for how to set up that landing page, but in general it's best to have a content program in place to regularly publish content that you want to rank for. If you are a small business that targets a specific city or geographic area, consider building content based on popular searches happening for that area (e.g., best restaurants in Rosemont, Illinois, or best restaurants near O'Hare Airport) or adding pages about your business on websites that rank for those searches. When I did a search for things to do near O'Hare airport, I saw TripAdvisor ranked on the first page (Figure 9.2). In this case, you should consider adding a page about your business on TripAdvisor and then contact other sites that are ranking high for that search and see what you need to do to get a presence on that page.

   You can also conduct a localized keyword research. If you're using Google's free Keyword Planner tool (discussed in Chapter 2), you can find popular searches happening in your target market and then create content around those content topics. You can edit the location at the top left to find specific keyword topics for a city or metro (Figure 9.3 and Figure 9.4).

   The output will be a list of terms and their respective search volumes in that market (Figure 9.5).

Figure 9.1: Wix.com small business template example

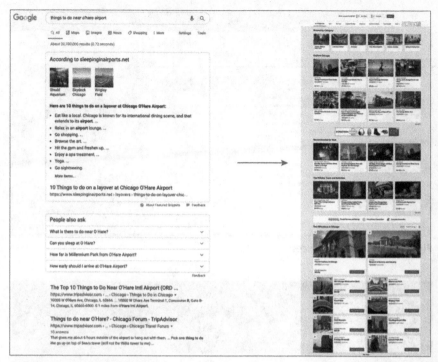

Figure 9.2: Trip Advisor example

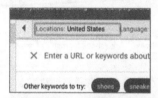

Figure 9.3: Localized keyword research

4. **Begin building links to your website and content:** Depending on what phrase you want to rank for, consider employing the link building techniques I outlined earlier. Consider local directories, complementary businesses' websites, service partner websites, municipal websites, or city/government sites that are within your local area.

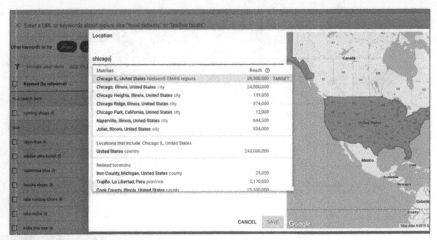

Figure 9.4: Location choices

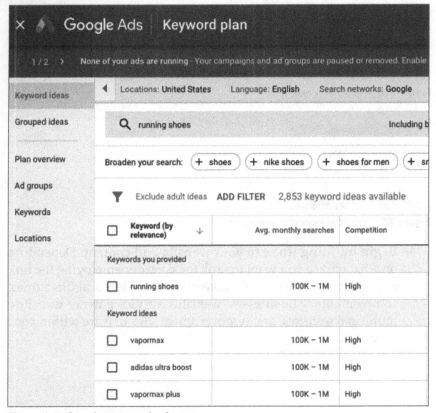

Figure 9.5: Search terms and volumes

5. **Promote your content:** If you are building location-specific content, consider employing content promotion or content discovery tactics such as links to your content or paid content promotion through content promotion vehicles like Google or Outbrain that can target down to a local market or contextually by keyword. Additionally, contact your local news sites and see if they offer custom ad or content opportunities that can promote your business and website. If there are relevant sites that rank for the terms you are targeting, consider contacting them to see if they offer custom content programs where you can essentially rent a page on their site or have another presence that ranks.

6. **Create and promote your social media pages:** Not only are social media pages such as Facebook great for a social media presence, but they also allow companies to communicate directly to customers. You can promote offers, collect feedback, and run localized ads or sponsored updates. Consider having an active social media presence on the biggest and most relevant social media sites, such as Twitter, Facebook, LinkedIn, and Instagram.

7. **Start an email database and regular newsletter:** Depending on your business, consider collecting emails on your website and offer free advice and other utility content. Since you're a local business, consider offering relevant information about your market as well. This allows you to stay in front of your customers by offering valuable content. This also provides an avenue for you to provide any announcements and promotions.

8. **Offer promotions and coupons:** Coupons and promotional codes offer a great way to get customers. If you are using a promotion, be sure to have a web page that speaks to it and have all your marketing materials link to that page when possible.

9. **Run localized pay-per-click (PPC) through Google Ads:** While not necessarily an SEO tactic, running localized ads on Google Ads allows you to target specific markets and ZIP codes. Consider setting up an Ads account and running some test ads to capture people searching for your services in your target market. Once you set up an account, you can call Google for step-by-step help.

10. **Set up a local directory page:** In my opinion, this is one of the most critical, if not the most critical, to your online local business presence. Be sure to set up, verify, and claim pages for your business on business directories, like Google My Business and Yelp.

These directories offer many search and traffic benefits and offer you the ability to promote your promotions and collect reviews and other information. Additionally, these pages are critical to ranking in voice search results. They also offer dashboarding tools where you can learn about how much traffic your pages are getting and other metrics. Additionally, these pages tend to be pulled into general search engine results and can link to your website as well. Where possible, make sure you "claim," or verify your ownership, so no one but you can edit the information. Claim your page by setting up a Google My Business account and adding a location to your account. Here are the high-level steps:

a. Visit GoogleMyBusiness.com and click Manage Now (Figure 9.6).

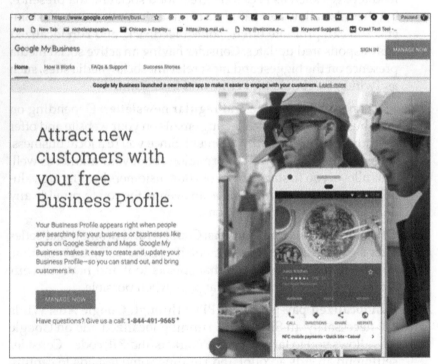

Figure 9.6: Google My Business

b. Set up an account to manage your business (Figure 9.7).

c. Once you have set up your account, log in, look up your business, and claim your listing if it's available (Figure 9.8).

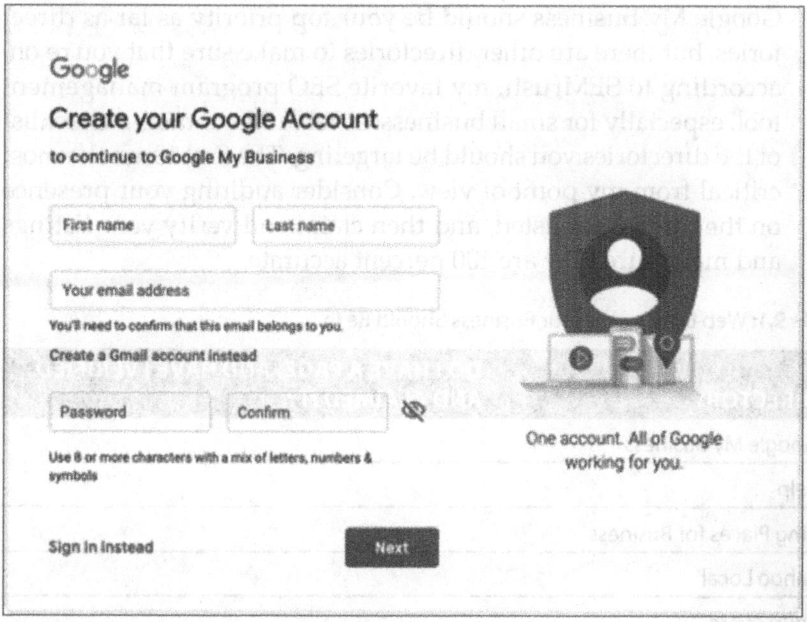

Figure 9.7: Google My Business setup

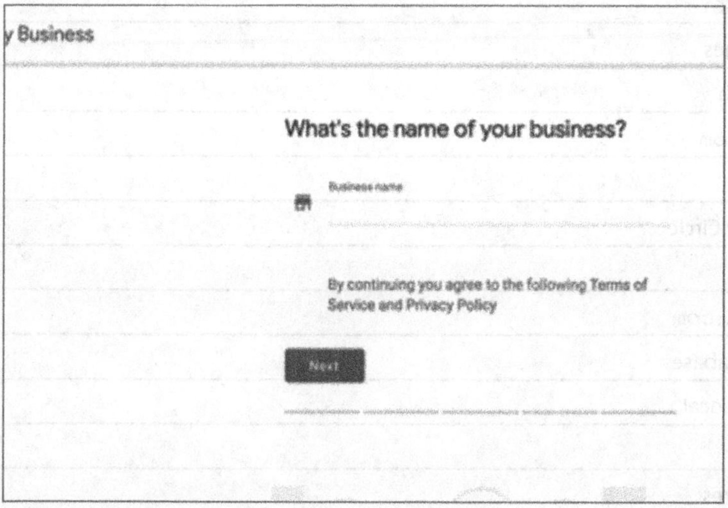

Figure 9.8: Claim Your Listing on GoogleMyBusiness

    d. Once you claim your business, you can make edits and complete your listing page.

Google My Business should be your top priority as far as directories, but there are other directories to make sure that you're on, according to SEMrush, my favorite SEO program management tool, especially for small businesses. Table 9.1 contains a checklist of the directories you should be targeting. The first 10 are the most critical from my point of view. Consider auditing your presence on the directories listed, and then claim and verify your listings and make sure they are 100 percent accurate.

Table 9.1: Web Directories Your Business Should Be In

DIRECTORY	DO I HAVE A PAGE, AND HAVE I VERIFIED AND CLAIMED IT?
Google My Business	
Yelp	
Bing Places for Business	
Yahoo Local	
Foursquare	
Facebook	
MapQuest	
Superpages	
Citysearch	
Local.com	
YP.com	
Merchant Circle	
Cylex	
EZlocal.com	
Local Database	
ShowMeLocal	
iGlobal	
CitySquares	
Local Pages	
LocalStack	
YellowMoxie	
Get Fave	

DIRECTORY	DO I HAVE A PAGE, AND HAVE I VERIFIED AND CLAIMED IT?
Tupalo.com	
Avantar	
Property Capsule	
Navmii	
Where to?	
ChamberofCommerce.com	
USCity.net	
YellowPagesCity.com	
AmericanTowns.com	
8coupons	
eLocal	
GoLocal247	
YaSabe	
YellowPagesGoesGreen	
PointCom	
ABLocal	
Opendi	
VotefortheBest	
2FindLocal	
My Local Services	
Credibility Review	
Insider Pages	
Yalwa	
Brownbook.net	
Bizwiki	
AroundMe	
Hotfrog	
PR.Business	
FindOpen	

Bonus: Interview with Small Business Expert

To get a better idea of how a small business can overcome digital challenges, I interviewed Nitin Hemmady, small business consultant and managing partner of I0n Creative at i0ncreative.com. The full interview is provided next, but the key takeaways of the interview are the following:

- Common challenges for small businesses when executing marketing initiatives tend to be budget, skill set, and lack of digital marketing strategy.

- Small businesses should use a website platform that allows them to develop modern websites in a flexible and low-cost manner (Wix, Squarespace, WordPress, etc.)

- Paid search, SEO, and content marketing can be extremely beneficial to capturing sales for small businesses, and businesses should consider running those programs through a marketing partner with experience in their business category.

- Richer content assets that go beyond text (i.e., video content), voice search, and AI are upcoming trends that small businesses should be honing in on.

Nick Papagiannis: Why don't you just describe what your role is with supporting businesses, and small businesses specifically, and your experience.

Nitin Hemmady: I'm managing partner of I0n Creative, which is a digital marketing agency. We help small businesses technically, and then we help them with growth by providing them with the digital marketing strategies that they need. My main focus is to allow small businesses to grow and flourish digitally, including e-commerce, web development, and also SEO, SEM, and then SMS.

NP: From your perspective, what are the big online challenges you're seeing from a small business perspective when it comes to technology and digital marketing?

NH: The first challenge that I see is that small businesses don't have a huge budget for their website. They don't have the technical resources. When I look at a small business, the first thing is the website, right? That's kind of the small business's story. So, if that's not performing well, if it's not driving home a message, if it doesn't look modern, that's the business's first challenge.

The second challenge is designing effective digital marketing strategies by leveraging paid advertising and content. Businesses, because they're so engrossed in trying to do what they do, they sometimes ignore these pieces, which can hurt them.

NP: What kind of solutions do you usually recommend to your clients to solve business challenges? Like what kind of digital marketing products or solutions?

NH: What I recommend is first picking the best website platform that can allow them to develop or allow them to have something that looks very modern, something that performs really well, and something that's really easy where they don't need a whole lot of resources to constantly update the site, because I think, back in the day, that was a huge problem, where people were just messing with HTML. And now, we have products out there. There are many, many different content management systems that we can use, both open source and enterprise, that we recommend to clients. There's Wix, there's Squarespace, and there's WordPress, as well as other types of CMSs that are financially feasible and don't require a whole lot of resources to maintain. So, from a technology aspect, I recommend a good website using those CMS platforms.

The second thing (once the business has their website and they're able to effectively market) is to do paid search and organic search and social media campaigns. These will allow them to be seen by people searching for all kinds of things on the Internet or social media.

NP: As far as solutions, are there any best practices outside of the website that you also want to mention?

NH: Besides having that website that's performing well, it's all about content, so they need to constantly update their content, and make sure the content that they are providing is highly relevant to what they want people to search for and then eventually come to their website. So, content is something, whether it be a blog, or some kind of information that's relevant to the business. That's really important.

The second thing is paid search campaigns. They're very effective. I think businesses were—in the beginning, during the whole paid search thing—they were a little hesitant, but now, it's kind of a necessity to compete. Depending on your region, there are businesses competing with each other. So, targeted, focused advertising is very effective, and it's absolutely necessary. So we put that together for small businesses. The small business ends up thanking us later, right? Because they're starting to see traffic grow; they're starting to see more conversions at the end of the day.

And also, Google Analytics, or some kind of analytics platform, is important to monitor who's coming to their website, where are they coming from, and what are people searching for. Also, what kind of devices are being used to reach them. That's really important information to have. And then, there are all kinds of other complicated facets that you can utilize within those analytics platforms, depending on the business need.

NP: You mentioned content. Do you recommend other types of content outside of just text or web pages? Things like videos?

NH: Absolutely. Custom content, like video content, that's highly relevant, that's entertaining, and that's going to be eye-catching is highly effective for a business. I mean, every time we go to a website, we see a video. We see a commercial. And now, I'm kind of okay with that as a user. I'm okay with seeing a commercial, and some of them are kind of entertaining. And now, small businesses can design their own professional commercials. . .and then, put it out there for the public to see. So, it's pretty amazing what can be done outside of just like a blog post or content on a website. So, media like video is highly recommended and highly relevant in today's marketing.

NP: It sounds like you really make the case for small businesses to leverage a vendor like yourself, to create these strategies, versus trying to do them themselves. I feel like your knowledge of the industry and your team can help them create the assets and strategy they need to really improve their business and bottom line. You would agree with that, right? Versus them trying to just do that themselves?

NH: Absolutely. They need professional scaffolding to help them. Because at the end of the day, you're trying to minimize your expenses and maximize your conversions. If you go out there into this vast world of digital marketing and try to go off on your own and do these things, you might end up spending a little bit more money than you wanted, and you might not get the kind of conversions that you want. Also, you might not get the data that you're looking for. So, it's highly recommended that a small business, if digital is not their forte, that they get an agency to help them think through strategy and then go off and implement it.

NP: I'm trying to prepare small businesses for changes on the horizon. Technically, everything is changing so quickly. Are there any trends that you think a small business marketer or owner should watch over the next five years or so, and prepare for?

NH: Besides the video content, which is really going to generate a lot of traffic, I think voice search is a big one. A lot of different companies are getting into that. And voice search is convenient, and it can really help minimize the time a user spends in actually searching. So, users can just use natural voice commands to search for something that is relevant to them without having to click 20 times to get the answers or to get the results that they want. I think voice is going to be really important. That's the biggest technology challenge that businesses need to keep their eyes on.

Quiz

1. Fill in the blank: For small businesses to succeed online and in general, they must have a certain business _____.
   a. Mind-set
   b. Acumen
   c. Customer service
   d. Relationship

   Answer: a

2. According to this book, which of the following are important traits to have for a small business to succeed online? (Choose all that apply.)
   a. Eagerness to learn
   b. Open mind
   c. A strong staff
   d. Thorough understanding of competitive landscape
   e. Thorough understanding of the principles of marketing
   f. Easy processes

     g. Accepting bitcoin and alternative currencies

     h. Enthusiasm about your business, products, and business category

     i. Strong work ethic

     j. Feedback mechanisms

     k. Dedicated marketing budget

     Answer: a, b, d, e, f, h, i, j, k

3. Which of these is considered a feedback mechanism that businesses should always utilize?

     a. Online product or business reviews

     b. Social media comments

     c. Surveys

     d. Online chatter

     e. All the above

     Answer: e

4. Which of the following are common problems for small businesses online? (Choose all that apply.)

     a. Not ranking for searches on search engines

     b. Limited products

     c. Lack of online reviews or negative online reviews

     d. Bad location

     e. Low Traffic

     f. Low sales

     g. Insufficient accounting practices

     Answer: a, c, e, f

5. According to this book, which are some of the steps to improving SEO for a small business? (Choose all that apply.)

     a. Create an SEO-friendly website

     b. Work with influencers

     c. Start a content program

     d. Set up directory pages

    e. Work with competitors to start an association

    f. Offer promotions

    g. Install website analytics

    Answer: a, c, d, f, g

6. Fill in the blank: Setting up, verifying, and claiming local directory pages are _____.

    a. Some of the most important or critical things a local business can do online

    b. Relatively important, but not necessary

    c. Not that important at all

    d. Less valuable than most SEO tactics online

    Answer: a

7. Which one of the following is the most important directory online for SEO?

    a. Google My Business

    b. Yelp

    c. Yellow pages

    d. City Search

    e. All the above

    Answer: a

8. What are other tactics a small business should consider online?

    a. An email newsletter

    b. Localized paid search or PPC programs

    c. Social media pages and advertisements

    d. Localized content promotions and content discovery programs

    e. All the above

    Answer: e

9. When building links for your local business, consider obtaining links from sites that are _____. (Choose all that apply.)

    a. Highly rated

    b. In your local area

    c. Partner sites

    d. Municipal or government sites with .gov extensions

    e. Sites from outside countries

    Answer: a, b, c, d

10. As a small business owner, it's important to look at marketing as an _____ and not an _____.

    a. Expense, investment

    b. Activity, option

    c. Activity, expense

    d. Investment, expense

    e. Option, expense

    Answer: d

Creating Your Optimization Path

Now that we have discussed all the various areas and practices of SEO and content marketing, it's time to bring everything together and provide guidance on how to create your custom strategic plan to achieve full optimization of your marketing programs and business and to yield the most amount of free traffic as possible.

As I have said throughout this book, search engine optimization should not be limited or segmented out into its own thinking or practice. If your goal is to be a business with a strong organic presence and traffic, it's pretty important to focus on these key areas:

- Building and executing an SEO and content vision throughout your company
- Understanding which search engines to focus on
- Establishing your research channels
- Taking inventory of your assets and platforms
- Understanding who your true competitors are
- Knowing how SEO and content can help solve business problems

- Providing a positive brand search experience
- Understanding your industry and the program considerations and risks
- Having a detailed optimization project plan in place

Without these, it can be difficult to execute SEO and content programs to their fullest potential. Addressing each of these can ensure that your business is optimizing its marketing programs to their fullest and bringing organic traffic levels to the highest levels possible. It's important that you have the following in place:

- **Executive mandate:** It can be difficult to get everyone on the same page and to prioritize SEO and content marketing above their own priorities. Having an executive mandate can help foster this culture change.

- **Process-minded culture:** As we discussed in earlier chapters, SEO and content marketing are dependent on process. They have their own processes but also can be inserted in existing processes across the company. It's critical that you develop a process-centered culture, especially when executing your optimization project plan.

- **Cooperation with IT teams:** IT teams are critical to implementing SEO recommendations and content. It's critical that you have a cooperative relationship set before moving forward with your programs. Additionally, when taking inventory of your owned media assets, IT will have a lot of knowledge of your web assets.

- **Cooperation with the total marketing team:** Oftentimes, marketing specialties are siloed (print, social media, broadcast, etc.). It's important to be able to get their buy-in and cooperation to get an understanding of all your marketing programs, since they can benefit from SEO and be useful in your content marketing programs.

Building an SEO and Content Vision Throughout Your Company

Simply understanding SEO and content marketing is not enough. It's important to build a vision for how these two sciences can help your specific business. A vision or strategy cannot be built without the right foundation. When building a vision, first and foremost, it's important to do a little self-reflection as a brand, marketing team, business owner, or anyone else involved in moving the needle for a company.

The key question to ask yourself is if you understand the value of SEO and content as outlined in previous chapters. Having a decisive and strong understanding of the value of SEO and organic content is critical from an execution perspective.

Additionally, you as a marketer will have to likely sell and educate important decision-makers along the way, when pushing forward with SEO and content initiatives. Here are some ideas of how to address the issues:

▪ **Selling decision-makers:** Decision-makers can be all different types of people in various positions of power, including an IT manager, a finance manager, or other employees who are involved in managing a business. Selling decision-makers can be daunting but is critical to reforming processes and attitudes that may hinder your ability to implement SEO and content processes. It's important to understand your audience and what pieces of information they value. Oftentimes, marketers must embrace an ROI mentality when it comes to selling ideas to decision-makers. When dealing with decision-makers, it's best to provide an estimate of the impact your SEO and content initiatives might bring from a business level. From my perspective, it's always best to use the basic formula *ROI = (Increase in sales − cost of SEO initiative) / cost of SEO initiatives* to prove that SEO and expanding content can increase traffic and or sales.

▪ **Providing workshops and education sessions:** To implement an SEO and content vision across your company, education will be key. Personnel involved with executing marketing initiatives must all have a foundational understanding of SEO and content and the value it brings. Be prepared to conduct ongoing workshops that provide attendees with a basic understanding of how SEO and content can bring value to the company and their job performance. Be sure to use case studies and competitor information to show how each science is benefiting competitors or the industry. It's important to simplify SEO and content marketing so that users can perform their regular duties without any additional burdensome tasks. If you complicate their job, they will most likely not use SEO and content marketing. When I pull together workshop content, my presentations typically focus on the following questions and areas:

▪ How does SEO work?

▪ Why is content important?

- What is the standard SEO and content process?
- How does this apply to you?
- Are our competitors doing it well, and what can we learn from them?
- What are some best-in-class case studies or examples?

- **Conduct an opportunity audit across disciplines:** Do some analysis around the various departments of your company that help execute your brand product and services. This can include a public relations team, sales team, and even IT teams. Once you get ahold of all the different departments that your company has, consider meeting with each one of them to identify their processes and see if there's any way search and content can help elevate their performance. If possible, set up a time to interview the leaders of each department with the understanding that you are an SEO and content expert who can help make their jobs easier and more successful. Here are some basic interview questions to help you collect the information needed to conduct your opportunity audit:

  - What would you say your subject matter expertise lies in?
  - Does your job or team result in the production of any content whatsoever in any format?
  - What are the ultimate goals of your department, and what metrics are they evaluated by?
  - Do you work closely with any other departments?
  - Does your department have team members that rely on Google searches for information?
  - Do you understand what search engine optimization and content marketing are and how they can help benefit businesses?
  - Does your company website have any kind of information on your department? If so, how is this information valuable to them?
  - Does your department contribute to the company blog or other content?
  - How does having more customers, business traffic, or sales directly benefit your department?

- Are you or is anyone available to help create content for company content channels?
- Can you provide a process breakdown of your most common processes?

After getting answers to these common questions, it's important to take those answers and analyze areas of opportunity and ways that that department can help execute SEO and content programs. Take those answers and follow these best practices to incorporate them by doing the following:

- Determine whether the discipline understands the value of search engines and content from a customer acquisition and branding perspective. If you feel they don't understand that, be sure to schedule a workshop with the team to walk through how it works and why it should be important to them.

- Identify what content opportunities there are by seeing what kind of content they can create that can be used in your content strategy.

- Look at their common processes and identify if there is an opportunity to enhance the performance of these processes by integrating new steps that emphasize content and SEO best practices in them.

Understanding Which Search Engines to Focus On

The search landscape continues to grow, with new search engines continuously popping up. Depending on the size of your business and your goals, it might make sense to have a multi-search-engine approach. These days, many people consider different sites to be search engines. In the past, search engines were limited to Bing, Yahoo, and Google, but now there are many different types of search engines available, depending on what content users are seeking. As you can see from the jump shot study shown in Figure 10.1, 94 percent of searches are happening on a Google-owned property. This includes YouTube, Google Maps, and Google Images. That being said, it's still important to always find out what other search avenues are available to capture traffic to your content. Additionally, it's important to consider your business model and your website type to determine which search engine should be the top priority. For instance, if you're selling products on your website or are an e-commerce site, it's important to consider Amazon as a key driver of traffic because it's considered a top search engine for

products, according to an eMarketer study (`https://www.emarketer`
`.com/content/more-product-searches-start-on-amazon`).

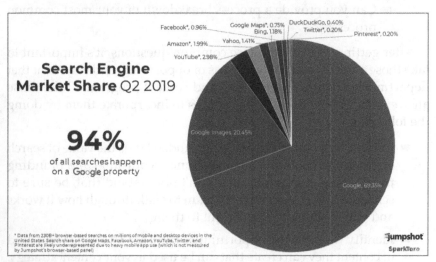

Figure 10.1: Search engine market share

If you're a small business that's not selling products, the best search
engine to optimize around is Google. It's important you do some self-anal-
ysis to determine which search engine is important to your business
and which search engine should be the top priority for you to optimize
around. Most of the time it'll likely be Google, but there are situations in
which it might make sense to focus on others. Additionally, Bing powers
Yahoo's search engine, so if you optimize well for Bing, you will likely
rank well for Yahoo too. DuckDuckGo is a relatively new search engine
that emphasizes a user's privacy, which is helping it gain traction. With
all the controversy around privacy, it's important as a marketer to keep
a watchful eye on your traffic reports to see if DuckDuckGo increasingly
gains momentum as a go-to search engine.

Optimizing for each search engine can be complicated, but fortunately most search engines provide a list of quality guidelines that they
use as part of their ranking algorithms. These guidelines are published
and available for the general public to reference as part of their website
strategies.

As discussed in previous chapters, it's important to use a website
analytics tool that collects information on users coming to your website
and content. Most of them provide insight into which search engines are
currently driving traffic to your website. Figure 10.2 shows an example

of Google analytics and the report data it provides on the top search engines coming to a brand's website. To view yours, all you have to do is select Acquisition ➪ All Traffic ➪ Source/Medium.

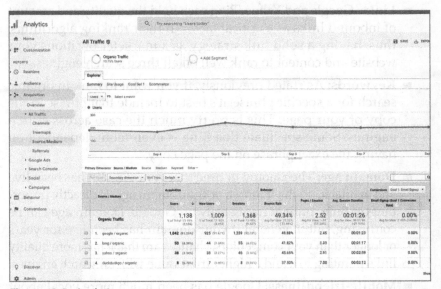

Figure 10.2: Analytics

If you are seeing a smaller ratio of traffic from each search engine, as compared to the previously mentioned study, consider optimizing the traffic for those search engines. Additionally, each search engine has its own "quality guidelines" that lists practices to avoid because they are viewed as spam and might compromise your ranking.

Optimizing for the Big Three Search Engines at the Same Time

The quality guidelines are long for each of the big three search engines (Yahoo, Bing, Google), so users should understand how difficult it can be to rank for all three at the same time. For most businesses, it almost always makes sense to focus on Google because it controls the largest market share, while at the same time optimizing elements to also rank other search engines or elements that they find valuable.

Since Bing and Yahoo have a partnership that allows for Bing to control the search engine results on Yahoo, it makes sense to focus on them as one unit.

There are a lot of similar focus areas across the big three search engines. Optimizing the following areas can help you perform better on each of the three engines:

- **Links:** Google and Yahoo/Bing each hold the quality and amount of inbound links as a critical factor in their ranking algorithms; thus, having a solid link strategy as a marketer positions your website and content to rank well on all three search engines.

- **Keywords:** As stated previously, if you want to rank in organic search for a specific phrase, it's best to include that phrase in the copy of your page. This is pretty much the case across search engines. Some speculate that Bing is even more dependent on having the exact phrase on the page copy.

- **Domain age:** The amount of time that your domain has been live and available on the Internet, or the domain age, is directly important on Bing, but not necessarily on Google. Domain age can be confusing, but in general if your domain has been live for years or longer than your competitors, chances are that it has more quality links pointing to it and a higher trust value with all search engines.

- **Mobile-friendliness:** Google has been much more vocal about having a mobile-friendly website and content, whereas Bing and Yahoo haven't been as explicit. As we have discussed, Google introduced the first mobile update, which incorporates mobile friendliness as part of its ranking algorithm. Since all search engines value user experience, it's important to emphasize mobile friendliness when trying to rank any of them.

- **Standard technical aspects of your site:** It is important to have the basic technical elements of your website, as outlined in Chapter 2. These include the following:
  - HTML tags (title, description, canonical, Schema.org)
  - Page speed
  - `robots.txt`
  - XML sitemaps
  - Proper redirects
  - URL structures
  - Long-form content

- **Location pages:** If you have multiple locations or stores, be sure to set up pages for each of your locations on both the Bing Places for Business and Yahoo Local Listings directories (similar to Google My Business).

Establishing Your Research Channels

In "Data Informed Content" in Chapter 5, "Data-Informed Creative," I discussed the various data sources you can use to establish research on your users, products, and business. As you build your optimization path and plan, it is important to identify solid research venues like these. Understanding the data can help provide insight on opportunities that can help your brand performance and connections with your target audience. Here are the tips that you should consider when trying to establish your research channels for creating and continuing along your optimization path:

- **Conduct a data channel audit:** As discussed in Chapter 5, there are many different forms of research and data available, depending on how your business is set up. It's important that you conduct some internal research to determine all the plausible data channels that you have at your disposal. Data channels can range from providing data on your audience, brand performance, and current content in SQL performance. Work with your analytics expert to determine all the different data points available.

- **Understand how often this data can be provided to you in real-time:** Sometimes data will have to be pulled manually, and sometimes it is pulled automatically. Since user needs and behavior change quickly and require real-time business strategies, it's important to understand how difficult it is to have this data.

- **Summarize your business state, opportunities, and weaknesses:** Whether through a traditional SWOT analysis or something less formal, it's important to establish an understanding about what business opportunities there are and how you're fairing.

- **Correlate how SEO and content help your business outcomes:** Once you discuss your weaknesses and opportunities, figure out how SEO and content can help you alleviate issues. Later in this chapter we'll discuss common issues and the ways SEO and content can provide a solution to them.

- **Establish goals:** As is the case with many business projects, it's important that you establish goals and your optimization plan. Goals are critical to evaluate the success of your efforts and, in the end, the success of your brand and business.

- **Consider building a reporting process or dashboard that can help summarize data:** Real-time data or close to real-time data is extremely critical to providing quick solutions and results. Consider how you can develop a real-time or close to real-time reporting process. The process should provide digestible summaries and implications to help you craft SEO and content solutions.

- **Establish a process to take action on insights:** Once you have the data, have summarized the issues, and have identified the solutions, it's important to take action. Having a defined process on implementing the solutions is critical in your optimization planning.

These are the key steps for establishing a solid research process and channel to inform your optimization path on an ongoing basis. Be sure to establish a formal process as part of your execution plan.

Taking Inventory of Your Assets and Platforms

A key step in optimizing your presence is to get a sound inventory of all the content assets, web platforms, and offline assets you own and have the ability to modify. These assets are essentially your owned media. Forrester Research, one of the most popular business and technology research firms in the world, says in its blog article "Defining Earned, Owned, And Paid Media" that the role of owned media is to "build for longer-term relationships with existing and potential customers." Additionally, owned media is different from other media channels because it allows a brand to have full control over it. Optimizing your owned media or content can yield exponential and long-term business benefits; thus, optimizing it should be your top priority because it can cost much less than running paid media advertisements. Additionally, your paid and earned media are used in conjunction with your owned media, and traffic often converts on your owned media. So it's best to ensure that it's set up in the most effective way possible. Table 10.1 shows a breakdown on the roles of each channel and the benefits and challenges of each according to Forrester.

Table 10.1: Media Channels and Their Benefits and Challenges

MEDIA CATEGORY	OWNER-SHIP	EXAMPLES	ROLE	BENEFITS	CHALLENGES	COSTS
Owned	Brand	Company website	Build for long-term relationships with customers, with the potential to capture new ones	Control	Takes time	Low to none
		Blog		Cost	Must be built correctly and in line with search engine guidelines	
		Instagram account		Longevity		
				Flexibility	Requires ongoing maintenance	
		White paper		Organic search engine presence		
		Catalogs		Customized and detailed data analytics		
Paid	Partner	YouTube ads	Captures an audience in venues outside of your control and certain need states	Immediacy	Cost	High
		Search ads		Volume	Ads are less trusted	
		Display ads		Control	Temporary	
Earned	Customers	Reviews	Leverages customers' points of view and influence to capture audiences and build awareness and consideration	Credibility/trust	No control	Low
		Comments		Highly influential	Can be negative	
		Chatter		Cost		
				Low effort		
				Provide research and feedback for your brand and products		

Conducting Your Owned Media Audit

It can be difficult to get your arms around all your different assets that fall into the owned media category, but it's important that you understand all your owned assets because your SEO strategy should reference as many of those items as possible. The more assets you have to use in your SEO and content marketing programs, the better performance you will see. Oftentimes, search results are limited by the number of content assets you have available. Additionally, SEO and search keyword data and other learnings can help inform strategies for your other marketing programs and content, whether it's online or offline.

To help you get an idea and conduct an owned media audit, Table 10.2 contains a starter checklist of common items that fall under the owned media category.

Table 10.2: Owned Media

OWNED MEDIA ASSETS	LINK TO ASSET
Dedicated website	
Microsites (products, campaigns, category)	
YouTube channel	
Resource content (e.g., recipes, help content, tips content)	
Image gallery pages (Flickr, Instagram, Pinterest)	
Blogs	
Twitter	
LinkedIn page	
Mobile apps	
Google Local page and other only directory pages	
Device-compatible websites	
News sites	
Amazon.com brand page	
Web pages on other domains (dedicated page on WebMD)	
Discussion forums	

OWNED MEDIA ASSETS	LINK TO ASSET
Books	
Newsletters	
TV channels	
Video series	
Conferences	
Newsletters	
Emagazines/magazines	
Gaming or game channel	
Ecards/gifts	

Auditing for Content Formats

In addition to having an understanding of your own media assets, it's important to have an inventory list of the different types of content. As I discussed in previous chapters, the more search demand and data indications there are about a topic, the more comprehensive and richer your content response should be. Since that's the case, it's important to understand all the different types of content you have in your arsenal that you can repopulate into your strategies. Table 10.3 contains a starter list of content types for your consideration.

Table 10.3: Content Formats and Types

CONTENT TYPES	LINK TO ASSET
Videos	
Articles	
Website copy	
Tweets	
Newsletters	
Magazines or emagazines	
White papers	
Case studies	
Books or ebooks	
Infographics	

Continues

Table 10-3 (*continued*)

CONTENT TYPES	LINK TO ASSET
Photos	
News stories	
Discussion forums	
Product reviews	
Presentations	
Webinars	
Podcasts or MP3s	
Music playlists	
Gaming	
Utilities or tools (e.g., calculators)	
Look books or style guides	
Catalogs	
Resource content (e.g., recipes, help content, tips content)	
Press releases	
Review content	

Identifying Your True Competitors

One of the most critical steps in solidifying an optimization plan is identifying who your *true* competitors are in the world of search and content marketing. Oftentimes, the competitors for search are not the same as the ones your organization typically views as your competitors. One of the best ways to determine who your competitors are is by simply doing a search for your product category or service.

For instance, if you are a brand selling tires online, doing a search online (Figure 10.3) for tires may show that there are a lot of websites vying to rank for that search.

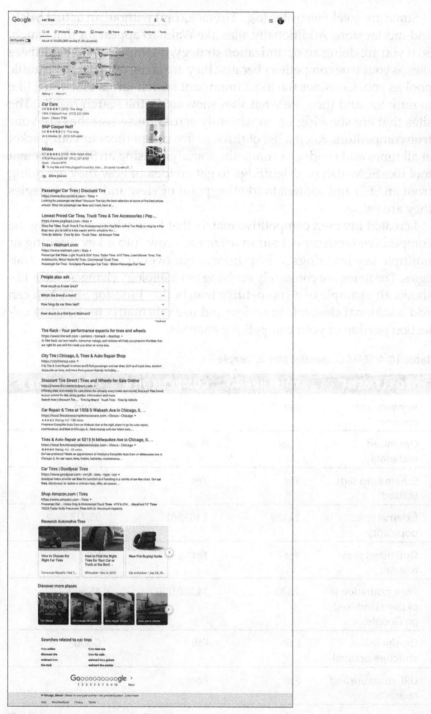

Figure 10.3: Search results for *tires*

Some are solely websites (e.g., Tirerack.com) without an actual brick-and-mortar store. Additionally, sites like Walmart appear for that search. So if you are doing an optimization strategy, it's important to view these sites as your true competitors because they are going after the same traffic pool as you. Consider the most important search terms that you'd like to rank for, and then see what sites show up in the search results. The sites that are showing up consistently across those searches are your true competitors. Keep a list of three to five competitors in your pocket at all times and conduct a competitive analysis using an SEO or content tool like SEMrush or BrightEdge to get an idea of how they are doing from an SEO and content marketing point of view and what strategies they are using.

I created my own competitive matrix that I use when evaluating the competitive landscape. I summarize each row into a key learning or multiple key learnings to help inform our overall optimization strategies. The items are constantly evolving as technology changes. Table 10.4 shows an example of a competitive matrix that I use for SEO. You can add additional elements to review and use this matrix for the data collection portion of your competitive analysis.

Table 10.4: SEO Competitive Matrix Sample

SEO ELEMENT	YOUR BRAND	COMPETITOR A	COMPETITOR B
Keyword-rich content	Fair	Fair	Good
Optimized metadata	Poor	Poor	Good
Schema.org tags utilized	Yes	Yes	Yes
External link popularity	21,189	1,192,161	95,217
Optimized press releases	Yes	Yes	No
Page saturation (# of pages indexed on Google)	2,120	14,100,000	45,500
On-site link structure optimal	Fair	Fair	Good
URL structure and redirects	Fair	Poor	Good

SEO ELEMENT	YOUR BRAND	COMPETITOR A	COMPETITOR B
Domain age	1999	1996	2001
Page rank	2/10	5/10	4/10
Page load time desktop)	82/100	52/100	77/100
XML sitemap used	Yes	Yes	Yes
Page load time (mobile)	46/100	52/100	54/100
Facebook followers	5,466	28,632	133,509
YouTube	Yes	Yes	Yes
YouTube subscribers	110	3,963	102
YouTube video views	471,700	3,497,050	325,278
Twitter use	Yes	Yes	Yes
Twitter followers	559	14,800	1,807
Twitter following	271	54	83
Accurate and verified Google My Business Center listings	Yes	Yes	Yes
Positive brand search results	Yes	Yes	No
Mobile-friendly site	Yes (Subdomain)	Yes (Subdomain)	Yes (Responsive)
Amazon brand page	Yes	Yes	Yes
Amazon content optimized	No	No	No
Blog/newsletter	Yes (Subdomain)	Yes (Subdomain)	Yes (Subdomain)
Mobile App	Yes	Yes	Yes
App Store Optimized	No	No	No

I also use a smaller matrix for doing a content competitive analysis (Table 10.5).

Table 10.5: Content Competitive Matrix Sample

CONTENT AREAS	YOUR BRAND	COMPETITOR A	COMPETITOR B
Nonbranded website content available	Fair	Fair	Good
Content published frequently	Daily	3 x Week	Monthly
Content has strong call to action	Yes	Yes	Yes
Content topics are in demand and mapped to search data and other data	No	Yes	Yes
Offer many different content types (video, infographics, slideshows, etc.)	Fair	Fair	Good
Content topics rediversified across multiple topic categories	No	Yes	Yes
Content promotion in effect	No	Yes	Yes
Text content optimized for SEO	Poor	Poor	Good
Content unique	No	Yes	Yes
Content offer utility	No	Yes	Yes
Content visual	No	Yes	Yes
Content length longer than 300 words	No	Yes	Yes
Content fresh	No	Yes	Yes
Content unique	No	Yes	Yes

A competitive analysis should answer these questions:

■ What search terms are they ranking for versus mine? As you can see from the SEMrush keyword coverage chart in Figure 10.4, Pepboys should be the top competitor to go after if you are a tire seller online.

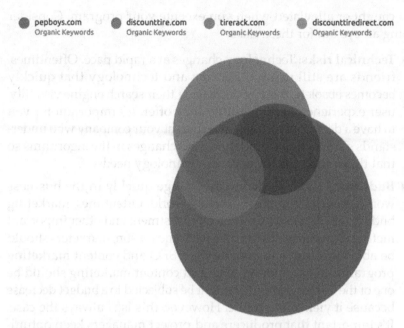

Figure 10.4: Keyword competitor coverage chart from SEMrush

- How are my competitors doing on a technical level from an SEO side of things (e.g., load time, tags)?
- How much are content or web pages getting indexed on Google?
- What content types do they have on their website?
- What kind of link building strategies are they pursuing?

At the end of the day, your competitive analysis should identify what opportunities there are in the competitive landscape and how to catch up and get ahead of your competitors. Be sure the deliverable allows you to walk away with a lot of useful insights and next steps for your brand.

Knowing and Managing Risks

It's extremely important to understand that just knowing SEO and content marketing and process isn't enough for your path toward full optimization. I've seen many programs get compromised despite having all the pillars in place because of a lack of risk management and not addressing program issues as they arise. There are a lot of things that can go wrong, if not caught or alleviated when you execute your program. Consider keeping an eye out for these risks:

- **Technical risks:** Technology changes at a rapid pace. Oftentimes, friends are still using platforms and technology that quickly becomes obsolete, thereby decreasing their search engine visibility, user experience, and the utility they offer. It's important for you to have a dedicated technology expert at your company who understands search engine guidelines and changes in the algorithms so that they could quickly address technology needs.

- **Budgetary risks:** Budgets can change quickly in the business world, especially in the marketing world. Oftentimes, marketing budgets are dictated by return on investment and other important metrics. If budgets do decrease for some reason, marketers should be able to continue to execute their SEO and content marketing programs. In my opinion, SEO and content marketing should be one of the last line items that might be subjected to a budget decrease because it yields free traffic. However, this isn't always the case. It's important that producers and project managers keep optimization plans on budget and continuously watch the pacing of costs throughout the optimization program. In many cases, budget is addressed in the project manager's status report. It's important that project managers are equipped with sufficient reporting tools around costs so that SEO and content marketing maintain a strong return on investment.

- **Personnel risks:** Personnel risks are important to minimize because team members come and go. It's important that your optimization plan accounts for multiple roles and subject-matter experts and has backup plans should a team member decide to leave the project.

- **Process risks:** As we will discuss, process is critically important when building and executing your optimization plan. It's important that you look at ways to standardize processes throughout your marketing programs, especially SEO and content marketing processes. Having everyone abide by the same process improves quality, keeps costs lower, and assigns ownership, all of which make execution more effective.

- **Knowledge and goal-setting risks:** Goals can make or break programs. It's important that goals are realistic and attainable because if they are not met, oftentimes the programs are deemed a failure and are terminated. Goal setting can be tricky, so it's important that the people setting the goals have approval by the necessary subject-matter experts, in this case SEO experts and content marketing experts. An executive who doesn't understand the sciences should not be setting these goals. It's important the team understands and accepts that.

- **Legal risks:** Legal risks are common, especially in the content game. It's important the team plays it safe as much as possible and avoids any legal infringements or controversies. Violating laws can result in hefty fines, terminated businesses, and other catastrophic events. It's important that legal guidelines are provided to content marketing teams to ensure the programs play it safe. Executive teams should be employing a lawyer who is available for any gray areas that need clarification.

Minimizing these risks throughout your optimization program can help keep your brand ahead of the game and on target. Be sure that a team member is always watchful of these risks and addresses them quickly as they come up.

How SEO and Content Can Help Solve Business Problems

When pulling together your optimization path, it's important to think about your brand's business problems and how SEO and content can be used to help solve them. Here are the common business problems mentioned in previous chapters and how SEO and content can help solve them.

Poor business sales: Brands aren't meeting sales goals.

- This is perhaps the most common issue and why brands typically use SEO and organic traffic strategies. SEO and content aren't a cure-all; however, what can help bring more traffic to your brand and improve conversions are sales. Depending on the problem, SEO strategies should be crafted to help increase performance.

Brand and target audience disconnections: Brands and target audiences are not connecting effectively in the way of expectations, purchase processes, and other areas.

- It's important to evaluate your brand presence and brand search results by identifying the most common searches around your brand to make sure you are providing users with the information they are seeking. While search data is a key data point in doing this, surveys and other analytics reports can provide additional insight as well.

Lack of awareness and consideration: Brands fail to be top of mind during the awareness and consideration phases.

- Oftentimes, brands lack the awareness among consumers, which can lead to less traffic and, in the end, fewer sales. Content and SEO can help improve your brand presence among high-volume searches in your business category. A sound content strategy and SEO strategy can help identify these content gaps and remove SEO obstacles, which in the end can help you intercept users at a much higher level of the purchase funnel and build awareness.

Poor processes and process management: Brands lack the processes needed for effective execution of marketing programs.

- When SEO and content processes are clearly laid out, they can help train employees to be more process-driven in their own disciplines. Oftentimes, SEO strategies, process templates, and deliverable templates can be repopulated and reformatted into other disciplines.

Stale skill sets: Team members don't evolve their skill sets and end up with stale skill sets, resulting in a compromised output.

- In the digital world, SEO, owned media, and content are often at the forefront and lead technology innovation are the necessary skill sets to optimize them. SEO and content point of views can help provide employees and teams with education around up-and-coming technologies and the necessary skill sets that they must build.

Heightened competition: Competition, especially online, has become extreme. Competitors come in many forms as well. This results in lost business for brands.

- As we said earlier in this chapter, your online competitors are sometimes your true competitors and not your traditional list of competitors. Online competition is fierce, and most categories and businesses can face significant competition. Employing SEO and content tactics can help brands get ahead of online competitors, which can in turn provide a competitive edge.

Uninformed creative concepts, content, and campaigns: It's still quite common for creative strategies and campaigns to build campaigns without solid data.

- As mentioned in previous chapters, consider using SEO data going forward to inform content and campaign ideas.

Unoptimized and non-search-friendly content: Brands are still creating content that's not optimized for search engines and are missing a large and impactful traffic opportunity.

- This is an extremely common problem, and adapting a solid SEO and content process can help ensure that content is capturing as much traffic and conversions as possible.

Building a New Brand Through SEO and Content

Sometimes, brands start from scratch. They're brand new and don't even have a website or other owned media. Short-term, it is extremely difficult to build a brand by solely using SEO and content marketing initiatives. SEO takes time. Google and other domains build up trust as time goes on for a domain, so it's important to think long-term when looking solely at SEO and content marketing to build brand awareness and sales. It also makes sense to employ high-funnel tactics and "Advanced Plus" content tactics outlined in Chapter 6 to build awareness of your business and traffic to your website.

If you can't do that level of content response, you need to think of organic tactics as a longer-term initiative whose results may not be visible for a year or more. If you have the budget, I would consider focusing on creating the following owned media assets and promoting them through paid media tactics:

- **Website:** Building a website with conversion features (purchases, ordering, etc.) should be your top priority. Additionally, be sure to have a blog or content hub with unique content around your product category to build search relevance to your website domain.

- **Amazon page:** If you are an e-commerce business, consider extending your presence to Amazon, eBay, Google Shopping, and other shopping platforms since your website will take some time to rank for your product searches. Additionally, users are increasingly going to these channels directly to seek products, so your presence is extremely critical.

- **Social media assets and content (Facebook, Instagram, etc.).** Building a brand following is critical and can provide organic traffic to your website. Seek out ways to build your following on all the major social media sites.

- **YouTube channel and video content:** YouTube is considered to be one of the top search engines these days. Consider building a brand page and post videos that can rank in search for your product category. Work with your SEO expert to identify topics that are trending in search. Once videos are created, consider a content promotion strategy with broad reach to get your videos and brand in front of your target audience.

- **Local search pages:** As discussed in our small business chapter, local search directory pages like Google My Business and Yelp are critical for retail businesses with brick-and-mortar locations. Be sure to use the directory sheet in Chapter 9 to identify the directories on which to create your business listing.

In addition to these owned media assets and a solid product offering, it's important that your business and leadership embrace a culture that's optimal for launching a successful brand online. While not an exhaustive list, consider incorporating the following into your team culture:

- **Content Production:** As I've been saying throughout this book, a brand's presence online is as big as the amount of content they have online. Be sure to embrace a culture that is constantly producing content ask of every member of your team to write blogs, articles, and social media content; create videos; and share content—the more, the better. Aim to produce an extremely high amount of content from the get-go. Additionally, provide tools (cameras, video, and audio equipment) and dedicated time for your team to come up with, write, and promote content.

- **Big creative ideas:** As I mentioned in the previous section, coming up with Advanced Plus content ideas or big creative ideas is critical to building awareness and traffic to your new brand. Consider large scale partnerships and initiatives based on data that create buzz and get in front of as many consumers as possible.

- **Sizeable investment:** Starting a business online these days requires investment, from the standpoint of time and money. It's critical that you are prepared to spend a significant amount of money to promote your business, content, and products via paid media tactics. Consider working with a paid media specialist to map out a media plan that can connect with as many people in your target as possible.

- **Long-term thinking:** Businesses need immediate results to keep moving and secure a greater investment. It can be difficult to keep your eye on long-term results, but it's critical. Many short-term businesses will be in the red financially, as they spend money to boost marketing, product development, and brand awareness. Additionally, as we said before, it takes time to rank for high-funnel searches on the engines, so if search is a goal, be prepared to wait months and even years to rank for competitive and highly searched phrases.

- **Relevant skill sets and expertise:** Starting a business can be difficult, but expecting yourself to know everything and execute everything will almost always result in flawed programs and can compromise results. Be sure to tap into freelancers or contractors with different marketing expertise who can help you put your plan together.

- **Product evolution:** Be sure to always look to improve your product with new features and benefits. Offer surveys and pay attention to user data and online reviews that can help inform the direction of your product. It's important to address pain points and enhance benefits to keep your product popular.

- **Having a thorough understanding of the competitive landscape:** As we said earlier in this chapter, having the right list of competitors in your industry and product category is critical. Oftentimes, your actual competitors are not the ones you think they are. Be sure to have a thorough understanding of what types of tactics and content your competitors are employing and learn from their ideas and exploit their lapses.

These are just some of the cultural mind-sets a new business should embrace and promote internally in order push forward successfully. Constantly evaluate your culture and embrace these marketing principles as you move forward with your new business, as they can optimize your brand's performance.

Prioritizing Locations, Demographics, and Countries

Targeting the right people with your marketing strategies can be critical to achieving optimal brand performance. As a brand, it's important to make sure you have a solid idea of who your target is, by conducting thorough research and developing detailed personas. Some high-level benefits to doing this include the following:

- **Better ROI:** It allows you to steer your marketing campaigns and dollars toward the avenues and venues that reach your target.

- **More relevant messaging:** You are serving messages and content that are more relevant to users, which can result in an improved customer experience and yield more conversions.

- **Better brand image and authority:** Having a clear target allows you to offer users with valuable content to them and allows you to be a true partner and authority in their world.

Brands that offer a broad spectrum of products may have a difficult time identifying who their target is, but oftentimes it can be the person who ultimately makes the purchase decision in the household. Once you get an idea who that person is, it's important to solidify their profile by understanding their

- Offline behavior
- General interests
- Preferred websites
- General preferences
- Hobbies
- Day-to-day responsibilities
- Age
- Location

Locations

Your website and search data can provide some simple insight into what users (and their location) are looking for in your brand and website. One of the easiest ways to see this data is in Google Analytics.

The Google Analytics Audience ➪ Geo ➪ Location report allows you to see the locations of the users coming to your website. As you can see from Figure 10.5, the United States is driving the most traffic to the site.

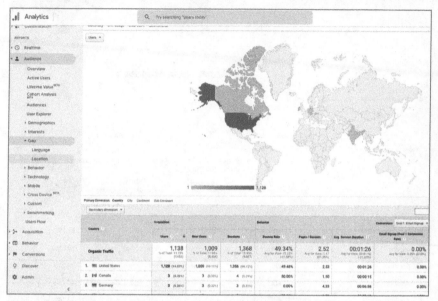

Figure 10.5: Audience/Location report in Google Analytics

If you click the United States link, you can see the states that are driving the most traffic (Figure 10.6).

And if you click into each state, you see what cities in those states are driving the most traffic (Figure 10.7).

This allows you to see if your localized marketing strategies are driving traffic and allows you to steer marketing programs to cities that make sense for your goals.

Google offers another tool, called Google Trends, which allows you to identify top priority markets. The tool can break down to a market level, where popular searches are happening. Figure 10.8 shows an example for the term *Adidas*. As you can see, Greece is the most popular area where users are searching for that term. Just like Google Analytics, you can keep drilling down to the more detailed market level. If you are seeing a disconnect with where popular searches are happening for your brand and the location of your website visitors, consider altering your marketing strategies toward the Google Trends chart, since it indicates a nonbiased view of where consumers care most about your brand.

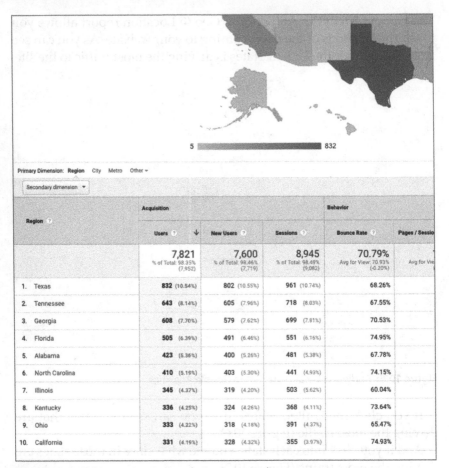

Primary Dimension: **Region** City Metro Other ▾

Secondary dimension ▾

Region	Acquisition			Behavior	
	Users ↓	New Users	Sessions	Bounce Rate	Pages / Sessio
	7,821 % of Total: 98.35% (7,952)	**7,600** % of Total: 98.46% (7,719)	**8,945** % of Total: 98.49% (9,082)	**70.79%** Avg for View: 70.93% (-0.20%)	Avg for Vie
1. Texas	**832** (10.54%)	**802** (10.55%)	**961** (10.74%)	68.26%	
2. Tennessee	**643** (8.14%)	**605** (7.96%)	**718** (8.03%)	67.55%	
3. Georgia	**608** (7.70%)	**579** (7.62%)	**699** (7.81%)	70.53%	
4. Florida	**505** (6.39%)	**491** (6.46%)	**551** (6.16%)	74.95%	
5. Alabama	**423** (5.36%)	**400** (5.26%)	**481** (5.38%)	67.78%	
6. North Carolina	**410** (5.19%)	**403** (5.30%)	**441** (4.93%)	74.15%	
7. Illinois	**345** (4.37%)	**319** (4.20%)	**503** (5.62%)	60.04%	
8. Kentucky	**336** (4.25%)	**324** (4.26%)	**368** (4.11%)	73.64%	
9. Ohio	**333** (4.22%)	**318** (4.18%)	**391** (4.37%)	65.47%	
10. California	**331** (4.19%)	**328** (4.32%)	**355** (3.97%)	74.93%	

Figure 10.6: U.S. state view in Google Analytics Audience report

Gender

Gender is another key data point when building your target and understanding if your marketing programs are connecting with them. Google Analytics provides a breakdown of gender of your website visitors as well (Figure 10.9).

Also, if you click the gender, you can get an idea of the age breakdown as well (Figure 10.10).

City ?	Acquisition			Behavior		
	Users ? ↓	New Users ?	Sessions ?	Bounce Rate ?	Pages / Session ?	Avg. Sess Duration
	832 % of Total: 10.46% (7,952)	802 % of Total: 10.39% (7,719)	961 % of Total: 10.58% (9,082)	68.26% Avg for View: 70.93% (-3.76%)	1.71 Avg for View: 1.74 (-1.90%)	00:01: Avg for V 00:0 (-15.
1. Dallas	212 (25.18%)	200 (24.94%)	251 (26.12%)	69.32%	1.57	00:0
2. Houston	99 (11.76%)	93 (11.60%)	108 (11.24%)	65.74%	1.72	00:0
3. Austin	70 (8.31%)	64 (7.98%)	86 (8.95%)	67.44%	1.83	00:0
4. San Antonio	40 (4.75%)	39 (4.86%)	43 (4.47%)	79.07%	1.23	00:0
5. Fort Worth	32 (3.80%)	32 (3.99%)	36 (3.75%)	69.44%	1.56	00:0
6. (not set)	15 (1.78%)	14 (1.75%)	15 (1.56%)	80.00%	1.27	00:0
7. Amarillo	11 (1.31%)	10 (1.25%)	11 (1.14%)	100.00%	1.00	00:0
8. Cypress	10 (1.19%)	10 (1.25%)	10 (1.04%)	70.00%	1.70	00:0
9. Tyler	9 (1.07%)	9 (1.12%)	9 (0.94%)	88.89%	1.33	00:0
10. Allen	8 (0.95%)	8 (1.00%)	9 (0.94%)	55.56%	1.67	00:0

Figure 10.7: City view in Google Analytics Audience report

Figure 10.8: Google Trends global popularity view

Similar to location, be sure to compare your marketing program efforts with what gender and age are driving website visits. If there is a disconnect, be sure to align your content and SEO efforts toward the audience and target you want to capture.

Figure 10.9: Gender breakdown in Google Analytics

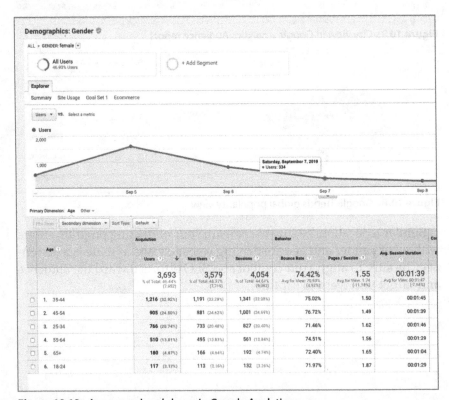

Figure 10.10: Age range breakdown in Google Analytics

Providing a Positive Brand Search Experience

When someone searches for your brand, the results page is called your *brand search results*. From an SEO side of things, this results page can be even more important than your website home page. Therefore, it's extremely important to always monitor the first page of your brand search results, since these results typically capture 90 percent of the traffic that searches for your brand. I often see negative reviews, press, and irrelevant sites cluttering up brand results, which creates a negative consumer experience and may result in lower traffic and sales.

Your brand results page should aggregate all your owned media assets. These include your website, social media pages, YouTube videos, blogs, news releases, location pages, mobile apps, reviews, and any other web listings that you built.

Figure 10.11 shows an example of a great brand results page.

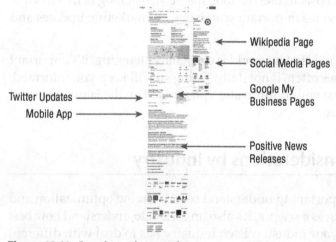

Twitter Updates
Mobile App

Wikipedia Page
Social Media Pages
Google My Business Pages
Positive News Releases

Figure 10.11: Brand search example

Staying in Tune with Search Engine Changes

If you don't have an SEO expert on hand, there are many blogs and websites that offer updates and news on search engine changes. It's best to always monitor them for updates to search engine algorithms. My personal favorites are the following:

- Google Webmaster Blog
  - URL: https://webmasters.googleblog.com/

- This is Google's blog where the company announces important news for how it manages its crawling and indexing of websites, including search algorithm updates.
- Search Engine Land
  - URL: https://searchengineland.com/
  - A free online industry magazine that provides the latest search engine news.
- Search Engine Watch
  - URL: https://www.searchenginewatch.com/
  - Another free online industry magazine that provides the latest search engine news.
- SEMrush Blog
  - URL: https://www.semrush.com/blog/
  - While it costs to use the tool, the SEMrush Blog is free to view and provides important search engine marketing updates and news.

Since the SEO and content world is constantly changing, it's important to check these sites often, if not daily. Doing so will keep you informed, and you can adjust your optimization plan based on the latest news and algorithm updates.

Program Considerations by Industry

Not only is it important to understand search engine optimization and content marketing as a science, it's also important to understand how best to use them for your industry. Each industry has to deal with different challenges and opportunities when it comes to search engine results and content marketing. Depending on your industry, things can be extremely competitive or less competitive yet face different obstacles. Looking at the chart by Marketing Charts (source: eMarketer) in Figure 10.12, you can see what industries owned the greatest share of marketing dollars in 2018. A higher percentage indicates a more competitive industry, which can make it difficult for businesses with a lower budget. The same holds true for SEO and content marketing. If your industry is a high-spend category, your optimization plan must think outside the box and look to different methods to capture traffic.

Top US Digital Ad-Spending Industries 2018	
Retail	21.9%
Automotive	12.6%
Financial Services	12.2%
Telecom	10.7%
CPG	8.8%
Travel	8.0%
Consumer Electronics	7.8%
Media	6.1%
Entertainment	5.1%
Healthcare and Pharma	2.6%
Other	4.3%
*SourceMarketingCharts.com and eMarketer	

Figure 10.12: Industry marketing budget/spend breakdown

In my 20 years working in digital marketing, I've seen many trends that are consistent for each industry. Table 10.6 outlines the most popular industries and their respective SEO and content marketing considerations that marketers should take note of.

Table 10.6: SEO and Content Marketing Considerations by Industry

INDUSTRY	DIFFICULTIES	POSITIVES	CONSIDER DOING THE FOLLOWING
Real estate	Extremely competitive due to large number of real estate companies, but also real estate consumer sites like Realtor.com, Zillow .com, etc. Most sites in the industry show the same content, agents, and real estate listings.	Category is very search-driven and localized, so there is ample opportunity to intercept users.	Building content beyond real estate listings. Conduct research into your audience and see what topics or events provoke a move. Perhaps life stage, investment, home project, and city relevant topics.
Government	Regulation and legal considerations around content can restrict content. Technology tends to lag. Users are online interested when they need something.	Search engines reward .gov sites with a higher ranking; also the sites they link to tend to get stronger link value.	Prioritize on using the most up-to-date technology and using search data to see what people are searching for in your category. Consider adding content to your website that speaks to those topics.

Continues

Table 10.6 (*continued*)

INDUSTRY	DIFFICULTIES	POSITIVES	CONSIDER DOING THE FOLLOWING
Finance and insurance	Extremely competitive category. Very costly to do paid media as well. Most sites focus on life stage content and calculators and other utilities.	A very search-driven category, with a lot of opportunities to capture traffic.	Consider conducting surveys to determine what kind of content and tools your target audience would like to see you offer. Consider focusing on CRM and other organic channels that can help maintain customer base because acquisition of new customers is extremely costly.
Healthcare	Regulation and legal considerations around content can restrict marketing. A very competitive category can make it difficult to rank for search phrases. Depending on the site, search engines tend to favor the big content sites (Mayoclinic.com, WebMD, etc.) versus brand sites, which makes SEO difficult.	Users tend to go online to search for health topics and ailments.	Build SEO-friendly website content around conditions, ailments, and other topics your target audience may be searching for. Consider content partnerships with the big content sites (MayoClinic.com, WebMD.com). Optimize and add content on established domains that have high SEO domain value, like YouTube and other social media sites.

INDUSTRY	DIFFICULTIES	POSITIVES	CONSIDER DOING THE FOLLOWING
Retail/CPG	Crowded space online with major retailers already owning the space and have very strong SEO that makes it almost impossible to get ahead of them.	More and more users are shopping online and less in stores, making search and content great avenues to capture them.	Consider adding incentive content on your site (coupons, promo codes, gift cards, etc.). Focus on building your presence on the major product search engines like Amazon, Walmart, and other sites that rank for your product searches. If you have physical stores, be sure to verify and claim your Google My Business and other directory pages (Yelp, Yahoo, Bing). Manage reviews and work to mediate negative reviews.

Continues

Table 10.6 (*continued*)

INDUSTRY	DIFFICULTIES	POSITIVES	CONSIDER DOING THE FOLLOWING
Travel	Extremely competitive category. Advertisements can be expensive as well. Google has become its own travel search engine as well, trying to monetize the travel searches happening on the search engines.	Travel topics are frequently searched online. There are many sites available for partnerships that have strong SEO value from search engines.	Consider building up your social media following to promote your content and products. Build a presence and consider partnerships on the major content hubs (TripAdvisor, etc.) and publishers. Contact one of their sales representatives and consider specialized content partnerships with major travel industry brands and publishers. Consider paid media to promote your brand, which can yield more organic traffic. Consider broad content programs to boost awareness and traffic (TV, films, etc.).
Entertainment	Extremely competitive category; the Internet is saturated with more entertainment content than ever.	Many users tend to use the Internet for entertainment purposes these days.	Depending on your product or content, consider building a blog, mobile application to connect with users about entertainment topics and your product. Consider paid media to promote your brand, which can yield more organic traffic.

INDUSTRY	DIFFICULTIES	POSITIVES	CONSIDER DOING THE FOLLOWING
Education	Education continues to be a main driver of Internet use and activity. Due to search habits, many sites offer how-to and education content, even sites that aren't in the education category.	Users online are in a content consumption and learning mode, making them more receptive to educational content.	Consider building content on YouTube, which is a key venue for users looking to learn and educate themselves on topics. If you are promoting a product, consider creating content around the issues that your product can help with and reach your target audience using content discovery engines.
Business services	Key business decision-makers can be difficult to target in that search results are not custom to a person's job title or position.	Search and content can be a very low-cost method to capture sales.	Consider building content on your site that your target, business principles are interested in. Partner with trade sites and publishers to build custom content programs, to be housed on their websites if they have strong SEO. Use LinkedIn to run ads that connect with your target audience; consider contacting a sales rep at LinkedIn to discuss this and set up a customized program.

Continues

Table 10.6 (continued)

INDUSTRY	DIFFICULTIES	POSITIVES	CONSIDER DOING THE FOLLOWING
Auto	Extremely competitive from a search engine results standpoint; according to some sites, it's the most competitive category. There are many publisher sites, manufacturing sites, reseller sites, review sites, and automotive service sites that are all competitive for the same search.	Search and content can be a very low-cost method to capture sales.	Consider building content on your site that users are searching for. Also, conduct surveys to determine what kind of content and tools users would like to see. Consider partnerships with sites that have strong SEO value, (Autotrader.com, caranddriver.com, etc.).

Calculating ROI

Oftentimes, to get executive buy-in on projects and proposed initiatives, you have to provide a return on investment calculation to justify the cost and investment in the initiative. Here again is the typical formula for doing that:

ROI = (Increase in sales – cost of SEO initiative) / cost of SEO initiatives

Expected ROI

Calculating expected ROI is typically used to evaluate whether a project should go forward, using this formula:

Expected ROI = (Expected increase in sales – expected cost of SEO initiative) / expected cost of SEO initiatives

It is a much trickier ROI calculation because there are so many factors at play that affect search engine ranking and the project's success from a performance and ranking standpoint. The most difficult part of the expected ROI formula is calculating the increase in sales. Marketers should take extra caution when determining what this variable is.

Step 1: Identify Your Keyword Targets and Expected Ranking

The typical way to identify keyword targets and expected ranking from an SEO and content point of view is to identify a subset of search phrases that you'd like your content to rank higher for, along with their respective average search volume. The next step is to run a ranking report on those keyword terms to understand how high you rank for them currently.

The position you rank for a search phrase typically correlates to your click-through rate. According to a study by Advanced Web Ranking, the positions listed in Table 10.7 correlate to the click-through rates on mobile devices.

Table 10.7: Ranking and Click-Through Rate Correlation

RANKING POSITION	AVERAGE CLICK-THROUGH RATE (%)
1	23.08
2	13.82
3	9.55
4	7.25
5	7.5
6	3.43
7	2.3
8	1.82
9	1.41
10	1.08

Source for data: https://www.advancedwebranking.com/ctrstudy/

For example, if you are not ranking for a search phrase and you move to position 1, you can expect to capture 23.08 percent of the search clicks.

Step 2: Calculate Expected Traffic

The next step is to provide an estimated ranking that your project will result in. After that, based on the current position and expected position start, you can apply this framework:

$$(\text{Expected Click Through Rate}) \times (\text{average search volume for keyword}) = \text{Expected Traffic}$$

Step 3: Determine Number of New Orders

Once you determine your expected traffic, you can look at your conversion or order rate, assuming your Google Analytics is set up correctly and tracking it to determine how many orders or transactions you'll be getting.

$$(\text{Expected Traffic}) \times (\text{Conversion or Order Rate}) = \text{Expected Orders}$$

Step 4: Calculate the Total Expected Sales Increase

Once you get an idea of how many new orders you can expect, you can multiply your current average order value (also tracked in Google Analytics) by the number of expected new sales to get your total sales increase:

$$(\text{Expected Orders or Transactions}) \times (\text{Average order value}) = \text{Sales increase}$$

Once you get the total expected sales increase, you can reference the total costs of the project and apply the expected ROI formula discussed earlier to determine the ROI of the project.

Compiling Your Optimization Plan

Once you gather all the information presented in this chapter, it's important to start putting together an optimization plan that takes advantage of business and content opportunities and improves your SEO standing.

Why a Plan Is Important

Building a formalized optimization plan is the most critical piece of the SEO and content equation. It's not good enough to just have an informal list of tactics. It's more effective to actually put a presentation together with a timeline and other elements to ensure stakeholders are on board and everyone is on the same page. Having a strong optimization plan can make or break business results.

Having a detailed optimization plan communicates business problems and their solutions, team roles, tasks, and timelines. It also helps keep programs on track and ensures their execution by assigning ownership and expectations. It ensures everyone is on the same page and collectively agrees with the optimization path forward.

What Your Plan Should Include

Plans don't have to always follow the same format, but at the core, they should address the following:

- Target audience:
  - Who your audience is and if you are connecting with them currently
  - If you are currently capturing them and how to capture more of them
  - Journeys and need states
  - Content strategy
- Competitors:
  - Identify your competitors.
  - Identify how you compare against them (strengths and weaknesses), and what they are doing better than you from a content and SEO point of view.
  - Identify what content and SEO areas you can improve on and action items.
- Opportunities:
  - Highlight important opportunities and weaknesses that your research (discussed earlier in this chapter) identified.
  - Your top three priorities and goals (e.g., improve brand search results, increase traffic, improve sales, etc.)
  - All your areas that need focus to improve organic performance (website, blog, Amazon, etc.)
- Your custom optimization project plan should be created and owned by the team's project manager or producer:
  - The plan should outline the plan forward to help alleviate issues and improve performance in your category.
  - The plan should list the business problem, the solution, tasks, deliverables, timelines, and task owners.
  - Table 10.8 shows an example of a simple optimization project plan.

Table 10.8: Optimization Project Plan Example

PROBLEM	SOLUTION	TASK	TASK OWNER	DUE DATE	DEPEN- DENCIES
Lack of traffic	Build new content	Content brief development	Brand strategist	1/1/20	
Lack of traffic	Assess current content strategy	Content diversification analysis	SEO	1/8/20	
Lack of traffic	Assess current content strategy	Optimize existing content	SEO/ copywriting	1/31/20	
Lack of traffic	Build new content	Formulate new content ideas	Creative director/ SEO/ copywriter	1/15/20	Task 1
Lack of traffic	Fix SEO issues on site	SEO audit	SEO	1/15/20	
Lack of traffic	Fix SEO issues on site	Update HTML code and fixes	SEO/web developer	1/22/20	Task 5
Lack of traffic	Fix SEO issues on site	Q/A fixes	SEO	1/29/20	Task 6
Lack of traffic	Optimize Amazon pages	Review product page titles and copy	SEO/ copywriting	2/7/20	
Lack of traffic	Optimize YouTube Pages	Review video titles and copy	SEO/ copywriting	2/14/20	
Improve conversions	Conduct landing page testing	Create landing page testing list	SEO/UX/ copywriting	2/21/20	
Improve conversions	Improve navigation and site flow	Create new navigation designs	U/X		

- Ongoing research/measurement:
  - Articulate specific business and marketing goals that the optimization plan should help achieve.

Once the plan is solidified, it's time to move forward.

Quiz

1. Building an SEO and content vision throughout your company requires the following, except which one?
   a. Workshops and education sessions
   b. Selling decision-makers
   c. Conducting an opportunity analysis across disciplines
   d. Mandating change

   Answer: d

2. When providing SEO and content workshops, it's important to highlight which of the following?
   a. How SEO works
   b. What content is and why it's important
   c. How each process works
   d. How they apply to your audience and can make their job easier
   e. How competitors are using them and best in class examples
   f. All the above

   Answer: f

3. Which are important tech advances happening that brands should prepare for and optimize their presence on?
   a. Conversational commerce
   b. Artificial intelligence
   c. Next-generation CRM
   d. All the above

   Answer: d

4. True or False: Conducting an opportunity analysis is a key activity when trying to encourage SEO and content initiatives across your business.

Answer: True

5. Fill in the blank: If you are a small business, prioritizing Google as your top search engine makes the most sense because _____.

   a. It encompasses 94% of searches.

   b. It's the easiest search engine to optimize for.

   c. It doesn't value domain age as much as the other search engines.

   d. Links aren't important to Google.

   Answer: a

6. Fill in the blank: DuckDuckGo is a relatively new search engine, gaining in popularity because it emphasizes _____.

   a. More relevant results

   b. A mobile-friendly results page

   c. A user's privacy

   d. Only websites with a strong reputation

   Answer: c

7. The main elements that the big three search engines look at include all of the following except which one?

   a. Links

   b. Keywords on copy

   c. Basic HTML tags

   d. Clicks to your site

   e. robots.txt files

   Answer: d

8. Benefits to owned media include the following:

   a. Brand controls entire platform

   b. Cost efficiency

   c.　Longevity, offers long-term traffic opportunities

   d.　Organic search engine listings that rank when someone searches for your brand

   e.　All the above

Answer: e

9.　True or False: Conducting an owned media audit is not important because it helps you understand all your assets and because your SEO strategy should reference as many of those items as possible.

Answer: False

10.　Fill in the blank: Oftentimes, the competitors for search rankings are _____ as the ones your organization typically views as your competitors. One of the best ways to determine who your competitors are is by _____.

   a.　Not the same, asking your marketing team

   b.　The same, asking your CMO

   c.　Not the same, doing a search

   d.　Exactly the same, doing a search

Answer: c

Case Studies

In my 20 years or so in this business I've completed a few hundred projects, all with different scopes and deliverables. Many of them have faced the issues that I've outlined in this book and failed to overcome them, so they were not as successful as they could've been.

However, there are many that were extremely successful because we removed all the obstacles, the client cooperated, and we developed good SEO and content practices. It's important to understand that these case studies worked well because the sites had a proactive and responsive IT and website management team that quickly implemented everything we created. Additionally, the clients invested in the three pillars of good SEO in the way of content publishing, tech improvements, and link strategies.

I will outline some of these successful projects in this chapter. It's important to understand that good results are achievable when best practices are followed.

How to Keep the Success Going

There are many projects that were not successful for reasons outside of the client relationship. Additionally, there have been several updates with Google over the years that have made some of these practices and rankings obsolete.

It's important to understand that maintaining positive results on an ongoing basis requires many different things. These include the following:

- A cooperative and responsive IT and brand team
- Skilled SEO experts
- Ongoing content production
- Strong analytics and regular reporting
- Effective and well-thought-out content, SEO, and link strategies
- Broader paid media and marketing initiatives

Why Case Studies Are in This Book

When I was writing this book, I wasn't sure if I should show actual work results, but I've come to realize that case studies are valuable and should be included. Additionally, this book is ultimately about growing free, organic traffic to your brand assets. Case studies will help you, as a reader, understand the effectiveness of the steps and optimizations outlined in this book. Some broader benefits of case studies include the following:

- They are often used to sell ideas in sales meetings.
- They help explain how to apply processes effectively.
- They help demonstrate scenarios using steps outlined in this book that showed effective outcomes.
- They showcase results of effective processes to students and other audiences that are learning about the topics throughout this book.

The following are some cases that I chose to highlight from varying industries.

Automotive Brand

A brand was entering the automotive maintenance industry and was looking to boost awareness and name visibility. The key performance metric was website traffic. A plan that outlined the process shown in Figure 11.1 was activated.

Figure 11.1: Automotive brand SEO process

The site audit findings were remedied and fixed. With a new, SEO-friendly website, a content analysis was done.

There were significant content gaps based on the topics discovered, and we addressed them by doing the following:

1. Expanded content (articles, infographics, video) on the website and blog with an emphasis on high-funnel, product category topical content, with heavy search volume.

2. Optimized existing content and HTML tags.

   a. Revised HTML tags.

   b. Positioned the site to rank for voice search results and quick answer results.

3. Incorporated SEO reviews and data into blogging and content calendar.

4. Established a link acquisition strategy.

The results were increases in traffic, inbound links, keyword rankings, and quick answer and voice search rankings.

- Monthly organic traffic increased 500 percent from the beginning of the campaign to the peak of the campaign.

- Link popularity increased more than 8000 percent.

- The site began ranking for Google quick answers and voice search queries because of the built-up trust value and valuable content that the team created helped build and optimize. All were pulled into Google voice search results.

Financial Services Brand

A popular consumer-facing financial services brand was suffering from low brand awareness. Traffic to their website was at an all-time low. A plan that outlined the process shown in Figure 11.2 was activated.

Figure 11.2: Financial services process

The site audit findings were remedied and fixed. With a new, SEO-friendly website, a content analysis was done. We identified the trending searches in their category according to Google's keyword tool (Table 11.1).

Table 11.1: Financial Category Relevant Searches

CATEGORY	SEARCHES PER MONTH
Search topic category 1	15 million
Search topic category 2	11 million
Search topic category 3	4.6 million
Search topic category 4	4.1 million
Search topic category 5	1.6 million searches per month
Search topic category 6	250,000 searches per month

The team conducted a content gap analysis and emphasized the need for content diversification. Current traffic was mainly brand and basic category traffic. A content diversified approach could provide exposure to many more searches and clicks. The team estimated the total organic impressions and clicks could be in the millions.

We pulled together a content response suggestion based on the search demand of each topic.

Because of budgetary reasons, the client focused on employing the medium demand content responses, which included the following:

▪ Each quarter, we created several videos to be populated on YouTube, and each month, we created almost a dozen articles for their website.

▪ We built a YouTube channel to house videos.

▪ We embedded relevant videos on their website in relevant articles.

▪ We employed content promotion tactics via their email newsletter and existing paid media programs.

The results were increased traffic and awareness.

- Brand searches increased more than 30 percent from previous year, indicating greater brand awareness.

- SEO traffic became the highest on record, with an increase from the prior year over 100 percent.

Auto Insurance Brand

SEO was engaged to help increase traffic around the auto insurance category. The client and the SEO team agreed to two goals: to increase traffic by at least 30 percent to key auto insurance entry pages and to improve the amount of #1 rankings around auto insurance terms.

To achieve the goals, we did the following:

- Provided a technical audit of the site and made content recommendations that corresponded to high-performing "auto insurance" category terms. The team reviewed high-performing paid search keyword terms as part of the strategy.

- Worked with the client's IT team and legal team to implement recommendations.

- Worked with the client to employ an off-site link building campaign around two targeted priority keyword terms: *auto insurance* and *car insurance*.

The results were increased traffic and the keywords ranking #1 in search results.

- Total visits to target pages increased 125 percent from the baseline, exceeding the goal of 30 percent.

- The final month of the project showed a traffic increase of 342 percent to the auto insurance category page (Figure 11.3 and Figure 11.4).

- The amount of number #1 rankings increased by 30 percent.

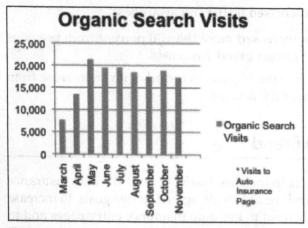

Figure 11.3: Auto Insurance brand total traffic results

Auto Pages				
	Baseline Organic Traffic	October Organic Traffic	November Organic Traffic	Percentage Change from Baseline
home.asp	427,710	484,606	423,000	-1%
auto_insurance.asp	2,494	12,501	11,018	342%
ins_auto_type.asp	1,172	1,512	1,503	28%
grndthft.asp	829	462	446	-46%
SteerClear.asp	772	1,675	1,407	82%

Figure 11.4: Auto insurance page results

Major Coffee Brand Website Redesign

A major coffee brand tasked our SEO team to provide SEO support and strategy into the development and quality assurance (QA) phases of a full website redesign. There were two goals.

- Ensure SEO site compliancy by working with the IT team and development vendors to police site construction and integrity
- Ensure all existing external search equity (domain age, links, etc.) is passed adequately to the new site

We provided several SEO deliverables across the entire project. Specific deliverables and tasks included the following:

- Provided keyword recommendations and best practices for web page content

- Delivered creative feedback on design layouts, wireframes, and sitemaps
- Created and added metadata tags into copy decks
- Provided custom prelaunch and postlaunch SEO site audits; some issues had to be escalated because recommendations were not implemented by development vendors
- Provided 301 redirect recommendations for top-priority pages (based on most search traffic/rankings)
- Link building program around two of their top-priority keywords

The results were increases in organic traffic, sales, and rankings. We saw the following successes (Figure 11.5 and Figure 11.6):

- Site moved from #10 to #3 for the term *coffee* on Google
- Organic traffic increased 130 percent from 36,062 in October to 86,066 visits in November, when metadata was finally implemented (in late September)
- Organic sales increased 170 percent from $50,390 in October to $136,998 in November
- Organic traffic increased 200 percent from baseline (before site was released)

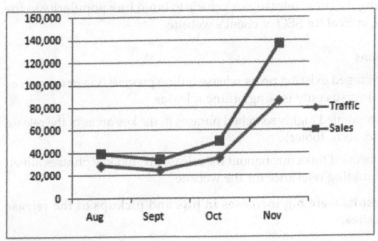

Figure 11.5: Coffee search traffic

August	represents the baseline month	
Month	**Total Organic Traffic**	**Total Organic Sales**
Aug	28,558	$39,614.00
Sept	24,656	$34,534.00
Oct	36,062	$50,390.00
Nov	86,066	$136,998.00

Figure 11.6: Coffee search sales results

Press Release Case Study

A paper brand had two annual press releases they would drop every year and used a newswire service to help increase the circulation of the releases. The performance of these releases was pretty flat year over year and was measured by the number of hits, i.e., views of the releases. The SEO team was brought in to provide SEO recommendations on the content of each release and to increase text links in the release to the brand's website. As a result of the SEO optimizations, each release saw significant increases in total views of the release, attributed to increased search rankings and more sites picking up the release and reposting it.

Challenges

- Increasing the reach and visibility of press releases
- Using the press release as a vehicle to build link popularity to the site, critical for SEO of client's website

Solutions

- Leveraged existing press release online process (via prnewswire. com) versus only issuing offline releases
- Incorporated highly searched phrases in the key areas of the release (title, body, footer)
- Embedded links throughout the release around key phrases aimed at building relevance for the website

The results were big increases in hits and pickups of the release on news sites.

- A St. Patrick's Day release saw a 45.6 percent increase in the number of hits versus the previous year's unoptimized releases.
- The Annual Report release saw a 72.7 percent increase in the amount of hits versus the previous year's unoptimized releases (Figure 11.7).

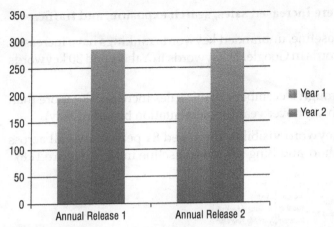

Figure 11.7: Year over year PR pickups

Major Women's Clothing Retailer

A major women's clothing retailer was in need of improved SEO performance, specifically improving the site's ranking numbers from a nonbrand perspective. The team applied the three pillars of SEO mentioned in this book and saw dramatic organic results.

Challenges

- Increasing overall organic search visibility, particularly for unbranded organic terms.

- Removing duplicate domains. Many instances of duplicate domains as well as roadblocks in implementing 301 redirects and URL changes existed.

- Increasing content. There was a general lack of content on main landing pages.

Solution

- Devised a solution with the internal IT team to redirect or remove more than 100 duplicate domains.

- Provided optimized copy, title tags, meta tags, and a method to add content to landing pages.

- Targeted specific terms with link building to garner strong gains for highly searched unbranded keywords.

The results were increased sales, search exposure, and traffic.

- Since the baseline, unbranded keywords rankings have increased by 16 keywords in Google, 24 keywords in Yahoo, and 30 keywords in Bing.

- August through December organic sales increased by more than $1.8 million year over year (implementation began in May).

- Targeted keyword visibility improved 84 percent overall across Google, Yahoo, and Bing since the baseline in May (Figure 11.8).

Keyword	% Increase in Sales YoY	Google Ranking Increase	Yahoo Ranking Increase	Bing Ranking Increase
women's sweaters	100%	+21	+28	+29
women's apparel catalogs	100%	+5	+19	+1
women's dresses	88%	+16	-	+28
long skirts	100%	+12	-	+7
petite clothing	100%	+15	+9	-
knit jeans	56%	+23	-7	-1
knit pants	100%	+20	-3	+16
women's dress pants	100%	+9	+15	+28
women's petite clothing	100%	+5	+13	-

Figure 11.8: Increased keyword rankings for important product category terms leads to increased sales

- Organic traffic increased 17 percent year over year.

Conclusion

These case studies provide evidence that applying the SEO and content marketing principles outlined in this book will result in meaningful performance improvements in the way of search engine rankings, free or organic traffic, better user experience, and overall better brand performance. While results sometimes take time because of implementation obstacles, it's important to have an ongoing strategy that combines SEO and content marketing. Doing this will result in free traffic and can offset the money spent on your total marketing budget.

Index